Made in the USA
Middletown, DE
17 October 2023

Enneagram

for

dummies®

A Wiley Brand

Enneagram

by Jeanette van Stijn

A Wiley Brand

Enneagram For Dummies®

Published by: **John Wiley & Sons, Inc.,** 111 River Street, Hoboken, NJ 07030-5774, www.wiley.com

Copyright © 2021 by John Wiley & Sons, Inc., Hoboken, New Jersey

Published simultaneously in Canada

For general information on our other products and services, please contact our Customer Care Department within the U.S. at 877-762-2974, outside the U.S. at 317-572-3993, or fax 317-572-4002. For technical support, please visit https://hub.wiley.com/community/support/dummies.

Wiley publishes in a variety of print and electronic formats and by print-on-demand. Some material included with standard print versions of this book may not be included in e-books or in print-on-demand. If this book refers to media such as a CD or DVD that is not included in the version you purchased, you may download this material at http://booksupport.wiley.com. For more information about Wiley products, visit www.wiley.com.

Library of Congress Control Number: 2020951380

ISBN: 978-1-119-77112-8; 978-1-119-77113-5 (ebk); 978-1-119-77114-2 (ebk)

Manufactured in the United States of America

SKY10023515_122220

Contents at a Glance

Table of Contents

Introduction

For many years now, interest in the Enneagram has been growing exponentially worldwide. Maybe you've already heard of it at work, at a seminar, or from friends or relatives. The Enneagram as it is described in this book is about 20 to 30 years old, is a popular and recognized method of gaining insight into your personality, and has become an increasingly common tool across a broad spectrum of professions.

The Enneagram became popular because many people felt a need for a greater sense of self-awareness as well as a desire for increased personal development. They also wanted to better understand the people around them — their partners, children, parents, bosses, colleagues, and others. Why do people do what they do? Why is it that certain people clash so severely? The Enneagram reveals the answer. The Enneagram is a compassionate method that enables people to gain not only greater insight but also a better understanding of each other and of why things happen the way they do. The Enneagram helps people build bridges between themselves and the other people in their world.

About This Book

The goal of this book is to offer you a clear, concise, practical, and — above all — *comprehensible* overview of the world of the Enneagram. It should also encourage you to try the Enneagram for yourself. This is a book for you if you see your life as a journey on which you still have a lot to discover, experience, and learn. If that statement describes you, you might be interested in the answers to the following questions:

>> What is the Enneagram?

>> What can you do with the Enneagram?

>> What is the "language" of the Enneagram?

>> How do personality structures develop?

>> What are the Enneagram personality types?

>> How can I apply the Enneagram to my everyday life?

>> Is there just one way to do the Enneagram?

>> Does the Enneagram have a spiritual component?

I wrote this book for two reasons. First, the Enneagram has personally given me a lot — in fact, I have no trouble saying it has changed my life. I have fewer difficulties with my own, personal "stumbling blocks" and am finding increasing amounts of freedom in the decisions I make. One outcome for me was that I sold my share in my organizational consulting firm to dedicate myself fully to the Enneagram. I want everyone to have this decision-making freedom and inner peace.

The second reason is connected to the first. At the seminars, training sessions, and workshops that I hold on the topic of the Enneagram, participants often ask which book I can recommend as an introduction to the topic — a book that offers an easy way to start, a convenient overview of the possibilities out there, and exercises for further development. You're holding this book in your hands.

Foolish Assumptions

This book was written for people who want to use it for their own, personal development as well as for professional users who are interested in this tool for their work. What consultants who delve deeper into the Enneagram often have in common is that they come in professional contact with people trying to function — sometimes unsuccessfully — in their environment. They can use a tool that gives them quicker insight into the characteristics of people with whom they work. This affects managers, mediators, coaches, personnel managers, relationship therapists, pastors, organizational consultants, management trainers, team builders, lecturers, physicians, entrepreneurs, and many others.

About the Examples

WARNING

All examples mentioned in this book give an impression of the tendencies shown by many people who recognize themselves in a certain type. I don't mean that all people who recognize themselves in that type work exactly the same way. The reality is much more differentiated. For that reason, it can easily happen that you recognize yourself in the mechanisms of a type but not in the example I present for that type. Maybe it works differently for you. Even if you recognize the mechanisms, you're still a unique individual!

Instead of the selected examples, I could have mentioned many others. The examples are meant for illustrative purposes only and don't fully represent the types in their infinite variety. I selected the examples from the ones I collected in 12 years of intensive work I've done with people as part of my Enneagram practice, especially from the comments many people made during Enneagram workshops.

The Various Enneagram Movements

The Enneagram is distinguished by different movements. The existing books were usually written from the perspective of one or another of these orientations. In this book, I identify each of the major movements and give proponents and course participants from various schools of thought a chance to speak. This should give you an impression of the world of the Enneagram. As a trainer, I am often asked in what way the various movements differ. I always start by saying that I, of course, come to the Enneagram from a certain perspective: I first encountered the Enneagram via Helen Palmer and David Daniels, who introduced me to the principles of the Enneagram many years ago in San Francisco. As I've already mentioned, I got a lot out of this meeting. It had a profound effect on how I see things, and as such, I regard that educational experience as a great success. It formed the foundation of the approach to the Enneagram and the development method described in this book. However, I still think it's important to mention the other movements. (Many roads lead to Rome, you know.) I hope this book will help people who have recently started being guided by the Enneagram to find suitable seminars and lecturers.

How to Read This Book

Like all *For Dummies* titles, the structure of this book lets you skip the chapters that don't apply to your situation. In the chapters you read, you can also limit yourself to the parts you find interesting. Check out the table of contents or the index for subjects of special interest to you. Also notice the icons placed strategically throughout the text; they're designed to help you choose what you want to focus on. (You can find out more about the icons later in this introduction, in the section "Icons Used in This Book.") You'll notice sidebars in some chapters — I use those to add extra information for interested readers.

How This Book Is Organized

Enneagram For Dummies is organized in six parts so that you can start by looking at the big picture of Enneagram and then walk through its method, its application, and its history.

Part 1: Getting Started with the Enneagram

In Part 1, you discover what the Enneagram is. I also address the fact that, generalities aside, all people are fundamentally different. In this part you see how the Enneagram model differentiates between nine patterns for thinking, feeling, and acting. Discovering your preferred patterns is already a first step on the path toward self-awareness — and to personal development. Because *that's* what the Enneagram is about: giving each person the opportunity to develop their personality. You just have to know how!

Part 2: Examining the Enneagram Types

The elements that make up each Enneagram type are the starting points for the Enneagram method. In this part you discover that all nine types consist of the same elements but that the content of these elements differs from type to type. The basic pattern of thinking, feeling, and acting emerges as a mechanism with not just one but nine different contents. After your first brief encounter with the Enneagram types in Part 1, you now get more detailed information on how various thought patterns work, how people's thoughts and feelings influence each other, and what predictable patterns will arise from these interactions. Here we explore how people function on a psychological level.

REMEMBER

The Enneagram doesn't claim that there are only nine types of people in the world. That would be ridiculous! Each person is unique — this is why there are just as many types as there are people in the world.

Part 3: Working with the Information You Get

In this part I slow it down a bit and help you digest what you've read so far in this book. You may have come across a number of technical terms as well as details about the various personality structures and the nine type mechanisms. In Part 3, I provide you with examples of what you can actually do with everything discussed so far. After all, that's what this is about. The possible applications that you read about here are meant to guide and inspire you. You can already start using them right now, before tackling the more intensive path toward personal development that I introduce in Part 4. In Chapter 11, you can read about general applications in the workplace — applications appropriate for a number of different work environments. In Chapter 12, you get the chance to look at applications for managers to use when mediating conflicts. Chapter 13 deals with applications in the kind of one-on-one work situations experienced by coaches, therapists, (corporate) social workers, and others.

Part 4: I Know My Type — Now What?

You can read in Part 4 what the path of development and self-realization might look like and what you can do for it. You will gain insights into your learning and the course of learning that you have already (subconsciously) completed. You will discover that what you have learned so far by falling down and getting up again is probably no coincidence. You'll find out about the difference between learning and developing on a psychological level and about functioning on different levels and states of consciousness. Even when it comes to human development, many roads lead to Rome. You will also get to know two paths of development based on spiritual traditions: the *via negativa* and the *via positiva.* In various sections, you'll find tips on your personal development and self-observation, along with tasks. You will read what you can practice to continue developing yourself. The last chapter covers the spiritual Enneagram. Even if you aren't interested in spirituality, I recommend that you read this chapter because it too contains valuable, "worldly" tips for your personal development.

Part 5: The Roots of the Enneagram

In Part 5, you'll discover that internal work is timeless and find out the origins of the word *therapist.* You will read how you can consider the Enneagram from this perspective and what it contributes to the image of the psychological Enneagram. In this part you'll read about the origin of certain perspectives that you encountered with the spiritual Enneagram in Part 4. I will walk you through the more recent history of the Enneagram in the West, and then you can read about the different currents or schools that exist now. This knowledge might help you make a more informed decision on which type of Enneagram work fits you and will help you progress. You will learn a few things about different Enneagram currents and the tradition of this internal work throughout the centuries. The Enneagram also has the tradition in which wisdom is passed from one person to the next, from one generation to the next. You will see that *the* Enneagram doesn't exist, that it remains a work in progress. And, you'll see how this situation preserves it as a consistent source of meaning for individual people — for people like you and me.

Part 6: The Part of Tens

I close this book with a mainstay of the *For Dummies* series: The Part of Tens. I decided to populate this part with ten possible applications for the Enneagram and ten book recommendations — in the hope that the Enneagram can inspire you to even greater heights.

Icons Used in This Book

In the margins of this book you'll often find icons used to call attention to specific information. Here's what each icon means:

REMEMBER

This icon refers to information that I want to particularly emphasize and that is absolutely worth reading. Maybe you want to highlight these particular passages or store them away in your mental memory banks for later reference.

TIP

This icon indicates a good tip or hint or some practical information. Don't skip these!

TECHNICAL STUFF

At first, some terms related to the Enneagram might sound strange. The information next to this icon explains technical terms. Before you know it, you'll sound like a pro!

WARNING

This icon warns you against possible problems or frequently occurring errors.

PRACTICE

This icon points you to different exercises to deepen your knowledge about your type or about the Enneagram itself. If you're looking for exercises, watch for this symbol.

EXAMPLE

This icon offers you a practical example so that you can remember the subject even better.

Beyond the Book

In addition to what you're reading right now, this publication comes with a free, access-anywhere Cheat Sheet that offers a number of tips, techniques, and resources related to the Enneagram. To view this Cheat Sheet, visit www.dummies.com and type **enneagram for dummies cheat sheet** in the Search box.

Where to Go from Here

Though some people will open up *Enneagram For Dummies* and read just the bits about their own type, I hope that the many opportunities offered by the Enneagram will touch you and inspire you to use it in a more active fashion. *For Dummies* books are structured so that you can read them chapter by chapter from beginning to end, scroll right to the end, or jump around between the chapters that happen to interest you most at the moment. Are you looking for basic knowledge about the Enneagram? Then look at Parts 1 and 2 of this book. In Chapter 4, you'll find specific information on how to discover your type. If you want to use the Enneagram at work or as a manager, open Chapters 11 and 12. Do you want to use the Enneagram as a professional companion? Go ahead and jump to Chapter 13.

Everyone is warmly invited to delve deep into *Enneagram For Dummies* and reap the rewards. I wish you much success and joy in the process!

1

Getting Started with the Enneagram

» Discovering the Enneagram's personalized prisms

» Managing yourself

» The psychological and spiritual sides of the coin

Chapter **1**

The Enneagram in a Nutshell

The personality types in the Enneagram are denoted by numbers: Type 1 to Type 9. In other symbolic designations, the number 0 stands for . . . the jester, or the dummy! Here's the good news: When you look into the meaning of 0 as a symbol, you see that it stands for the original completeness, the paradisiacal original state, and for connection, a new or repeating cycle — one you can enter into without needing any experience.

The 0 is also the basis of the Enneagram's symbol. The Enneagram serves as a development path to completeness, connecting with yourself and with others, and getting to know the unrevealed state within you. In short, the Enneagram is all about becoming aware of what is dormant and subconsciously present within you. The 0, or the *dummy,* is also called "the spirit who wants to gain experience" and is guided by curiosity and desire. Without a preconceived plan, they spontaneously travel along paths that are full of surprises — carefree and open. They're like the lovable child in you. They're not basing everything on reason, so they can play, laugh, dream, and just have fun as a totally free person. In other words, if you want to have more fun in your life, make friends with your inner dummy.

Think of *Enneagram For Dummies* as the Enneagram for those who want to be truly free — for people who want to have more fun in their lives and who want to avoid being hindered by their limitations. Or perhaps I'm talking about people who are simply fed up with spending more time struggling than having fun in life. The jester is often depicted with a knapsack, which symbolizes the package of untapped knowledge within you. The Enneagram is a tool for discovering and learning to benefit from the unused knowledge you carry inside.

Let's Get Going!

Seeing the word *Enneagram* might bring to mind a complicated method, peppered with inexplicable terms. You start with an explanation of the Enneagram. What's the starting point? Where do you go from here?

What is an Enneagram?

The word *Enneagram* comes from the Greek words *ennéa*, which means "nine," and *grámma*, which is translated as "writing" or "something written or drawn." In its modern manifestation, the *Enneagram* is a symbol consisting of a circle on which nine points have been drawn (see Figure 1-1) and various meanings assigned. Some say that the Enneagram summarizes the progress of processes (the *process model*), and others use it to describe nine different states in which you can find yourself as a human being. To tell the truth, the Enneagram doesn't actually exist. (Well, it exists as a symbol, but not as an unambiguous system of meaning.)

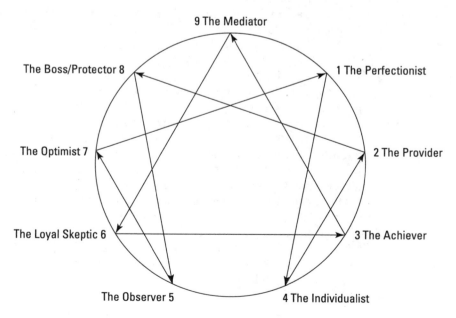

FIGURE 1-1:
The Enneagram.

The meaning of the Enneagram symbol covered in this book is as a model that summarizes nine personality structures. In Enneagram jargon, you refer to the personality structures as *types*. When I talk about the Enneagram in this book, I'm talking about the psychological and spiritual aspects of types.

Gaining an understanding of human differences

Every person is different, which is something you probably notice often when dealing with others. That's nothing new. The question is *how* people differ, which is more difficult to understand. The Enneagram provides insight into this aspect of your life. Many people already acquainted with the Enneagram have gained not only an understanding of how people are different but also a better understanding of other people — that is to say, a better understanding of others' *differences*. I think that's one of the fantastic things the Enneagram offers: It provides a bridge between people.

Nine prisms to view the world

The Enneagram distinguishes between nine personality structures. These can be seen as nine different prisms that are viewing the same reality — nine prisms through which reality is perceived differently. The prisms filter what is seen and what available information enters, and how it's processed internally. In psychology, it's called *selective perception.* You observe selectively. Once you realize this, you immediately understand the pointlessness of all the "is so!/is not!" conversations you may have experienced in your life (with yourself or with others). This is usually a matter of both people seeing different things due to looking through different prisms. As a result, it's possible that what one person has perceived or experienced is true, *and* that what the other person has perceived or experienced is also true. The only conclusion you can then draw together is that you have perceived or experienced things differently. This is a first step toward understanding others and toward respecting them and what they have seen or experienced differently.

People like different things about the Enneagram

EXAMPLE

I asked a number of people what appeals to them about working with the Enneagram, and I got the following answers:

>> The model is perfectly designed, and the method is meticulous.

>> It helps me adapt even more to the needs of others.

>> It's efficient and targeted.

>> It is profound and takes into account that every person is unique.

>> It's structured and put together well, and it brings wisdom.

>> It provides security and a clear model, and it's a reliable system.

>> It's a fascinating method that provides many options for perceiving people.

>> It provides truth about people and is a powerful method for growth.

>> It generates harmony in me and between other people.

Look at the list of responses people gave to the question of what appeals to them about the Enneagram. Is there an answer or answers that are more relevant to you to consider when judging something — for example, whether something is careful, profound, or safe? If so, it's not so much about whether you agree with the Enneagram, but more about whether one prism fits you better than the rest.

REMEMBER

This is a prime example of how the nine types give different answers. They focus on different aspects of the model because they think different things are important. That's how the Enneagram works.

The model . . .

People are curious about themselves. They might ask, "Why do I react one way in this situation and you act in another way? Why are you in such a hurry and I'm not? Why was I bored in that meeting and my colleague was an enthusiastic participant?"

The way your thoughts and feelings work is interesting. People have been trying to gain more insight into this process for centuries. You may know that the ancient Greek philosophers spent a lot of time contemplating their thoughts and thought processes. Reality is so complex that people try to understand and clarify it. They do this by representing aspects of that reality in models. Humans, and how they work together and function, are so complex that it's practically impossible to comprehend. Yet it's a human peculiarity that everyone wants to understand themselves better, to get to know themselves. People needed models that could make their complex nature more comprehensible. They created models to observe and understand their mutual differences. This is part of reality, which is described in some detail in the Enneagram. But it's just a model and therefore not reality itself. The reality is that everyone is a unique individual.

Although far apart in place and time, systems have been developed within different cultures around the world that are, upon closer study, amazingly similar at heart. Many people, for example, focus inward with meditation or prayer. For the purposes of this book, note that people in different places and at different times have come to the conclusion that you hinder yourself by adhering to familiar thought patterns and mental habits — patterns and habits that blind you to other points of view.

. . . and the method

The question now is, What are the benefits of understanding yourself and others? What's the fun of that? How does having this knowledge help you? Nothing changes from insights alone; they don't automatically lead to personal development. For that to happen, you need a practice in addition to a model that makes your inner life easier to understand. That's what the Enneagram also offers. Bookcases are packed full of literature about the Enneagram as a model, but what's less known is that the Enneagram also offers a *practice*, a method of self-development or self-management. One of my goals in this book is to give you an idea of what to do with this practice after you've finished reading.

The map of your inner self

Many models classify personality structures — most do it by describing externally observable characteristics: Are you more extroverted or introverted? Are you more of a leader or a follower? The Enneagram emphasizes something else: The personality structures are classified and described according to what happens within you as a human being. So the Enneagram is actually more of a map of your inner self.

You have to learn to read and use a map. Where are north and south? How does the map indicate a hiking trail, a river, and a bridge to cross the river? Reading a map also applies to the Enneagram. The first step of your journey using the Enneagram map is to become familiar with the language with which your inner structure is expressed in words. This first part mainly explains this language and focuses on what you mean when you use it.

Leveraging the Enneagram's 2-in-1 concept

The Enneagram's added value is that it offers a coordinated method of self-development built on top of the map of the inner self. Other methods of self-development generally offer exercises and tips that are pretty much the same for everyone. The beauty of the Enneagram's methodology is that there's a corresponding map in which differences between people are thoroughly mapped out. The path to self-development is different for each type on the Enneagram. The development path and what to practice are tailored to the peculiarities of each type. This is why working with the Enneagram is effective.

Many trainers, coaches, and other professionals have discovered the value of the Enneagram as a model. To put the Enneagram to practical use, you need instruments and a method. Because it's less well known that the Enneagram provides these tools, professionals often combine the Enneagram with other techniques. One example is the commonly used combination of the Enneagram and neurolinguistic programming (NLP.) (For more on this topic, check out *Neuro-linguistic Programming For Dummies*, by Kate Burton and Romilla Ready). Sometimes trainers and coaches who are skilled in other techniques then discover the Enneagram map. They therefore feel no need for the method that the Enneagram also offers. This book demonstrates the 2-in-1 concept and shows its corresponding possibilities and value. For example, precisely by practicing the method does the insight into the types continue to deepen. I hope that many professionals will embrace the method in addition to the model. It pairs well with other techniques and skills that they may already have acquired.

Seeing What the Enneagram Can Offer You

The main benefit that the Enneagram offers is a focused and easy way to learn more about yourself at a deeper level — to become more aware of how you think, what you feel, why you act or react the way you do, why something or someone can or cannot affect you, or why certain people have a particular effect on you. On top of all that, you can learn more about what effect you have on other people and how you come across to others and then, most importantly, where that perception comes from. Finally, the Enneagram can reveal to you what you're focusing your attention on, what you think is important deep down, what you desire, what you're looking for, or what you're avoiding.

Choosing to develop

Imagine that you're finally getting to know yourself. You learn to observe where you focus your attention, and you learn to perceive, from a nonjudgmental position, when and how your type manifests itself. You become more aware of things that you may not have known before. If you do become aware and notice when your type kicks in as your automatic pilot, there comes a time when you get to make a choice: Keep your type in charge, to carry out your habits as you have always done, or leave the habits behind. In doing so, you refuse to remain a captive to your type; you now have the freedom to not get caught up in it. That's a step in your development.

REMEMBER

There's more to come. This is just a taste of what the Enneagram has to offer if you choose to walk that path: awareness and ability to function with more freedom.

EXAMPLE

I'm a Type 1 person, and my type made me not only a captive of my type but also a captive of my work. If something wasn't good enough, I couldn't stop. It didn't matter what it was; only when it was perfectly in order could I stop and go to sleep. I worked through many a night. Because everything had to be done perfectly, stacks of work were always on my desk — many and high. Next to and under my desk, behind my chair, an extra cabinet that I bought just to hold the stacks. Can you picture it? It wasn't healthy for me, nor was it a joy for those around me. The Enneagram made me see not only those stacks but also, above all, how I created my own mechanisms and then chose to stop them. What helped me for months to make a real turnaround was asking myself the question, "Isn't it already good enough?" with every job. It was always good enough, and so I could teach myself to stop.

In this book you'll find your own question to help you make a change and to no longer be a captive to your type.

Committing to your inner work

I use *inner work* as a term for the work involved in personal development. It's not hocus-pocus; it's just plain work, but it's work done on the inside. Anyone can learn how to do inner work, but, as with anything you want to learn, it doesn't happen on its own.

REMEMBER

People are dealing with increasing demands at work regarding their personal and professional functioning. You'll discover that this inner work is also indispensable, even when it comes to professional development. It helps you face your limitations and overcome them and teaches you how you can better use your innate qualities. Wanting to develop yourself or certain aspects of yourself requires time and effort — but above all, your attention.

Stick with this development for a while because inner work can

>> Offer you fun in addition to depth, meaning, and inspiration

>> Provide you with surprising benefits that can be of great significance to you

>> Make you a happier person

That last reason is why I continue to use the Enneagram.

Benefitting from self-management

Of course, it sounds nice and enticing to become free, or at least freer, in your actions. You likely have a way to go before that happens, though. Let's be honest: You have to be convinced of the importance and the benefit of this concept before you'll be prepared to travel that path. Am I wrong?

It helps, then, to remember the possible benefits of development. Managing your personality becomes important when you want to

>> Reach your full potential

>> Enjoy meaningful and lasting relationships

>> Suffer less from your limitations

>> Work as part of a team as effectively and enjoyably as possible

>> Live a more visible and resilient life

>> Strive for changes and/or conflicts to ultimately be constructive

>> Pursue inner peace and balance

>> Live with less conflict and more harmony and connection

This list is somewhat long, but I think the point is clear.

TIP

Ask yourself these questions as you consider how important it is for you to develop: How can you benefit as a person, in your relationships, and at work? Do you have qualities within you or in your life that you want to be less bothered by?

Seeing the downside of developing without tools to help you

You may have noticed that people also develop in life without using tools. My life experiences mean that I also learned and unlearned lessons without the Enneagram. Without tools, this was a long, difficult, searching, and even painful path — a path of trial-and-error where, rather than know what you're doing, you're just trying something to see where it leads. If it turns out positive, you can repeat it; if not, then you no longer do it. That's how you gain life experience. After I started working with the Enneagram, I was able to develop much more purposefully and faster.

There are many different ways to travel. If you want to go from the Netherlands to Spain, for example, you can start walking south and you might eventually end up there — as long as you have enough time. Or maybe you don't make it there. The chances of finding Spain are better when using a map of the route. Then you might take the occasional wrong turn, but at least you can rely on the map to get back on track. Now if you find an even more efficient way to travel, you'll probably arrive even faster. This is what the Enneagram offers: an effective (targeted) and efficient way to travel on the inner path to development.

Examining some practical applications

The Enneagram is versatile. It can be used in all situations where good personal functioning is important, as well as in situations where good interaction between people is vital. Personal functioning can include how you function in your work, in relationships (private ones and work ones), and in raising your children. There are numerous applications in the workplace.

Table 1-1 offers specific examples of the possibilities for development with the Enneagram and the areas where they can be applied.

TABLE 1-1 **Development Possibilities with the Enneagram**

Development Possibilities	Areas in Which They Apply
Leadership qualities	Coaching
Communication skills	Education and training
Collaboration skills	Team-building
Emotional intelligence	Conflict mediation and management
Management skills	Therapy and counseling
Social functioning	Change processes in organizations
Sales qualities	Mediation

Psychological? Or Spiritual?

The division into specialist disciplines as they're known today has not been around that long — more specifically, the boundaries between subjects like philosophy, theology, and psychology. These specializations have become increasingly, and more strongly, distinct in recent decades. This distinction didn't exist before the modern era. Humans and how they function has been a subject of study and reflection for thousands of years. For most of that time, the distinction between the psychological and spiritual aspects wasn't even made. The Enneagram itself isn't that old, but the knowledge contained within it about people is. So this knowledge existed before the division into specialist disciplines. Some claim that the Enneagram is spiritual, and others emphasize the psychological elements that can also be recognized in the Enneagram. I personally see no distinction; in developing yourself, the psychological and spiritual go hand in hand. It happens whether it's your intention or not. By working on one, you'll notice that it has an effect on the other. They're not separate from each other. It depends on what you mean by spiritual or psychological aspects. The next few sections take a closer look at this topic.

What's psychological about the Enneagram . . .

The Enneagram provides a description of your inner self. This description of the Enneagram types usually begins with the qualities and limitations of a type, what that type focuses on, and what your regular "thinking, feeling, acting" pattern looks like. This is also called the *psychological* Enneagram. It's a description of the personality structure. Psychologists (including Freud) call it the *ego.* In spiritual terms, it's also called the Lower Self. In the Enneagram, this description of the ego/Lower Self is the type, or the Enneagram of passions and fixations.

The functioning of people at the psychological level is what you perceive when people are captive to their type. This applies to most people. The term *captive to your type* means that you actually have no freedom of choice — not in what you think, what you feel, and how you act. The lack of freedom of choice is caused by people not knowing themselves well. As a result, they have little awareness of themselves and of their automatic patterns of thinking, feeling, and acting. When you're not consciously aware, you're on automatic pilot; you don't want to get angry, for example, but you definitely do get angry. You can't help yourself; it just happens. That is a lack of freedom of choice. You function from your Lower Self; your ego is in charge.

. . . and what about the spiritual?

The Enneagram offers a method of development; it's a transformation model. *Transformation* is a word used in spiritual circles, and it concerns the transformation from the Lower Self to the Higher Self. (In psychological terms, that would mean moving from functioning at the ego level to functioning as a free person. It's where the ego no longer has control over you.)

But what is spiritual? It's such a broad concept and also quite personal, with many different views or interpretations. Many see spirituality as equivalent to a religion and believing in a God. For others, including myself, these are matters that are not necessarily connected with each other. One example is Buddhism, where believing in God is not part of the spiritual doctrine. Some nonreligious people lead spiritual lives. Conversely, not everyone who is part of a religious group follows a spiritual way of life.

Spirituality is, in a broad sense, how people experience themselves as part of a greater whole, when they feel a connection and unity with everything or seek to realize it within themselves. I also see it as when people welcome the Higher Self into themselves. This Higher Self may be God or Allah or even the Higher Self that is present within you. This can be the desire to live following your true self, your essence, and it's based on higher values or virtues. An example of the latter is when people choose to live out of love. Love is the highest value on which they base their lives, and they strive for it above all else. The goal that people pursue — especially the ways in which they articulate that goal — differs from person to person. People who believe in God may formulate their aspirations in this life in order to feel closer to God. People who don't believe in God articulate it as something akin to becoming free. How one pursues this goal may make little difference at its core because if the goal is to feel closer to God, then the question is, "What stands between you and God?" If the goal is to become free as a person, then the question is "What stands between you and being free?" The answer is the same: You alone stand in the way: your ego.

Two sides of the same coin

The psychological and spiritual aspects are two sides of the same coin. In spiritual traditions, the Lower Self, or ego, is always investigated and interrogated, precisely because this is the beginning and therefore the starting point for transforming into higher values. It's perfectly plausible that the reason a spiritual orientation arose in people is due to the daily observation that people suffer mainly from the ego. Many people want to suffer less, so humans have been searching for the How for thousands of years. What can people do to suffer less? Only the language in which things are expressed is different. In these differences you can see the changes on earth from place to place over the course of time.

With the development of science in recent decades, people's mental well-being (or lack thereof) has become a specialized field of psychological research. The methods of development in this case are called *therapy*. It's not difficult for the spiritual practitioner to recognize in various other therapies the core of what is practiced in one's own spiritual practice. The guru is now called a *psychotherapist*, one who also focuses on meaning and the pursuit of developing higher values in the client — simply because it makes everyone happier as people!

The psychospiritual Enneagram

It's not a case of either-or; the Enneagram has both psychological and spiritual elements:

>> The psychological map charts your inner self — your ego.

>> The spiritual side maps your Higher Self.

>> The method provides insight into how to move from one to the other — the path of transformation from the Lower Self to the Higher Self.

>> Above all, the Enneagram extends the invitation to every person to achieve the Higher Self within themselves by learning to face the Lower Self within themselves. One is not separate from the other!

Being human

The Greek word for "human" or "humanity" is *anthrôpos*, which, in the ancient Greek sense, stood for "he who looks up" and "he who is destined to the higher." Being (or becoming) truly human was about opening oneself to the higher, but also to others and caring for the well-being of others. It meant being a good person.

WHATEVER WORKS FOR YOU!

The fact that you picked up this book and are reading it may indicate that you're also on a quest — a quest for your own development or a quest based on your profession. Maybe you're looking for a tool that can help you, your customer, or your organization and employees. This quest might have many different reasons or goals, but you're reading this *Enneagrams For Dummies* to gain insights quickly as well as an overview of whether the Enneagram might mean something to you — and if so, how.

I tell you in the main text what the Enneagram is and what it has to offer — the model and method side, and the psychology and spiritual side. Those are the perspectives from which I wrote this book.

The Enneagram is nothing more or less than one of the many means of transportation on the journey to development. It's a tool for self-management. For me personally, this tool has helped me so much that I enjoy helping other people benefit from it as much as I do. Everyone is different, however, and what works for me might not for work for someone else. Perhaps the most important advice is to go discover what works for you!

The path that the Enneagram offers is learning to relax your type and welcoming your true self and the higher virtues you have within. At the end of the path, your ego or your type is no longer in charge. The Enneagram provides a path to life based on awareness. You then have knowledge of yourself and your own limitations and qualities, and with knowledge of others, but also becoming more receptive to what is there and what's present in you and in your life — a life with more balance, more tranquility, more joy, more wisdom, more peace, and more love.

A Helpful Summary

Here's a final overview as you prepare to start your journey

What is the Enneagram?

>> Symbol with various meanings

>> Symbol in which your psychological and spiritual structures are summarized

>> Map of your inner self

>> Model that distinguishes nine personality structures

>> Method of practice for personal development

>> Method in which the path of development is different for each of the nine types

The benefits of using the Enneagram for development

>> Getting to know yourself and discovering who you are

>> Getting to know others and discovering how they're different

>> Acknowledging recognition, acceptance, and appreciation for yourself and others

>> Allowing compassion for yourself and for others

>> Building a bridge between people so that they can have more understanding of, and for, each other.

>> Fostering meaning and appreciation of your life (including your past, your parents, and your ex, for example).

>> Connecting with yourself, which leads to connecting with others

>> Gaining an inner balance and becoming less easily unbalanced by outside forces

>> Experiencing inner peace

>> Becoming a freer person, with your happiness less dependent, or no longer dependent, on people around you or on situations, for example

>> Having more fun and pleasure in your life

IN THIS CHAPTER

» Tips before starting with the Enneagram

» Examining your internal workings

» Eliminating stereotypes and categorical thinking

» Getting to know the nine Enneagram types

» Prepping yourself for the road ahead

Chapter **2**

Before You Get Started

R ight off the bat, I need to stress something: No single Enneagram type is better than another. The Enneagram approach doesn't judge when it comes to types; it only aims to deliver an appropriate and detailed description of the various ways in which people act in life. In this short (yet quite thorough) introduction, you get to know nine types of people who deal with the events that life throws at them — that's nine descriptions of how they see and experience the world. You may recognize yourself in one of the descriptions, but keep in mind that you might not be a one-to-one match with your unique personality.

A Heads-Up

Before getting to know the Enneagram, check out a few notes I've put together on the best way to learn about it — including the best way to use this book as fully as possible.

What's in a name?

One of the ways in which you can see that the Enneagram makes no judgment about types is that the types themselves were originally designated by numbers. When I talk about Type 3, for example, you probably have no idea what this term means and thus you have no judgment about it. It's a name, nothing more or less. But how would you see it if I talked about the Enneagram Boss/Protector type or the Perfectionist type? You'll likely instantly form an image of this person, and probably a judgment. As soon as people wrap an item inside a word, they call up a mental image of that item, often — unnoticed and unintentionally — along with a judgment. They consider the item good or bad, nice or not nice, and so on. Words have a positive or negative charge, whereas numbers are neutral. Some people, however, think that using numbers as names is annoying, precisely because the numbers are neutral and meaningless. No image appears, which makes it harder at first to remember the names. That's why various trainers have named the types. Once these names call up images, they're easier to remember when starting out with the Enneagram.

REMEMBER

Every name is a drastic abbreviation of a type's nature and complexity. Each name refers to only a limited characteristic of a personality structure. Just like people themselves, the personality structures are complex and multilayered, which is why they can't be easily captured in a name. Furthermore, you'll never come across two of the same people, not even two who recognize themselves in the mechanisms of the same Enneagram type. The Enneagram is only a map of the personality; the landscape itself is always unique and different from the map. Maybe you and I recognize ourselves in the Perfectionist type, for example, but that doesn't mean we're the same person. The name *Perfectionist* indicates that both of us probably value perfection, but there can be a world of difference in how we fulfill our perfectionism and where we aim our desire for it. Billions of people live in this world, and each one is unique, after all.

Seeing what's working inside of you

Descriptions of personality structures often consist of long lists of characteristics. Person A, for example, is described as extroverted, dominant, and direct, and Person B is seen as introverted, shy, and reserved. These descriptions probably evoke images in your mind, and maybe you also know people whom you would identify as Person A or Person B. You can list the characteristics of each of the nine Enneagram types in the same way. They refer to *external* properties — behaviors or aspects of attitudes that other people can perceive from the outside.

The descriptions of the Enneagram types, however, are much more detailed because they're more about the mechanisms working inside of you. That's why they can rarely be seen from the outside.

People who recognize themselves in the same type — making use of the same internal mechanisms — often express the type differently in their actual behavior. Also, conversely, two people who see themselves reflected in different types can behave similarly. In those cases, different motivations or drives lead to the same behavior.

HELP — I DON'T WANT TO BE CATEGORIZED!

Many people dislike designating personality structures by numbers. They associate this process with getting a serial number — it makes them feel that they're being put into a category. In response, Helen Palmer, a major figure in the world of the Enneagram, says that the Enneagram doesn't set out to categorize anyone; it's merely an aid you can use to discover which category is keeping your personality type imprisoned. You can free yourself from this category on your own. And by the way, you don't have to typecast yourself, so to speak, in order to work with the Enneagram. The goal is to expand your self-awareness, to get to know yourself better. After you read the descriptions of all the various types, ask yourself: What part of this do I recognize in myself? How does this work in my case? Am I exactly like that or a little different? This is also a way to get to know yourself better and become more aware of your limiting behaviors. If you're interested in determining your type on your own, you can find tips and exercises throughout this book that will help you on your way.

EXAMPLE

How this apparent contradiction works itself out can be illustrated in a brief example. Mary (Type 1), Louise (Type 7), and Margaret (Type 9) avoid conflicts rather than face them head-on. (Another way to refer to them is *conflict avoiders*.) However, they tend to avoid conflicts for different reasons. In Mary's value system, for example, "one just doesn't do conflicts." Louise's conflicts are nothing to laugh about; they're simply painful and, as such, are situations she wants to avoid. Margaret is afraid of destroying her relationship with whoever is the cause of the conflict.

The motivations behind all three people's desire to avoid conflict are quite different, but they all lead to the same behavior. This is why you look not at the behavior itself in the Enneagram but rather at the driving forces behind that behavior. In the Enneagram, the underlying *motivation,* or driving force, is considered more important than the behavior itself, because recognizing this drive is the starting point for further development. The approach for learning to deal with conflicts in a different, more productive fashion varies for each of the three. For them, it's not about handling conflicts per se, but rather about uncovering the actual reason they avoid conflicts.

REMEMBER

The word *type* crops up time and time again in this book, and you'll also come across the term *type mechanism*, which refers to the internal mechanism of a type. You can find out more about type mechanisms in Part 2.

You're not a type — you have a type

Admittedly, the distinction is slight between being a type and having a type. But no matter how slight, the distinction is still important. It's connected to the difference between your nature — your true self — and your ego. Your nature, or *true self* (as the word *true* indicates), is what you truly are at the core. Your ego, or your type, is also called the *false self:* It's what you believe you are. It's an incorrect identification; in the development of their own identity, human beings started believing that they're endowed with particular characteristics: I am shy, for example. Even if your ego is useful to you (more on this topic later in this chapter), people define themselves by what their ego tells them they are. If I'm truly convinced of my shyness deep inside, I will behave accordingly. This increasingly reinforces the behavior, and I resign myself to it, telling myself, "That's just how it is." Now any prospect of further development has vanished and I'm simply stuck. If I say, "I often feel shy" or "I need some time until I feel comfortable," that's a different story. Then I don't identify with the shyness, which in itself grants me some space.

Using the Enneagram as a tool

The Enneagram is a tool or an aid for developing yourself. You should use it that way. In other words, use it for yourself! As with other tools or techniques of self-development, it occasionally happens that people who grapple with it are primarily interested in changing the people around them. The thing is, no one is happy if they are pushed into something, and any attempt on your part to do so will surely backfire. You can encourage people to join you on your path only if they're already open to further development. The best way to do this is if you become a source of inspiration because others see how you benefit from your method. My mother always told me, "If you want to improve the world, start with yourself." That's what I call "living by the Enneagram."

Dealing with stereotypes

A *stereotype* is created when someone puts a label on people based on biases. Unfortunately, the personality descriptions offered by the Enneagram are well-suited for this purpose: "Now I know your type; now I know who you are." This is a quiet shift in focus: Rather than learn more about the types, you end up seeing other people exclusively as their type. In this respect, here are some examples of such type stereotypes:

> Perfectionists have tidy apartments.

> Your apartment is tidy, so you must be a perfectionist.

Therefore:

You can't be a perfectionist because your apartment is an absolute mess.

I see the internal mechanisms of the Perfectionist type in myself, but my apartment certainly isn't tidy. Yet what's so bad about stereotypes? First, they lead to no good outcome and solve no problems. They're superfluous. Second, they don't let the many small details of the Enneagram type mechanisms come into effect. Certainly, some perfectionists — perhaps even many — have tidy apartments. That's not what this is about. Other types may also prefer a tidy apartment, for different reasons. Perfectionists can keep an apparently messy household because they just don't consider tidiness important or because tidiness doesn't correspond to their sense of order. With stereotypes comes the likelihood of missing the mark.

Finally — and most importantly — stereotypes never do justice to the individual being labeled. No one likes having stereotypical biases attached to them — even if the biases are essentially positive. At a meeting, for example, I was told by a stranger: "What I like so much about you perfectionists is that you hold on to things consistently." This woman didn't know me and still stuck this label on me because she knew something about perfectionists and because my Enneagram type was listed on my name tag. Although I recognize myself in the type mechanism of the Perfectionist, I definitely don't "hold on to things consistently." It's annoying that other people attribute such things to you, especially if the attribution is incorrect or the other person barely knows you.

LETTING GO MEANS DEVELOPING

You developed your personality structure — your type, in other words — as a child because it was important for your development. Without the development of a healthy internal structure, you may find yourself subjected to disorders that reach the point where it isn't possible to act independently in society. At the same time, people tend to exaggerate the characteristics of their type to the point that they become pitfalls and restrictions. Then it's time to free your true self and let it take control. Your type is a false identification. You *have* your type, but you are not your type. What you are is something that will never leave you — you are what you are. If you have something, it stands to reason that you can also let go of it — in every situation, as often and as long as you want. Liberation here means freeing yourself of this identification, thus creating a space for further development.

YOUR DEVELOPMENT IS MORE IMPORTANT THAN YOUR TYPE

Any knowledge about the type mechanisms includes recognition that strengths and weaknesses are type-related. This is why you can predict which strengths you're more likely to see in one type than another. But the nice thing about the Enneagram is that, as a dynamic model, it assumes, and even aims toward, your continued development. Alice, who originally had a type that avoids conflict, can learn to confront others. Stan, whose tendency is to dominate the room, can learn to listen more to others. But some people can also be less characterized by the weaknesses of their types because those who have influenced them already took care to teach them certain concepts in this respect. Margaret, for example, says, "Helping others was important in our family." She demonstrates a lot of Type 2 behavior, although that isn't her own type mechanism. I also often see that people develop in exactly the area representing their greatest weakness and also the weakness that bothers them the most. Because they pay a lot of attention to this weakness, they can also compensate well. For that reason, I always tell people to use the Enneagram with great reservation and caution when it comes to employee recruitment. A person's development and learning capacities are more important than their type.

Using your type as an excuse for your mistakes

Tina recently learned about the Enneagram and discovered that she can see a lot of the Type 3 mechanism in herself, which helps her understand the criticism she used to receive from her project team. That's good, but now she keeps referring to it as an excuse: "I'm sorry for getting impatient, but I'm a 3, after all, and I care about speed" or "I'm sorry that I'm not considerate of your feelings, but, as a type 3, I don't have much talent for this."

It is precisely because you get to know your type and reach more self-awareness that these are no longer excuses for you. Because you now have a deeper insight and have become conscious of your strengths and weaknesses, you also get pointers on where to start developing your strengths and overcoming your weaknesses. Knowing about your type, in other words, is no excuse to stand still with your type's weaknesses and especially not to let them simply run wild.

Don't believe the hype — try it yourself

In the Enneagram tradition, your own experiences are vital — this is not about blindly believing in something. That's why, in the practice described in this book, the focus is on developing your own observational and analytical skills. A good starting point for this task is to not just adopt something out of hand but rather to explore it yourself. You can also find this advice in the Bible: "Prove all things; hold fast that which is good." (1 Thessalonians 5:21). This is the path toward self-awareness and development. Give it a try!

May I Introduce You to My Type?

So that you can develop an image of the nine Enneagram types as quickly as possible, the following sections offer nine summaries of the various internal mechanisms associated with each type.

Type 1: The Perfectionist

Mary is a perfectionist who has (subconsciously) established standards for herself to decide what is acceptable and what is not — to decide how things should be and how they should not. Being furious, for example, is not acceptable. She sees fury as an undesirable emotion and thus suppresses her rage. Instead, Mary is often annoyed — when other people don't behave the way they should or the way it was agreed on or the way you'd expect any responsible adult to act. To make sure that Mary herself knows explicitly that she's behaving properly or doing something well, she sets the bar high. When you do something perfectly, after all, you don't run the risk of being wrong and being criticized, because being criticized definitely bothers Mary. She is so critical toward herself because she sees it as a way to prevent herself from doing something wrong. Her attention is thus directed toward perfectionism and avoiding mistakes. As a result, Mary has a nose for improving whatever can be improved.

Type 2: The Provider

Roy cares a lot about being accepted and appreciated. He achieves this goal by having a strong orientation toward other people and by being considerate toward others (more than toward himself). He has developed a feel for the needs of others in order to better assist them. He notices when someone needs help, and being useful makes him feel good. Roy has developed many talents that he uses to serve others. Many of these talents are in the organizational and social areas. He is active in many groups and committees, at his children's school, at the sports club, and so on. Roy has less talent for accepting anything from anybody, especially if he believes that he didn't earn it first.

Type 3: The Achiever

As a child, Tina already realized how much she enjoys being the center of attention and drawing applause whenever she succeeds at an endeavor. Unconsciously, she arrived at the belief that she is loved for what she does, not for who she is. For this reason, Tina is strongly oriented toward achievements so that she can be successful — the best in every effort. She has also experienced things not improving by themselves but rather because her efforts are needed to bring about a successful conclusion. Tina has developed habits such as working hard, competing, and building up and maintaining a good image. She has a nose for getting into (or creating) situations that bring acclaim. She has a preference for projects because those tend to have a finish line — and a chance of applause at the end. She won't join projects and teams with a low chance of success or where acclaim can be gained only after investing a lot of time and effort. The faster she finishes the items on her list, the sooner she will succeed. That's why Tina likes efficient solutions and efficient work.

Type 4: The Individualist

Tim often has the subliminal feeling of being incomplete, as though something is missing in him and his life. He thus has an unconscious longing for greater fulfillment and for being complete. His attention is drawn to the positive and attractive, to that which he longs for in the future as well as in the past. Tim lives less in the here-and-now because that only bores him and lets him know what he's missing. In his need to be seen, he tends to distinguish himself from others. He often has the sense that others don't understand him. On one hand, this fills him with sadness and loneliness, though on the other hand, he feels superior — as though he is special. After all, he has a lot more depth, which only makes it natural that others can't understand him. At the same time, Tim longs for a deeper connection with others; this is one of the many contradictions that he has to battle internally. He has a distinctive emotional life; he experiences high peaks as well as deep valleys, but this is exactly what gives him the sense that he's living intensely and meaningfully. His mantra is, "I feel; therefore, I am."

Type 5: The Observer

Alice has the need to understand life and people, to get to the bottom of any mystery about them. She is guided by this need because she finds life strenuous and is uncertain how she can participate fully in it. As a child, she was already an outsider, observing social relations, yet not feeling free or uninhibited enough to participate in them spontaneously. By watching how others handled social situations and trying to understand and sort things in her mind, she wanted to control both the situation and herself. Alice has developed the habit of keeping a low profile. When she makes herself less visible, people demand less of her less often. Having knowledge gives Alice the pleasant feeling of being independent of others, which is how she protects herself against intrusive questions and expectations. Her reasoning ability is her most important tool in life, but she doesn't quite know how to handle feelings. They cause unrest and chaos in her mind. Alice loves the seclusion of her room and her apartment. When she feels overwhelmed, she feels the need to withdraw. She likes intellectual problems; facts and figures; and analysis and structural thinking.

Type 6: The Loyal Skeptic

Ian has experienced internal and external insecurity since childhood. He doesn't like unpredictable situations. The prism through which he sees the world lets him sense where the danger lies and where the risks are at any moment. That's why he became accustomed to being vigilant. If you're alert, you see the danger ahead; you're less likely to be caught off-guard. Because of this alertness, Ian often imagines problems where none exists. On a human level, he tends to wait and see. He unconsciously remains suspicious until someone has proven themselves to be trustworthy. The greatest source of the insecurity, by the way, is Ian himself. Deep inside, he has little confidence, let alone self-confidence, which is why he often has doubts — about himself as well as his (yet to be made) decisions.

Type 7: The Optimist

Louise sees herself reflected in the Optimist type. At some point, she learned that life can limit you, take away your freedom, and be painful. Louise doesn't like that. The habits she has developed to deal with this fact-of-life consist of avoiding pain and keeping open many options and possibilities. Even if these options and possibilities exist only as mental images, they still give her a sense of freedom. Louise likes it when life is easy. Her attention is drawn to pleasantness and possibilities. A positive experience that takes place on the way is more important than the destination. Louise often has a full schedule. When she speaks with people, she quickly becomes fascinated by them, and what they say gives her new ideas. Louise thinks that it's more exciting to start things than to finish them, which means it's often hard for her to keep her mind on the matter without being distracted by new and fascinating distractions. Louise is an optimist who immediately sees the positive side of situations. Sometimes, she grows tired and occasionally wishes for a Tune Out button she can press to relax.

Type 8: The Boss/Protector

Stan experienced the schoolyard as a jungle, a place where the strong survive and take charge, at the expense of the weak. So he felt unprotected as a child. He sees the world as tough and unfair. Even before he was ten years old, he decided he would belong to the group of strong kids and protect himself. Fighting is a natural part of Stan's existence, including the battles against the injustices of the world that he finds he cannot accept. He also feels a strong need to protect others, although that need doesn't necessarily extend to everyone. In this regard, he tends to extend his protection only to those he feels actually need help, such as children, animals, the elderly, and the sick. He abhors the victim mentality, where people present themselves as weak and dependent and yet, to Stan's way of thinking, are perfectly capable of taking good care of themselves. He often sees the world in black-and-white terms. He has his own truth and tends to deny or ignore the truth of others. He often comes across as in-your-face and confrontational.

Type 9: The Mediator

Margaret feels good when she can participate in whatever is happening at the moment. Feeling relaxed and in harmony is important to her — more important than her own opinions, her own views, and her own plans, for example. When she is around others, all of these fade into the background for her; she can — temporarily — forget all about them. She isn't aware of this — it just happens. No matter how firmly she sets her mind to doing many things for herself on a Saturday — as soon as a girlfriend calls or her partner makes plans, Margaret's plans are forgotten. She has the great strength of being able to consider many viewpoints and see situations from all sides. Because she avoids confrontations, she already sees a confrontation if she doesn't agree with someone's opinion or suggestion. When that happens, it's easier to follow another person's wish, thus preserving harmony. Given Margaret's habit of quickly acquiescing to others, she has difficulty perceiving what she herself truly wants. She needs space and time away from others to come to herself, find her own point of view, and arrive at what she wants from life.

Numbers, archetypes, names

Keep in mind that the nine personality structures were originally designated with numbers. To make the types easier to recognize, later authors added archetypal interpretations to the numbers, such as the Provider and the Observer. This was intended to make it easier for people to get started with the Enneagram.

In this book, I'm designating these types a bit differently. I've just introduced nine people to you: Mary (Type 1), Roy (Type 2), Tina (Type 3), Tim (Type 4), Alice (Type 5), Ian (Type 6), Louise (Type 7), Stan (Type 8) and Margaret (Type 9).

You'll get to know them even better in this book — they play the lead roles here. When I explain the theory, I write *Type 1*; when I provide an example, I write the nickname, such as *Mary*. This makes it all a little more personal.

REMEMBER

The examples in this book happened in real life, although the nine people and their names are fictitious. Any correspondence with reality is purely coincidental. I don't know any Marys with Type 1 or any Roys with Type 2.

Only the Sun Rises for Free

When you travel, you choose a means of transportation that fits you and your travel plans. If your destination is a sunny island, you take a plane; when you travel to a beach, you probably take a train or car. In my opinion, people who embark on the great adventure of personal or professional development face a similar choice. For this, you also need a means of transportation that you hope will fit you and your journey perfectly. But it's often not that easy to find. Information about biking or riding a train or a plane is generally accessible and the choice is usually easy. When it comes to a means of transportation that helps you with your personal development, however, this often turns into its own journey of discovery. The information isn't as open or clearly available. I see people on this journey of discovery who rush from seminar to workshop, from one method to another, to find a means of transportation that is most suitable for them. I hope that the Enneagram and this book take you to the destination you're aiming for.

From my own experience with others, I know that people like to take the path of least resistance and they prefer to find a quick solution — one that delivers fast and impressive results with little effort. But just like with diets, this is an illusion. Many diets and methods provide a fast, short-term result with low exertion, but this success rarely lasts long. Similar to miracle diets, people try out numerous workshops that often (but definitely not always!) promise effortless, fast results. Deep down, you may also be looking for a magic bullet. And so I want to be honest from the start: If you want to benefit from the true potential of the Enneagram, you won't reach your goal the day after tomorrow.

Working with the Enneagram requires dedication, effort, and perseverance before it gives you what you're looking for. That's why I like the term *internal work*, because it doesn't raise false expectations. But I can say sincerely that your efforts will be rewarded. Many people who took this path before you found out that it may not be the path of least resistance, though it is a lasting investment that has yielded a great return to many people — maybe a happy (or happier) relationship, to name just one example. If that's not worth an investment, I'm not sure what is.

Tips for Optimal Learning

What is the optimal way to learn? In this section, you can find tips that will help you in your studies of the Enneagram and assist you in adopting its method:

>> **Be curious:** Children have an enormous learning capacity. They learn by playing, due to their childish curiosity. From an early age, they inspect everything in the big, strange world in which they've landed. If you discover this childish curiosity in yourself (again), you will learn optimally.

>> **Have an open, receptive mind:** The more baggage you carry around — for example, from studies and experience — the more difficult it can be to maintain an open and receptive mind. Because I am so strongly specialized in the Enneagram, I notice how difficult it is for me to learn new methods. I would rarely succeed in this effort without consciously making myself open and receptive toward it. When you open up to your learning process, you become receptive to new kinds of considerations. Try something new before you instantly reject it — you can always still do that later. When you deal with the learning processes of other people, an open-minded attitude is also necessary to support others with their studies. An open, nonjudgmental attitude is one where you truly listen and let what another person is thinking or writing affect you.

>> **Keep an open, receptive heart:** When it comes to human behavior, learning involves not just the mind but also the heart. Nothing can grow without love, which is certainly true for you as well. You can absorb a lot of knowledge, but if you don't (learn to) look at yourself with leniency, forgiveness, and love, you will hold yourself back. When you deal with the learning processes of other people, this attitude is also necessary to support the others in their studies. An open heart, one filled with empathy, is necessary for you to sympathize with others, understand them, and honestly deal with their existence as human beings and their problems.

>> **Make an effort and apply yourself:** Nothing ever happens on its own. Get to work with this book, complete the exercises, and focus on the text every day. You'll soon notice a result — even if the result is the simple joy of engaging with this topic.

Mental Fitness

Did this section heading make you sigh in frustration? That's how I always feel when I hear the word *fitness*. I know that it's good for me to work out or exercise in some way. Afterward, I always feel better and more energetic. You can look at the idea of internal work in the same way: You're seeking fitness not for the body but rather for the mind and heart — *mental fitness,* in other words.

It goes without saying that people have to exercise and train for their physical well-being; it's no different when it comes to their mental well-being, and this won't happen on its own, either. Get up and join in! As with physical activity, getting started can be tough, but once you get a taste of it, you won't want to stop.

It's better together. See what you think of this idea: Start your mental fitness effort by training with someone else, where you can coach and support each other, such as a colleague, your partner, or a good friend. For me, it's stimulating that my girlfriend reminds me to go to the gym together. After Enneagram workshops, the participants often continue to meet up. In Chapter 5, you'll discover that support from others is a prerequisite for personal development.

Chapter **3**

All Good Things Come in Threes

Nine is the same as three times three,
and we all sing our own song for free.
Three times three is the same as nine,
and Mark, he sings his song just fine.

very person does indeed sing their own song in their life. The Enneagram is structured like this short verse: The nine personality structures are divided into three groups with three types each. The three types in each group have this-or-that in common. This chapter describes the three groups, or *centers.* You'll come across other groups of three in the Enneagram, as spelled out later in this chapter. They lead to ever deeper insights into other aspects of your human self — aspects that I tackle one at a time over the course of this chapter. This inner work helps you peel away your old and battered outer skin just as you would peel off the outer skin of an onion — or, if you'd prefer an image from the Eastern spiritual tradition, this work serves to unveil the true personality within you. With this in mind, this chapter looks at some of the basic points to have under your belt in order to carry out your further studies of the Enneagram as it applies to your own personality.

The Three Little Rules of Behavior

Behavior is clearly visible and can thus be readily observed. But — as you may often hear from other people — a person's behavior is often difficult to interpret, because people act differently in one situation than they do in another. So, behavior depends on the situation. That's why it isn't effective to use behavior as an object of self-observation. After all, it changes from situation to situation. This is why the Enneagram is used to explore what the behavior is based on. It's designed to answer the question, "Why does someone behave in a certain way?" In the Enneagram, that which spurs your behavior is referred to as the unconscious driving force, or underlying motivation. Dr. David Daniels formulated three little rules for determining this driving force or motivation — three rules of thumb you can use when exploring your personality:

>> The energy that drives behavior flows wherever your attention is directed.

>> Managing this attention and energy requires the ability to observe yourself.

>> You can learn self-observation, but it will never become a natural habit.

Recognizing the importance of attentiveness

The word *attention* probably makes you think of getting attention or paying attention — paying attention to your children or your work, for example. People are more or less conscious of this paying attention or getting attention on this level. It's important to pay attention to things that mean something to you. Just think about what happens when you don't pay attention to certain things sufficiently — often, something goes wrong, from the failure of a professional project to problems in a relationship. This is attention in action — be attentive, pay attention, get attention — these are all things people actively do.

The attention I talk about with the Enneagram and in this book refers to the attention inside you — attention at a deeper level. You aren't conscious of it if you don't discover it inside yourself. This attention lies on the level of your hidden drivers — your underlying driving forces and motivations. Here you find the things that you subconsciously and automatically direct your attention toward because you consider them important, even if you aren't aware of the importance you place on them. Exploring this attention and the unconscious goals it focuses on is one of the most important aspects of the Enneagram. One pillar of Enneagram practice is training your attentiveness — also referred to as *mindfulness* nowadays.

Monks who observed themselves throughout decades of meditation and discovered a lot about their interior mechanisms have conveyed the following information:

>> **You can't *not* direct your attention toward something.** Human attention always has a target. People aren't aware of this — it just happens. The "something" that your attention is directed toward is the object of your attention.

>> **Your attention is always directed toward a single object.** Neurobiological research confirms the observations by the monks: In the best-case scenario, you can quickly jump back-and-forth between things so quickly that it looks as though you were directing your attention toward everything at the same time. However, brain research shows that people quickly switch around — you're always directing your attention toward a single thing at a time.

LOVE IS PAYING ATTENTION; PAYING ATTENTION IS LOVE

Paying attention is a way of expressing love. If something or someone is important to you — so important that you can call it love — then this something or person will also be the focus of your attention. The love you express for something or someone can be expressed by specifically paying attention in the form of doing something for the object or person. Sometimes, it's less the activity itself than the way you direct attention to this thing or person. For many people, their own children are certainly the best examples. Studies have shown that a mother can recognize the crying of her own baby among a number of crying children. In the turmoil of a schoolyard, parents immediately find their children. Paying attention consists of truly seeing and truly hearing your child. As a result, the child in turn feels seen and heard. This is love that is expressed in paying attention, and from this attention, you can see the love.

With the Enneagram, this is considered the pure attention that arises from persons being connected to themselves and connecting with others from that position of strength. That's attention on a different level — not doing, but being (conscious attention, in other words). Every healthy person can learn to train the conscious self by developing and paying conscious attention. The first step consists of seeing where your attention is unconsciously directed. Recognizing inside yourself which Enneagram type best describes your patterns of thinking, feeling, and acting offers you a foundation from which to observe the unconscious objects of your attention. Those objects designate the place on which you focus your attention — the place that causes each respective type (and person) the most worry.

Love is paying attention; paying attention is love.

>> **Your attention automatically wanders from one object to the next.** You might have noticed that it seems extremely difficult to keep your attention focused on one object for a prolonged period. As soon as the next object appears, your attention automatically flies toward it. People are distracted — when you keep your attention on one object for a prolonged period, it's called *concentration* — and it requires real training. When you can hold an object (a thing or a person) in your thoughts, and maybe even visualize it, it's called *object constancy*.

Uncovering your underlying driving forces or unconscious motivations

REMEMBER

As reported by people who make an effort to observe and study themselves, each Enneagram type unconsciously and involuntarily has a preferred object that draws that type's attention. The focus of the attention is the core of the type mechanism, forming the foundation of the entire automatic pattern of thinking, feeling, and acting for the respective type. The object that is (unconsciously) considered so important is referred to as the underlying driving force, or unconscious motivation. The Enneagram revolves around getting to know your patterns of attention and exploring your individual emotional programming that ensures that you act reflexively in certain situations. When you react and act on reflex as triggered by your pattern of attention, you are guided by this autopilot mechanism. The aim of working with the Enneagram is to make you conscious of the autopilot and, on the basis of this conscious knowledge, take back control for yourself.

Energy follows attentiveness

During the Holiday season, the house that belongs to Tina (Type 3) is always the most beautifully decorated one on the street. She gets a lot of compliments for it each year, and it makes her feel good. They give her a good feeling, but, unfortunately, it doesn't last long. When the praise has settled, Tina immediately gets the urge to concentrate on something else that will also be applauded — because she has discovered that applause is important to her. Now, you might say: "What is wrong with someone enjoying their efforts to decorate a house for Holiday?" Nothing, of course. I'm a fan of Holiday decorations and you might be, too. But here the question is whether it is done freely — just because it brings joy — or whether it's based on the underlying driving force of the type mechanism. Tina realized that, for her, it's the latter. She sometimes tells herself to maybe do a little less this year, but she has a hard time limiting herself.

This is just one small example of patterns of thinking, feeling, and acting. These three aspects inside you can't be separated from each other. At some point, Tina (unconsciously) started to believe that accomplishments are prerequisites for being seen and loved. This is important to her because the praise makes her feel good. Because it makes her feel good, her attention and energy are unconsciously focused on receiving this applause. This is how thinking and feeling influence each other and are implemented in action — in this case, in an activity intended to attract applause.

Many people like to receive praise, but for some people, like Tina, this need plays an overpowering role in their daily lives. Her antennas for applause, so to speak, are constantly in reception mode. This driving force forms the pattern for her thinking, feeling, and acting and gives her life content. The Enneagram knows nine of these driving forces, each of which forms the foundation of a certain automatic pattern.

REMEMBER

Here's another example: Mary's attention (Type 1) is unconsciously and automatically focused on whether things are correct and appropriate. This is why she immediately notices when something isn't entirely proper or right. She has no trouble zeroing in on precisely what's the matter. As a result, she has a tendency to improve whatever seems awry. Her attention is therefore directed toward showing what is correct and what isn't. Her energy follows that attention and corrects what isn't appropriate. We call this *automatism* — her natural tendency to correct.

REMEMBER

You can see this as Mary's strength, but it's also a weakness. When you ask whether Mary is freely acting this way, you come to the conclusion that she is certainly not free. The corrections are so unconscious and automatic that you could call them compulsive.

Recognizing what holds your attention

It's difficult to start observing yourself when you don't know what to watch for. Tina discovered her most important underlying driving force after using the Enneagram to observe herself for some time and reflecting on her observations. All at once, several things became clear and visible to her. If this is your first encounter with the Enneagram and you're reading the book from the beginning, you might not have a clear idea in which of the nine types you will most recognize yourself. (See Chapter 2 for a review.) No worries: I'll help you take it one step at a time. If your curiosity gets to be too much for you and you want to get a first impression of your type, you can check out on the Internet some of the quick tests for finding out.

REMEMBER

Answering questions and clicking to see a test result won't add much to your self-awareness — and self-awareness is exactly the goal of working with the Enneagram.

Let's start here with the first step. In the left column of Table 3-1, you find a list of aspects you might unconsciously be focusing your attention on. The right column contains examples of where your energy is flowing in such a case. You should also ask: Do you recognize what your attention is automatically drawn to and which things you unconsciously put your energy into?

TABLE 3-1: Attention and energy

Attention Is Focused On This	Energy Is In This
What isn't correct isn't appropriate	Improving, creating order
The needs of others	Giving, helping
Applause, earning points	Reaching goals, completing tasks, achieving something
What's lacking	Comparing yourself with others, longing
The expectations of others	Observing from afar, holding back, and barely getting involved
Threats, risks, dangers	Being alert, recognizing and avoiding risks
What keeps you constrained, what isn't fun	Keeping options and possibilities open, having fun
Vulnerable, the seat of power and strength	Being strong and combative, protecting yourself and others
Disharmony, competing desires, plans, and points of view	Integrating, merging with others, avoiding and preventing conflicts

Managing attentiveness and energy

If you don't see it, you can't manage it. People don't want to see the things that they dislike deep inside. This develops into a habit, as a kind of self-protection, and then they actually *don't* see these things. They become blind spots. So, the first step toward self-management consists of observing yourself closely despite all this. Everyone can acquire this ability to self-observe. Of course, it's easier when you have instructions you can rely on. You learn to systematically question yourself with the goal of interpreting your perception. With this questioning, you recognize that you're observing something, but you ask yourself what is the meaning of what you see? What could it indicate? This systematic questioning is called *self-reflection*; some people also refer to it as an *internal dialogue*.

The descriptions of the Enneagram types function as a kind of mirror. They tell you a lot about the unconscious driving forces and their function. When you look into these mirrors, you will recognize certain things in yourself, but others won't necessarily click. Self-reflection helps make the unconscious conscious.

Self-observation — a natural habit?

Examples of natural habits are eating when you're hungry and sleeping when you're tired. Other habits that have crept into your life, you find so pleasant that you immediately miss them when you deviate from them. These are rituals like taking the dog for a walk or watching a sports program. Self-observation, however, will never become a habit, no matter how much you benefit from it.

On this topic, Georges (or Gregor) Ivanovitch Gurdjieff, who brought the Enneagram to the West, says that people are like robots. They act purely mechanically and are programmed toward automatic reactions. People are sleeping — that's how Gurdjieff expressed it. For the most part, humans aren't aware of themselves, nor of the effect they have on others or the effect of others on them. They mostly lack will and just react. Surviving is a way to react to the environment. Gurdjieff talks about forgetting yourself: Humans even forget their intentions.

Gurdjieff searched for truth all his life, traveling a lot in the process and spending a great deal of time among spiritual groups whose wisdom he explored. The idea of forgetting themselves, their "sleep," can be found in many traditions; Gurdjieff didn't invent it. Buddha, for example, is also referred to as the awakened one. This term describes the various states of being, such as the state of being awake or not being awake. Becoming aware or being aware can be seen as not sleeping. People engage in self-observation and self-reflection when they are suffering but forget them again when they feel good. This is why internal suffering is often associated with the function of waking up again.

Think about some small thing you intend to do — something you've wanted to do every day for a while. It doesn't have to be something useful. This is about the practice itself, about remembering this intention. This exercise is also part of mindfulness training. It helps to associate the intention with a certain time or place.

Maybe these examples will help when you search for your own intention:

>> Consciously smile at your mirror image every morning.

>> Every day before going to sleep, think about a person you love who is absent but whose photo you possess.

>> In the mornings, think about what you're planning for the upcoming day.

Observe how easy or difficult this is for you. It's only about perceiving and noticing it; this is not about a judgment!

Three centers of knowledge

Numerous spiritual traditions, in many places in the world and during various epochs of history, refer to three centers of knowledge: knowledge with the head, with the heart, and with the gut. In Plato's *The Republic* (Book IV, 6-18), he (427-347 BC) briefly describes a human's physical structure: first, the head, home to their thinking capacity, with logical or intuitive reason; second, the chest, "which concerns courage," the potential for inspiration, for heroism, perseverance but also rage; and third, the abdomen, the instincts and passions which are at the service of human nourishment and procreation. When they act according to plan, the associated capacities are called wisdom (head), courage (chest), and moderation (body). These are the three essential human virtues that belong to the head, heart, and gut. There are plenty of deviations from these virtues — vices, in other words. That's because, whereas on one hand, virtue signifies accordance with the developmental laws of humans and this accordance is only possible in one form, on the other hand you have innumerable ways to diverge from this one possible form of accordance — divergences that take the form of vice. (The latter point is taken from Konrad Dietzfelbinger's study *Mystery Schools: From the Ancient Egyptians to the Early Christians to the Rosicrucians of the Modern Age.*)

The nine Enneagram types are distributed to these three centers, in accordance with the three personality structures that act primarily from the head center, three from the heart center, and three from the gut center. People who are intensely involved in self-research have recognized this. The three types in the head center are Types 5, 6, and 7. (They are also referred to in abbreviated form as the head types.) The types in the gut center are Types 8, 9, and 1 — the gut types, in other words. The types in the heart center are types 2, 3, and 4 — the heart types.

The American psychologist Mary Horney (1855-1952) named three methods by which people try to overcome their fears in life: submissiveness (toward others), hostility (toward others), and differentiation (away from others). This corresponds to the Enneagram centers — namely, the heart center (moving toward), gut center (moving against), and head center (moving away). You can see this concept in Figure 3-1.

Just because someone belongs to the heart center doesn't mean that this person has more feelings or is more sensitive than the types aligned with other centers. Nor are the head types more intelligent. The decisive point is that, for the types of a particular center, the respective function (thinking, feeling, acting) is predominant and plays a significant role in the type mechanism in one way or another. An imbalance generally occurs between thinking, feeling, and acting. You should explore the centers and recognize them because they offer a reference point for self-observation. It often helps your development if you create more balance among your various centers.

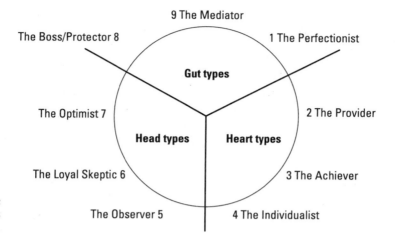

9 The Mediator

The Boss/Protector 8

1 The Perfectionist

Gut types

The Optimist 7

2 The Provider

Head types **Heart types**

The Loyal Skeptic 6

3 The Achiever

The Observer 5

4 The Individualist

FIGURE 3-1:
The three centers
of knowledge.

HEAD TYPES

The head types (5, 6, 7) are all directed toward understanding and explaining, analyzing, and developing practical ideas and concepts. Keep in mind that everyone sees the world primarily through some kind of mental filter. For the three head types, that filter lies in the value they place on independence, each in their own way. They also share an inclination to differentiate themselves (moving away). When something unsettling happens, for example, they tend to move away. The goal of this unconscious strategy is to minimize worries, gain control of potentially painful situations, and thus gain a sense of safety. This is carried out via the mental processes of deliberation, projection, conception, and planning.

REMEMBER

The head types often have a subliminal sense that something isn't right. This can (literally or figuratively) be a lack of space, safety, or freedom. This sense of lack can also be directed against oneself: feeling that you aren't good enough or thinking of yourself as incompetent or as a social-emotional failure. However, this perception might be quite far from reality.

EXAMPLE

The apartment where Alice (Type 5) lives is virtually a library. She reads four or five lengthy books each week. The people around her consider her to be an educated, intelligent person. Alice herself sees this differently. With everything that she reads and learns, she also discovers how much more still remains to read and learn. In the process, she finds out that she doesn't know enough of what one could know during one's lifetime and in the world.

GUT TYPES

The gut types (8, 9, 1) are either all focused on physical aspects, on activities, or on action or are focused on the exact opposite. They react to impulses and are either quite physically active and present or (again) not active or present at all.

They see the world through a filter of physical perceptions and unreflective instincts.

Gut types have an innate talent when it comes to listening to their bodies. Thoughts are experienced in the head, feelings in the heart, and perceptions in the body. These can be pleasant perceptions, such as the sun on the skin or the warmth of a touch, but also less enjoyable ones, like tension. The gut types value their autonomy, each in their own way. They share an inclination toward confrontation (moving against). When something happens, they have a tendency to fight it. Gut types use their personal position and strength to shape life the way it must be. They develop strategies to secure their place in the world and minimize unpleasantness. The idea of borders is a significant (unconscious) thematic for them, in the sense that they either don't actually experience boundaries or are unaware of their own boundaries.

Internally, gut types often experience a subliminal sense of resistance, especially when their (unconscious) boundaries are crossed. This resistance can be expressed in ways that seem either steadfast, passive-aggressive, or controlling. Just as the head types share a subliminal feeling of a lack or of personal failure, the three gut types often feel worthless or guilty because of some failure on their part. This is why their goal is often to be of value to others.

EXAMPLE

Stan (Type 8) instinctively perceives who has power. He wants to measure himself against that person, to pick a fight to garner respect and to see how they stand in relation to each other. This fight lets Stan experience his own strength, and that feels good. It makes him feel alive. When the situation calls for it, Stan can literally make himself bigger and stronger. And when he does that, the people in his surroundings often make themselves smaller. When he perceives his own power and strength, the danger exists that Stan no longer senses the power and strength of others. He underestimates his opponent, and this has caused him difficulties more than once.

HEART TYPES

The heart types (2, 3, 4) are all focused on themes of the heart: love, relationships, affection, the social environment, the people around them. They perceive the world through the filter of emotional intelligence. The three heart types value recognition, each in their own way. They want to pay attention or gain attention and be seen doing so. They like moving toward people. The strategy of heart types consists of adapting to the moods and feelings of others to gain a sense of connection with the other person. More than the other types, they trust and lean on appreciation and respect from others to maintain their sense of self-esteem and to feel loved. To preserve this appreciation and respect, they create an image of themselves that is meant to persuade others to accept them and see them as special. They are focused on a connection with others, on relationships.

This doesn't mean that heart types are always successful when it comes to making this connection. With their focus on relationships, they clearly perceive any lack of unity. They are oriented toward others and view themselves through the eyes of others; they imagine how others see them, what they think about them. For that reason, every heart type is interested in their image in a certain way and in making sure others don't end up having a bad image of them.

REMEMBER

Heart types often have a tendency to feel ashamed precisely because they always have their antennas up for how others see them.

EXAMPLE

Tim (Type 4) avoids goodbyes. He often leaves without even saying goodbye, for example. To him, the moment of leaving a beloved person feels as though they were being torn apart. He perceives the other person as a part of himself. The feeling of having a deep connection with the other is what keeps him alive. The moment that such a connection ends can therefore feel as though Tim's life itself were ending and he no longer has air to breathe.

The Rule of Threes

The *rule of threes* refers to the forces that are part of all processes. In many spiritual traditions, this rule is considered one of the universal laws of the cosmos, similar to Newton's third law of motion: For every action in nature, there is an equal and opposite reaction. The natural sciences define force as "everything that can change the speed of a body." The forces themselves are invisible, but humans experience their effect. Forces also have the energy to accomplish and complete something — to change the speed of a body, for example. As humans, we are part of the cosmos, so the universal laws also apply to us. Gurdjieff claims that each phenomenon is the result of three forces, but that nowadays people perceive and recognize only two of these laws. As examples of the two forces we know — forces that illustrate quite well our polar way of thinking — he cites the pairs negative-positive, action-reaction, male-female, yin-yang. Gurdjieff, for his part, thinks that a third force is always needed to bring anything into being.

Assume that two people have a difference of opinion. One shouts out "No!" while the other shouts "Yes!" If no third force intervenes, they will continue to shout "No! Yes! No! Yes!" because they're stuck in their positions. Nothing can set them in motion. And, as a result, nothing changes. Now suppose that a third person joins them, who neutralizes the "No! Yes!" and, for example, offers a creative solution, one that is acceptable for both "No!" and "Yes!" Only then does something happen.

Let's see what all the shouting is about:

>> **Active force:** active, positive, giving, male.

>> **Receptive force:** passive, negative, receptive, female.

>> **Reconciling force:** unifying, neutral, connecting, impartial.

Consider the famous Serenity Prayer:

> *God, grant me the serenity to accept the things I cannot change, the courage to change the things I can, and the wisdom to know the difference.*

You can find many versions of this prayer, though its origin and author are unclear. It's attributed to many people, from the emperor/philosopher Marcus Aurelius (121-180 AD) to St. Francis of Assisi to Nelson Mandela. The most likely explanation is that it was written by the theologian Reinhold Niebuhr (1892-1971) between 1937 and 1943.

This prayer can also be considered an example of the rule of threes. Here the active force is "to change what I can change," and the receptive force is "to accept what I cannot change." You can probably imagine what these two refer to. The third force is the reconciling force of consciousness or awareness. You can only evaluate the first two forces to know which to apply when you place them side-by-side. Humans perceive light because there is darkness, and vice versa. They think in comparisons; you can see differences by placing contrasts next to each other. The third force is needed to find and perform the right action. Back to the prayer: If you can't differentiate what you can and can't change, neither can you decide what would be the right course of action (changing things or accepting them).

It's helpful to research and recognize these three forces in themselves. If you want to keep developing but aren't making progress, only one or two forces are likely working inside you. In Gurdjieff's teaching, the desire for development is considered an active force, and the resistance of the ego (which doesn't want development) or the dormant state of the normal mental condition is the passive force. If only these two are present, it's true that nothing will change, exactly as in the "No! Yes!" argument. The resistance of the ego literally swallows up any energy there might be to become active. This leaves little energy left for growth. Self-management can also be referred to as energy management. You can learn to manage your energy so that you have enough energy available for further development and spiritual growth. Gurdjieff offers interesting lessons for the West on this topic as well. He writes that, in this regard, the unconscious has as many holes as a sieve and lets people's energy flow into all kinds of things. One example is speaking. It can be a leisurely activity, but also something that deprives you of a lot of energy. Have you ever experienced how tired you are after a phone call or a meeting? As if you were drained? According to Gurdjieff, you should see this as literally true. Is that bad? Not in itself, if speaking has brought you what you wanted. But have you also ever felt that you were completely exhausted and seen everything as a waste of time and energy?

REMEMBER

Your energy is like money: You can only spend it once. Energy that was wasted on useless chatter is no longer available to you for more important things — for yourself, for your development, for the people you care about. If your development is important to you, you need energy management. There's a good reason that the practice of many spiritual traditions includes being in silence. This allows you to return to yourself, save your energy, and recharge it.

Let's look one more time at the rule of threes. In the Enneagram, it's pictured as a triangle linking Types 3, 6, and 9. Point 3 stands for the active, positive force; point 6, for the receptive, negative force; and point 9, for the neutralizing, connecting force. This also corresponds to the characters and energy forms of people with types 3, 6, and 9.

In anticipation of my discussion of the spiritual aspects of the Enneagram (see Chapter 17), I list the higher or sacred virtues of these three types in Figure 3-2: faith, hope, and love. It's no coincidence that these virtues, praised by St. Paul in his First Letter to the Corinthians, are also an example of the rule of threes. (See? You've known about this rule of threes all along!)

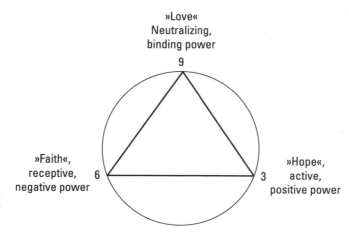

FIGURE 3-2: The rule of threes.

For St. Paul, the virtues of faith, hope, and love stand for something greater than these three words usually do in everyday language. The higher virtue of love is the greatest of all virtues: It comes first for Type 9, where the circle begins and ends. The Enneagram instructor and Franciscan priest Richard Rohr considers the holy virtues as an invitation from God, an offer of the unifying power of love, an offer to become receptive to faith, and an offer to hope actively and positively.

On the Path to Inner Freedom

The goal of working with the Enneagram is to discover your internal autopilot. When we know your personality structure, it's easier for you to consider this autopilot from the perspective of your internal observer. You can discover your personality structure on your own, but when you use the nine designs of the Enneagram, you can save some effort and get to know yourself much faster and more thoroughly. Your next step is to learn the basics of self-reflection — that internal dialogue with yourself that you use to interpret what has taken place inside of you. Then comes the challenge of being able to let go of your type as soon as it switches to autopilot. The path of inner freedom leads to personal mastery. For you, personal mastery means being alert, present, conscious, and in control of what is inside yourself.

Chapter **4**

Discovering Your Type

his chapter spells out an aspect of the Enneagram that will undoubtedly stimulate your imagination: getting to ask the question "Which type do I have?" Yes, the typology of the Enneagram does stimulate the imagination, but the goal here isn't just to find your type. Rather, it's to become more self-aware. Determining your type on your own is the way to go. The moment you recognize yourself in a type, you have already gained self-awareness. You can use some additional methods, such as various questionnaires, to help in this search as you determine your own type. In this chapter, you can find out everything you need to know in order to discover your own type, including information about type interviews and other aids for self-exploration.

Why Type Yourself?

Imagine a youth scouting group performing an outdoor exercise. The group has been dropped off in a wildlife area and have to find their way home. They have various aids for this purpose, including nine maps of various regions, and they first have to find out which map represents the surrounding area. The scouts initially study Map 1 for certain landmarks and then try to find them nearby. Map 1, however, is a nautical chart, so it isn't the one they need. Maps 2 and 3 depict cities, and the scouts are in the woods. After completing this initial process of elimination, four maps remain, all of which represent rural regions.

Eliminating the first five maps in this example is the easy part; now the second (and more difficult) round begins. The scouts now have to examine the nature areas on the maps and compare them with what they see nearby. In the end, they determine that one map fits their surroundings exactly. Using that map, they can quickly find their way home.

When you're looking at the right map, you can find your way much more quickly and easily. With the Enneagram, you distinguish nine different personality structures, each with its own development path. A characteristic that one type should deal with — a habit that should be acquired or discarded, for example — doesn't necessarily fit with another type. When you find your type, you also gain a valuable guide to what you personally should focus on.

Working with Types

At the point where you know which type you are, someone always asks: "Is it true that you have only one of these types?" Indeed, some Enneagram movements and trainers believe that each person has several types. They back up this belief with the logic of the quote "[N]othing human can be alien to me," borrowed from the Roman poet and dramatist Terence (195-159 BC). I'm inclined to share this opinion: Whatever emotion humans can experience internally — fear, anger, love, and joy, for example — are ones that I have also experienced, and you probably have too.

Other Enneagram authors believe that people can have several types because they're capable of developing the strengths of all types internally. I also share this positive perspective. People can learn about all this and develop it, yet such an expansive view isn't the essence — the crucial analytical level — of the Enneagram. Humans carry only one personality structure inside them that's at the level of the type mechanism.

For example, although I have occasionally experienced fear, I'm definitely not someone whose entire personality structure is built on fear and how to handle it. I experience true fear maybe once or twice per year. I remember an incident, some time ago, when someone suddenly stepped on the brakes on the expressway in front of me and I panicked.

For someone whose interior structure is based on fear, the fear and how to deal with it are daily companions. Fear is the essence of that person's pattern of thinking, feeling, and acting. The fact that I too occasionally feel fear is different from having this type structure. For many people, the belief that they simply have to have more than one type stands in the way of their development. My colleague

Hannah Nathans responds to this belief this way: "My eyes have only one color and I'm a woman (and not also a man), and if I don't dye my hair, it has one color for an entire lifetime. The truth is, the way that nature made us consists of limitations." Personally, I'm glad that I have only one type, because developing myself with the weaknesses of this type is already enough of a challenge. But I think it's nice that I can very well practice and develop the strengths of the other types.

Keep the following points in mind:

>> As you soon realize when you meditate, your attention can always be directed toward only one thing at a time. Humans unconsciously have a dominant preference for certain objects that draw their attention. This is the foundation and essence of the type mechanism.

>> The fact that you can develop all strengths inside yourself — that you have a development *prospect,* in other words — says nothing about your Enneagram type or where you're coming from. All types can certainly learn just about anything, but each type still has different things to learn. So the fact that you can learn something says nothing about the strengths you carry inside based on your type. Learning things doesn't turn you into another type. You still retain your own type mechanism, but continue to develop and, as a result, you don't let your type box you in.

>> "Nothing human can be alien to me" means that people can experience every human impulse. And it's true. All Enneagram types can experience anger and become angry, for example. But this isn't what the type mechanisms or the differences between the individual types are about.

In the end, imagine that the scout group would try to find their way home using only three maps. Would this lower number of maps help them? Would it be quicker? The essence of the Enneagram consists of making the development path more efficient.

Knowing which type you have

I certainly believe that you know best which type you have. After all, only you can look inside yourself. Only you can observe what you think, feel, and experience, for example. You might not yet know all about the Enneagram and the nine types, but when you receive the information you need, from this book or from a study course, you're sure to find your own type.

Finding your type isn't difficult. The Enneagram offers nine templates that you can use as a mirror. You look at every template and then ask yourself whether this might be the mechanism you recognize in yourself. So you move from one map to the next and determine which map fits you best. You observe yourself and ask, "Which part of this do I recognize in myself?" Then you begin a discussion with yourself, using the *inner dialogue*, or *self-reflection.* The Enneagram makes a point of offering many guidelines for self-observation and reflection because, when you start on the journey of discovering your own type, you also immediately start training and encouraging these two important skills on the way to further development. Maybe this inner dialogue already helps you discover the Enneagram type in which you see yourself reflected more than in the others. When you recognize yourself, you'll know your Enneagram type, yes, but more importantly, you'll have discovered and experienced things about yourself. You'll be more conscious of certain aspects of yourself and will have gained self-awareness.

Finding your own type means becoming active yourself

WARNING

When you do something yourself, you also learn something afterward — that's why you don't gain much when someone tells you that you have Type 1 or a questionnaire shows that you have Type 3. What does this info actually tell you? Maybe you *have* Type 1 and will now further explore yourself and learn something from it. In practice, however, I often notice that people to whom a type has been assigned by a third party don't do anything further with the info. After they know which type they have, why continue exploring?

Respecting every step of the journey

Here's another reason not to let other people assign you a type: One aspect of the Enneagram that appeals to me is the great respect this practice has for others. You broaden your perspective of "being other" and develop an understanding of it; and then you develop respect for the fact that everyone chooses and takes their own path, and for every development process taking its own shape and being unique. Above all, you acknowledge that each person is at a different stage of development and that none is better than the other. In my classes, I often ask the participants: "A baby is at the beginning of its life and still has to learn everything. Do you have less respect for the baby and the development stage that it's in? Do you love the baby less because it still has to learn everything?" On the contrary. That's exactly why humans think babies are wonderful.

Getting started

EXAMPLE

Your first step when it comes to finding out what your attention primarily focuses on — seeing what unconscious driving force or underlying motivation is responsible for your automatic habits — consists of questioning yourself.

Task 1: Take an inventory of your characteristics

You already have an image of yourself — an idea of how you act in life and what your strengths and weaknesses are in your job and your relationships. The first task on this journey of discovery is to write down three of your general characteristics, as shown in Table 4-1. Then ask two people who know you well whether they also see you the same way, what they see differently, and which characteristics they would add.

TABLE 4-1:

Write Down Your Characteristics

	What I See	What Person 1 Sees	What Person 2 Sees
Characteristic	1.	1.	1.
Characteristic	2.	2.	2.
Characteristic	3.	3.	3.

REMEMBER

In your continued work, when you determine which type mechanism fits you best, you may later notice that the characteristics entered here are less random than you might now believe. They are quite likely connected to your type!

Task 2: Recognize the archetypes

As you can read in later chapters, the Enneagram has different movements and instructors. Many of them have given names to the individual types. As a result, each type has different names in the literature. This is an attempt to express the essence of, or the most important characteristic of, a type. It can happen, of course, that different instructors each find another aspect of the type so important that they use it as a name. So the labels don't necessarily coincide, though the descriptions mostly remain the same.

Some people may already develop an idea of their type when they recognize themselves in a certain name. You use the different names for the Enneagram types as archetypes for finding your type. In Figure 4-1, you see boxes with designations for the various types. Ask yourself these questions:

>> Is there one or more box in which you (strongly) recognize yourself?

>> Are there boxes in which you don't recognize yourself, which you can exclude from the start?

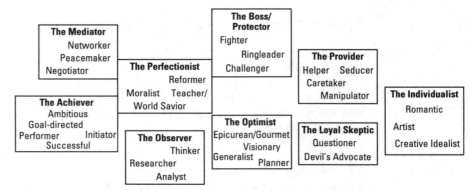

FIGURE 4-1:
Do you recognize
yourself?

The Mediator
Networker
Peacemaker
Negotiator

The Achiever
Ambitious
Goal-directed
Performer   Initiator
Successful

The Perfectionist
Reformer
Moralist   Teacher/
World Savior

The Observer
Thinker
Researcher
Analyst

The Boss/
Protector
Fighter
Ringleader
Challenger

The Optimist
Epicurean/Gourmet
Visionary
Generalist   Planner

The Provider
Helper   Seducer
Caretaker
Manipulator

The Loyal Skeptic
Questioner
Devil's Advocate

The Individualist
Romantic
Artist
Creative Idealist

Task 3: Recognize that strengths are easier to see

It's difficult to observe what your attention focuses on, especially when you're only starting out with the Enneagram. Recognizing your strengths is much easier. The strengths of the individual Enneagram types are no accident. They originate from the focus of a type's attention and their energy. The respective type considers these goals important and works on them. Accordingly, strengths in this area develop seemingly on their own. So the task for the self-observation is to read the nine strength descriptions in Table 4-2 and ask yourself these questions:

>> Is there one or more box in which you (strongly) recognize yourself?

>> Are there boxes in which you don't recognize yourself and can exclude from the start?

TABLE 4-2:   ## Do You Recognize Your Strengths?

Strong, forceful, determined, assertive, protective of others, virtuous, truthful, clear, to the point, firm	Openhanded and eager to help, generous, romantic, sensitive, appreciative, supportive, energetic, lively, expressive, obliging, tenacious	Educated, intellectually curious, aware, deliberative, calm in the face of crisis, respectful, "live and let live," reliable, ascetic, appreciates the simpler things, honors confidentiality
Honorable, careful, responsible, industrious, idealistic, independent, dedicated, makes an effort, does the right thing, holds high standards	Sensitive, empathetic, intense, passionate, idealistic, has a unique point of view, appreciates uniqueness, honors creative possibilities	Positive, inventive, imaginative, energetic, optimistic, inspiring, enthusiastic, loves life, recognizes intriguing possibilities
Thoughtful, warm, loyal, intuitive, sensitive, perceptive, honorable, has a good sense of humor, trusting of intimates	Quiet, adaptive, supportive, predictable, reliable, sensitive, stable, receptive, seldom judgmental, looks out for others	Efficient, goal- and solution-oriented, enthusiastic, ambitious, encouraging, practical, competent, holds strong leadership qualities

Task 4: See what your attention is focused on

You focus your attention on what's most important to you at an unconscious level — which might objectively *be* the most important. This is the *unconscious driving force*, or *underlying motivation*. It isn't easy at first glance to detect what lies behind this force, especially not in yourself. The question, however, is how are you supposed to be able to see something that's unconscious — a mental blind spot? How do you recognize the unconscious driving force behind an automatic habit? Start by looking in the mirror — the mirror represented by the boxes in Table 4-3 — and ask these questions:

>> Is there a box, or boxes, in which you (strongly) recognize yourself?

>> Are there boxes in which you don't recognize yourself that you can exclude from the start?

TABLE 4-3: **Where Do You Focus Your Attention?**

I focus on others — their plans, wishes, and points of view or anything else that distracts me; on keeping the peace; and on (not) being seen.	I focus on having power and control, fighting (in)justice, protecting others (all or nothing, the truth), and being able to gain or grant respect.	I focus on attractiveness in the future or in the past, elements of my life that I'm missing or separated from, desire and connectedness, and not being rejected.
I focus on the wishes and needs of others, being needed, being attentive and available, reciprocating, and being nice to others.	I focus on distinguishing between right and wrong, determining what can be improved and what has to stay the same, and being clear, careful, and responsible.	I focus on achieving a goal, carrying out efficient solutions, making myself invaluable to others, being the best person I can be, seeing myself through the eyes of others, and gaining the recognition I deserve.
I focus on rational solutions; knowledge to be gained; and facts, analyses, and (hidden) expectations that others may have of me, my time, and my energy.	I focus on what can go wrong or pose a danger; on drawbacks, risks, and secret plans; and on whom I can trust.	I focus on interesting, appealing, and positive ideas, options, possibilities, and projects; on fascinating concepts; and on any new beginning.

Finding an anchor to act as your type's good foundation.

The difficult part of finding your type is learning to interpret what you perceive. In determining your dominant type pattern, the important aspect is the degree to which you, for example, value perfection as a Type 1 and the extent to which that limits your freedom to act.

Christina is glad that her presentation turned out perfect and she earned the highest possible grade. But simply having created a perfect presentation and being happy about the good grade doesn't turn her into the Perfectionist Enneagram type. Most people appreciate a good evaluation of their work, including Christina. She didn't strive to create a perfect presentation and certainly didn't aim to earn the top grade. Nor did she work on it excessively. She isn't driven by outside success. The grade is the result of her simply having fun with the presentation. That Christina is capable of creating a perfect presentation doesn't make her an Enneagram Type 1, the Perfectionist.

Spending a great deal of time working on a presentation can likely be done only by someone whose attention is so focused on perfection that they can't stop as long as they see anything that can still be improved. The Perfectionist group includes people to whom perfection is the top priority and whose focus is therefore continually (at least several times a day) directed toward things that aren't good (enough) and must be improved on. Someone who simply delivers a perfect performance, like Christina in the example in this section, doesn't belong to the Enneagram Type 1 only because of this achievement. To determine whether you belong to this Enneagram type, you need to consider whether your attention is directed mainly toward perfection and improvement. Conversely, it's just as possible that someone has this Enneagram type but isn't actually capable of achieving perfect performances. What matters are the underlying driving force and the desired goal — not the actual implementation.

Finding your type can lead to various complications. If such complications were to occur, the support of an Enneagram trainer might help. Here are a few examples:

>> **Two types can show the same behavior or be similar to each other in certain respects.** You recognize yourself in this behavior but can't find out the underlying reason in your case.

>> **People who belong to the same type can appear differently to the outside world.** They might then recognize themselves in the type description but not in other people of the same type.

>> **You have acquired and discarded all sorts of habits in your life.** Maybe you were raised by parents who were of different types from you but conveyed their strengths to you. This makes it difficult to recognize what is actually at the core of your being and what you've acquired.

>> In books about the Enneagram, including this one, the individual types are described only in summary, which expresses the lowest common denominator of that type. The books present an average version of this type, so to

speak. This isn't really possible any other way because every type shows a great variety. If such books are to remain readable and fulfill their goals, the authors have to limit themselves by focusing on the common denominators rather than the exceptions. Reality has many more layers, and your version of the type can vary greatly from the average.

Working with Enneagram tests

In the world of the Enneagram, you will find many different analyses and many kinds of tests. Tests often appear in the questionnaire format, though they don't have to be that way. You'll also find others, such as the Stanford Enneagram Discovery Inventory and Guide (or *SEDIG test*), by Dr. David Daniels and Virginia Price.

Short but sweet

The good thing about the SEDIG test is that self-observation plays a role. As a result, the execution itself can contribute to your growing self-awareness. This simple test represents a first encounter with the Enneagram — a first bit of help on the way to finding your type, in other words. The SEDIG test is short and convenient, which is why many Enneagram trainers use it as an introduction in their workshops. After you get to discuss a short text about each type, you're asked in which one you most recognize yourself.

REMEMBER

The SEDIG test has been validated. When you recognize yourself in a type based on this test, you learn the likelihood of being this type and the likelihood that you will turn out to be another type in the end.

Measuring means knowing

You'll find on the Internet many Enneagram tests made up of a series of questionnaires. Some are good, and some are not-so-good. The goal is to distinguish one from the other. Psychology has developed in a direction in which tests are highly valued, where people apply the principle "Measuring means knowing." Psychology has also developed a heavily medicinal perspective, in which the right diagnosis matters. When it comes to physical illnesses, doctors need a diagnosis that's as precise as possible in order to determine the right treatment. The same applies to psychologists and psychiatrists. Testing and learning how to diagnose play a big role in psychological studies. Tests were developed to minimize, as much as possible, the risk of an incorrect diagnosis.

Good and not-so-good questionnaires

The test methods used in psychology offer the following reference points for recognizing a good questionnaire or creating your own:

>> **The test needs to test what it's supposed to test.** For the Enneagram, this means that the questions aim to research the underlying driving forces and the object of one's attention, not one's behavior.

>> **The questions avoid stereotypical images of a type.** The true goal is to also get the existing fine gradations and various manifestations of each type.

>> **The questions consider the differences that occur on the basis of the personal development status within the individual types.** Someone who is in a state that isn't spiritually healthy responds differently from someone who is in an average healthy state.

>> **The questionnaire considers the often unconscious tendency to provide socially desirable answers.** Rather than say what is really true for them, people sometimes say instead what they *wish* were true.

>> **The questions are worded so that they can effectively differentiate between types.** That means that the people who have a certain type have to be able to recognize themselves in the questions and that the people who don't have this type don't recognize themselves. The questions thus can't be too general or apply to excessively large groups of people. The question "Do you want to be popular among others?" aims toward a frequently occurring desire and thus isn't suitable for differentiating between Enneagram types.

>> **The questions differentiate according to the extent to which certain characteristics occur.** I have experienced fear now and then, for example, but I definitely don't see myself in the Enneagram type that's almost continuously dominated by a subliminal feeling of insecurity.

>> **The design of the test offers categories for answers from which you can clearly choose.** You aren't forced to choose between two statements in which you either don't see yourself at all or you see yourself in both.

>> **The test needs to test what it's supposed to test and gradually allows a congruent image to emerge.** The test delivers exactly one Enneagram type as a result, and if that's the correct one, it also appears as a result in the next one.

I could easily continue this list, especially if I were to also consider the scientific requirements for such tests, but that discussion doesn't belong in this book.

A few notes on the side

Like many of my colleagues and course participants, I've completed numerous Enneagram tests on the Internet multiple times. The result I received often wasn't the type in which I recognize myself. The same tests yielded different results at different times, although I hadn't become another person in the meantime. My colleagues and course participants report similar experiences — none of us would have found our Enneagram types by using these tests. Answering questionnaires is confusing to many people because they don't recognize themselves in the outcome or because a different result appears each time.

REMEMBER

When you answer a questionnaire, you easily, quickly, and playfully form a first impression — no more. Consider it a first step and keep in mind what you read about the essence of the Enneagram here: *The goal is self-awareness.* Train your capacity for self-observation and reflection, and learn to trust your perception and your judgment. Only you can observe and evaluate your inner self and determine which pattern corresponds most closely to you. Don't let various tests confuse you!

Chapter **5**

The Enneagram and the Narrative Tradition

In Chapter 4, I introduce ways to find your own type by showing you things you can do on your own: observing yourself or taking a test. In this chapter, you'll find out about two specific methods in the narrative tradition that you can use to gain knowledge and insight: the type assessment interview and the panel interview. You'll find out how they work and how you can benefit from them. Trust me: You can certainly gain important insights about yourself with the help of the type assessment interview and the panel interview. These methods were also originally used to gain insights about the nature of people and how this nature corresponds to the Enneagram types. (These methods are in fact how the Enneagram pioneers acquired their knowledge of the types.) This chapter starts with gathering and sharing knowledge in general, and then moves on to talk about the type assessment interview and the panel interview in greater detail.

Sharing the (Knowledge) Wealth

From ancient philosophers to modern science, observation and reflection have been, and still are, the recognized methods for gaining knowledge. Biologists go into the field to observe nature, anthropologists travel the world (by way of organizations) to study how people live in groups, astronomers observe outer space, and so on. The main idea is this: Look, look, and look again. But observation alone isn't enough. The philosophers also contemplated the thinking process itself and how one actually acquires knowledge.

Gathering knowledge in the narrative tradition

The monk Evagrius Ponticus (345-399 AD) was a scientist before the fact: He described how he explored the interior of the human mind. He regularly questioned other monks about their progress in the area of meditation and the obstacles they encountered. Using this qualitative study, he discovered the eight obstacles to peaceful meditation and labeled them *vices*, or emotionally charged thoughts. He observed that one monk was often disturbed by feelings of lust during his prayer, and another monk, more by pride. These vices are still differentiated in the Enneagram; they can even be considered cornerstones of the personality structure. The method used by Evagrius to acquire knowledge — namely, via interviews — is still practiced today when working with the Enneagram.

Helen Palmer primarily opts for this method (also in her seminars), and she calls it the *narrative tradition:* It's based on seeing people as experts for their own type. They themselves are best able to tell what they're like on the inside, how they see and experience things, and why they react the way they do. This is the most important source of knowledge about the types. Since the 1970s, when Palmer started her study groups, she has made audio recordings of panel interviews, and thousands of hours of material form the basis of her book *The Enneagram: Understanding Yourself and the Others in Your Life.* The same is true, by the way, of the examples I use in this book: The names are fictitious, but the stories are true.

Spreading knowledge in the narrative tradition

The panel interviews originated as a method to gather knowledge about the Enneagram types. Having panel audiences quickly proved to be an inspiring and instructive method for learning more about the types. This method turned out to be useful for learning new things, for both the study leader and the participants.

Enneagram trainers can, of course, explain all nine types (and talk endlessly about them). As experts, they have many interesting things to say. Enneagram trainers also have their own type — only on the basis of this type can Enneagram trainers share stories from within themselves and describe what life is like with Type X. Even the best trainer can't talk about the other eight types from their own, internal experience — they can only lecture about them. There's always a difference between an expert's explanation and an eyewitness report provided by someone about their own type. When people talk about themselves, their words are accompanied by their own facial expressions, aura, posture, and other characteristics. All this info often provides just as much information and insight into a type as the narrative itself, which makes the type easy to recognize and the story valuable. The narrative tradition has no abstract type definitions — you get the complete image of a real person of each type.

Working with type assessment interviews

People have to do a lot on their own when they work with the Enneagram. Can't everyone help each other? They certainly can. This prerequisite is one of four involved in personal development. (For more on people helping each other, see Chapter 15.) I mention one way people can help each other in Chapter 4, in the first task listed: asking someone else for feedback. This task revolves around the question "How do you see me?" or "Which words would you use to describe me?" Acquiring this kind of information can expand your self-awareness, which already becomes evident when people around you are bothered less (or not at all) by your blind spots.

A second option is to carry out a type assessment interview with a specially trained Enneagram coach. Your regular circle of friends and acquaintances can certainly help you find the information you need, but the task becomes more difficult when it comes to interpreting that information, especially if your circle doesn't know much about the Enneagram. A coach can help you with your self-reflection and help you interpret the information and insights you've collected about yourself using the Enneagram. To carry out this work, a coach has learned that, rather than consider an individual's behavior, they should assess the underlying layer of that person's type mechanism.

What is a type assessment interview?

In a *type assessment interview,* an Enneagram coach helps you recognize your Enneagram type. In effect, it's a diagnostic consultation. As indicated by the name, the coach interviews you. To start, this person asks a series of questions, mainly to determine which of the nine types can be clearly ruled out. The imaginary scouting group I talk about in Chapter 4, in their attempt to find the correct map to set them on the path toward home, categorically excluded all maps that showed terrain other than a nature landscape. A type assessment interview works the same way: Certain types can be quickly eliminated from the list of possible results. A second round of questions follows, targeted to those types that remain. These questions dig deeper and require you to observe yourself more and more closely. The Enneagram coach helps you see things more clearly by using a host of methods, most of which involve a large number of examples. You also must answer a recurring question about the degree to which you recognize something.

A type assessment interview is an intense discussion whose effects can last for days. It encourages contemplation as well as talks with your partner or friends. In many cases, such an interview yields new insights, even days later.

Doing your own type assessment interviews

If you want to learn how to conduct type assessment interviews, for your job or other reasons, I recommend that you complete a relevant course of studies. I was instructed by Helen Palmer and David Daniels by way of their Enneagram Professional Training Program. In Parts 5 and 6 of this book, you can find further information about interview training.

Doing panel interviews

A *panel interview* is another important method in the narrative tradition. Here's how it works: A panel interview includes audience members and a panel of between two and five people who recognize in themselves the same Enneagram type. The Enneagram trainer interviews the participants on the panel about various everyday topics: how they see certain events, what they think about them, and how they experience and react to various situations. The panels for all nine types are asked the same questions, and each panel answers completely differently.

BUT YOU'RE THE ONE DRAWING THE CONCLUSIONS

Enneagram coaches accompany you on your search by asking questions and reflecting on your answers. They help with the interpretation. They don't present you with a conclusion in the form of a decision about which type you have. They don't do this because they know that, ultimately, only you can determine which type you feel most accurately captures the *real* you. Coaches may suggest that you make a more detailed exploration of the types that eventually remain as possible options (usually two, and sometimes three). In the follow-up consultation, they will certainly explain why they believe that some types are good candidates and others aren't.

The hope is that you will learn a great deal about yourself during the interview. You'll learn self-observation and reflection and find out about the Enneagram as a whole — as well as its individual types. During type assessment interviews, I often find that people exclude a particular Enneagram type for themselves based on limited or incorrect images, sometimes as a result of stereotypes. The image can be presented in more detail in an interview so that a previously rejected type can ultimately become a possibility.

Nothing is self-evident

Everyone has their own, individual set of circumstances that they take for granted. Often, they aren't even aware of them. When the panel interview starts, some participants think that they're being pressed about trivial matters. Yet participants on the panel also have matters they've left unexamined — things they consider a given — and they often respond spontaneously to a query by saying that *everyone* does something like this, thinks like this, reacts like this. That's what makes panel interviews wonderful: You discover not only the things *you* take for granted but also the *completely different* things that others take for granted. And then you discover that what strikes you as normal — the group of beliefs you consider to be self-evident, for example — isn't normal at all for most other people. It may come as a shock, but it turns out that humans all assume quite different realities. This realization makes you aware of what it takes to build bridges to other people. The effect of these panel interviews on most participants is that they make a greater and more conscious effort to understand others and become attuned to them.

People of one type become increasingly alike

When the participants in the panel interviews for their type take their seats, you see diversity: men and women, older and younger people, and differences in terms of lifestyle, religion, origin, profession, and clothing. Then the interview starts and the participants tell their stories. In a fascinating way, this kind of panel interview shows how people with the same type have had similar experiences, list comparable examples, and share the same anecdotes. They have developed the same types of strengths and encounter the same problems in life and in their relationships. The people often recognize a great deal in the other participants. It can be a true revelation: "I'm not the only person to whom this happens constantly." Often, the participants in the panel give each other support and advice and have the desire to talk to each other afterward. In a wonderful way, the audience also increasingly understands how much the participants in the panel resemble each other in certain respects. This becomes ever more visible as soon as you learn to look past the external differences.

Learn from panel interviews

What is so instructive about a panel interview? Let's start with the participants. The panel interview invites people to observe themselves and report about their observations. This often spontaneously leads to self-reflection. As a panel member, you're encouraged to think about yourself. It's often a pleasant, accessible, safe, inspiring, and even playful method to learn, practice, and structurally apply skills such as self-observation and reflection. Participating in a panel is often an instructive experience for that person. It deepens self-awareness because you're asked to tell others how things work for you. In the attempt to share their experience in a way that others can understand, people learn by listening to themselves. In the end, the participants in the panel also learn from each other, maybe because a member has discovered their own blind spot that the other participants haven't noticed yet.

The audience of a panel interview learns a great deal about the psychology of people with a certain Enneagram type. People often have assumptions about what is happening inside someone else's mind. In difficult situations, people are often surprised or annoyed or feel powerless and ask themselves what might drive another person. A panel interview might present an Enneagram type that doesn't relate to you at all. When these people talk about what happens inside them, you get a chance to hear, directly from them, what motivates them deep inside — no hypotheses, no assumptions, and no theories about how they are, other than their own, authentic statements about how they experience their own truth and their own day-to-day lives and how they perceive the world.

Panel interviews arouse empathy

Simply by watching a panel interview, you create a greater understanding of the fact that people are different, and you help explain how they set themselves apart from others. Misunderstandings and communication problems, and the conflicts that arise from them, also become recognizable and visible. People with different Enneagram types generally can't understand each other well. After a panel interview, I'm often approached by people who suddenly recognize their father, sister, partner, or colleague in the type that was interviewed in the panel. They're delighted when they develop a slightly better understanding of what is happening in the other person and what is motivating them. They get the chance to hear something that reveals the hidden nature of someone they know, and it's coming from someone who isn't close to them, but rather who greatly resembles the relevant person.

REMEMBER

The narrative tradition (and particularly the panel interview) leads to a better understanding of other people. If you strive toward this understanding, you will find this method to be helpful in developing empathy for others. Empathy grows when you hear other people talk about their feelings of powerlessness, their weaknesses and frustrations, and their good intentions and efforts to learn, for example. Emotional intelligence can be learned and developed. I can't quite imagine a more effective, efficient, and pleasant method than this one.

NINE PERSPECTIVES OF REALITY

The world looks different to each of the nine Enneagram types. Remember that people differ from each other, and keep their differences in mind. Innumerable problems between people can be attributed to their inability to recognize the prism through which the other person views the world. Everyone has their own reality and is convinced that their prism is the only one that reveals the truth. This prevents people from recognizing another person's reality, and then they can't accept that reality. Realizing that your view of the world shows only one-ninth of reality can help you maintain an open-minded position and bring everyone the tolerance they need in order to be interested in another person's ideas. The panel interviews represent a podium on which the nine perspectives of reality equally find their place.

Attend a panel meeting

Would you like to attend a panel meeting? You can. You will certainly be able to find an opportunity on the Internet. If you want to be notified about the panel meetings that I organize, register at my website www.enneagram-nederland.nl/. In Germany and the United States, panel interviews are also a fixed component of studying to become an Enneagram trainer. You can find various kinds of contact information in Chapter 23.

2

Examining the Enneagram Types

Chapter **6**

What We Think About When We Think

For thousands of years, wise people have stated that the source of our human suffering is in our minds. Sayings such as "A person suffers most from what he fears the most" prove the point. Of course, some of these problems palpably occur. External circumstances influence people's lives, and they can hardly change. They can partially influence their health with a healthy lifestyle and by taking care of themselves, but that is no guarantee that they won't get sick. Diseases can just happen. This is compounded by the fact that when something happens to you, you influence to a great extent — unconsciously and unintentionally — the degree to which you actually suffer. People with an optimistic disposition suffer less from the things that barrage them throughout life than those who tend to take everything quite seriously.

Helen Palmer and David Daniels see the following as the starting point for the Enneagram:

It's the instinctive and limited nature of our personality and our personal reactivity that causes stress, conflicts, suffering, and weakness at work and in relationships. This personal behavior often recurs, unconsciously and automatically. This is why interacting with our personality and personal reactivity is fundamental for balancing out our professional and personal lives and filling them with serenity and meaning.

In this chapter, I help you take a look at the first building block on the path to a life filled with serenity and meaning: your thinking. Putting it in Enneagram terms, that means looking at the functioning of your head center.

My Mind Belongs to Me

PRACTICE

For a long period in my life, I honestly believed that my mind belonged to me — that I had a will, even a free will, and that I was directing my own life. Do you believe this too, or have you believed it so far?

Let's do an experiment. It goes like this:

> Sit upright on a chair, set your feet together on the floor, relax, and place your hands on the armrest or your thighs. Make sure that you're comfortable and relaxed. Close your eyes. The task is this — and it's important that you try it: *Think of nothing for one minute.*

I'm curious how the experiment worked — not so much whether you succeeded in this task but rather how you experienced the minute duration and what you felt. During training, participants often tell me, "It worked because I focused on my breathing" or "I suddenly heard all the sounds in the house that I usually don't hear" or "I kept thinking: Don't think, don't think" or "I thought I should focus, and then I realized that's a thought, too."

REMEMBER

Not thinking is a lot more difficult than you might imagine. Now the question is who or what is directing your mind if it's so difficult to perform a fairly simple task such as not thinking?

Here are a few important lessons from this experience:

>> **Apparently, you're not the only one directing what happens in your mind.** Thoughts come and go, wanted and unwanted, pleasant and unpleasant.

>> **You have or get thoughts, but you aren't your thoughts.** Those come and go.

>> **Apparently, something inside you perceives from the inside what happens in your mind.** After all, you can report how you experienced minute and what happened in your mind. So you perceive your think your thoughts.

>> **You perceive the outside world with your sense organs.** Science hasn't discovered yet how people perceive themselves internally, at least as far as I know. In spiritual circles, this is also referred to as the *internal observer:*

- *With the internal observer, you can register what happens inside you.* You need your internal observer, and train it, for the skills of self-observation and reflection. In psychology, this is called *introspection,* or an inspection from the inside.

- *With the help of the internal observer, you can learn to take control of what is happening in your own mind.* You can learn to consciously direct the content of your thoughts — to consciously focus your attention onto something or turn it toward something else instead.

- *Attention training is the starting point and essence of the Enneagram method for personal development and self-management.* But you haven't come to that point yet. You still need to get the lay of the land.

A Sixth Sense: The Internal Observer

Biologists might disagree, but anyone with a spiritual interest is certain that all humans possess another, internal sense organ: the internal observer. Why a sense organ? Eyes perceive what can be seen in the outside world; the internal observer can see and report what happens inside. You can discover it in the exercise at the start of this chapter, and maybe you've already encountered it.

REMEMBER

The internal observer appears as an important component of the Enneagram-based development method in different sections of this book. Here, I am describing it in more detail.

Another name for the internal observer is *witnessing consciousness.* It is indeed a different level of consciousness that you can awaken and use inside you. You encounter the internal observer again in Part 4, when I discuss the Enneagram development method and its spiritual aspects. Right now, I just want to hint at its importance: If you don't discover and train the internal observer, I don't think any kind of personal development and self-management are possible. That's how important it is. (For the whole story, check out Chapter 14.)

Helpful and nonhelpful thoughts

This idea of an internal observer isn't found just within certain spiritual traditions; in fact, this notion plays a huge role in psychotherapy. An example: Ian was in therapy because he suffered from anxiety. The anxiety increased because he saw more and more events that reinforced the sense of fear in him. The psychotherapist taught Ian to see and name the thought that triggered the anxiety. It was designated as a nonhelpful thought. Then the therapist helped Ian formulate a helpful thought. Now he has learned the technique of performing the following four steps whenever he feels afraid:

1. What is the nonhelpful thought?
2. Which feeling is part of it?
3. With which helpful thought can I replace it?
4. What effect does this have, and which feeling is part of it?

When the attention is directed toward helpful thoughts, the anxiety immediately subsides. In Chapter 1, I talk about the principle that some monks have discovered, stating that you can only focus your attention on one object at the same time. The technique I just mentioned follows this principle: You can't keep two thoughts in mind simultaneously (in this example, a negative and a positive thought). Just try it. In the best case, all you can do is quickly jump back-and-forth between two thoughts.

The four activities of the head center

The head center knows four kinds of activities, or functions: remembering, thinking, planning, and imagining, as shown in Figure 6-1. (You may also see them referred to as the *categories* of the mind.)

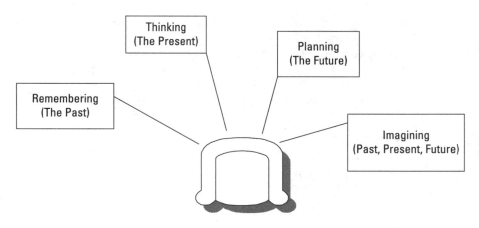

FIGURE 6-1:
The categories of the mind.

Remembering, thinking, and planning are linked to time. When it's about the past, the process is called *remembering*; when it's about the present, it's *thinking*, and when it's about the future, it's *planning*. People also use the activity or function of imagining during all three other functions.

Imagining is the activity of the head center in which you use your imagination. With the aid of your imaginative skills, you picture things that don't exist, and have never existed, in reality. They only exist in your mind and seem very real there. When you plan your vacation, for example, you use your imaginative skills to picture what the destination might look like. You create an image in your head. Every time you access a certain memory and experience it again, your imagination is active. This way, your memory is adapted every time you experience it anew. You also use the power of your imagination when you think and plan. Sometimes, it's difficult to differentiate between imagination and reality.

REMEMBER

Every healthy person is familiar with these four activities. The content of each activity — what's inside the memory, the thought, and so on — is different from one person to the next. The differences are influenced by what a person's attention is primarily focused on.

Trapped in your own fixations

TECHNICAL
STUFF

First and foremost, your attention is always directed toward an object. Then there's the fact that you have just four functions in your head — you remember, you think, you plan, or you imagine. You have no other mental flavors. It follows, then, that the content of the memory, the thought, the plan, or the fantasy consists of what you focus your attention on, in accordance with your type. Whatever you unconsciously consider important has a privileged place in your mind; this is called *mental focus*. You adapt to this object that has taken up residence in your head; it constantly occupies your thoughts. If this effect is strong, it's also referred to as a *fixation*. Your type forces you to fixate on certain thoughts, making it difficult to see or hear other things, aspects, or perspectives. Nor can you take another person's issues into consideration when you're fixated. Even if someone says something helpful, it doesn't get through to you.

The nine objects of attention

Your personality is primarily tuned toward information that supports and confirms your version of reality. You can compare it to radio stations: If you listen to a public news station, you hear something different from what's on a regional weather broadcast. Each of the nine versions of reality is a systematic deviation that shows you only an excerpt from the possible, 360-degree-spanning reality.

This short list spells out where the attention of the individual types is focused, what they're fixated on, and which part of reality they mainly perceive:

>> **Type 1:** What is right, what is wrong, what can be improved, what is someone (or what am I) doing correctly or incorrectly?

>> **Type 2:** Who or what needs my help, where and how can I serve others, how do I attract appreciation and confirmation, do people think I'm nice, or what is needed?

>> **Type 3:** What do I need to achieve, who or what needs my input, and how can I ensure that I draw applause and am seen as the best?

>> **Type 4:** What is missing in my life and in my relationships, what am I separated from, and what do others have that I don't have (and vice versa)?

>> **Type 5:** What does someone want or expect from me, who or what is invading my privacy and taking up my time and energy, and can I (or do I even want to) offer something to others?

>> **Type 6:** What can go wrong, where is there any danger, where are the risks and what do they look like, whom or what can I trust, and what is the secret plan?

>> **Type 7:** Which options and possibilities are out there, what is pleasant and what isn't, who or what is limiting me, and how do I keep my freedom and my space?

>> **Type 8:** What is true and what isn't, who or what is unfair, what needs my protection, and how do I attract respect, power, strength, and control?

>> **Type 9:** Who or what is threatening the harmony, how can I avoid discord or restore harmony, what does the other person want, and what can I do so that you continue to be happy and nice?

REMEMBER

The individual types attach particular importance to these issues, which are the primary focus of their attention. This happens unconsciously so that most people don't even know how important these questions are to them. They're even less aware of the fact that these things matter much more to them than others. To you, it may seem self-evident; after all, anything that matters to you must also be important to other people.

To each their own fixation

Another term for *fixation* is *mental focus*, or *world view*. This can be understood as the typical content filling someone's mind or this person's ardent and frequent concerns. I don't mean that you can't think of anything else, but if someone quickly responds to an issue or touches a sensitive chord, the focus that arises first and most strongly depends on the type.

EXAMPLE

Stan (Type 8) unconsciously believes that concepts like truth and justice are vital. Whenever he remembers an incident, he also focuses on identifying the (un)truth or (in)justice in the memory. It's likely that his imagination colors the image even further to confirm his perception. He is similarly focused on (un)truth and (in)justice when he thinks and plans. Stan unconsciously perceives this dimension and analyzes it. His mental focus can be so strong that it can be called a fixation. When falsehoods and injustices occur in Stan's perception, his mind begins to fixate on "revenge."

A specific, associated reaction forms mentally in that area where the attention is focused on (the fixation that can trap a type). Experiencing injustice triggers revenge — this is how the mind of Type 8 works (so Stan isn't alone). The other eight Enneagram types also have their fixations. In Figure 6-2, you can see which fixation belongs to which type.

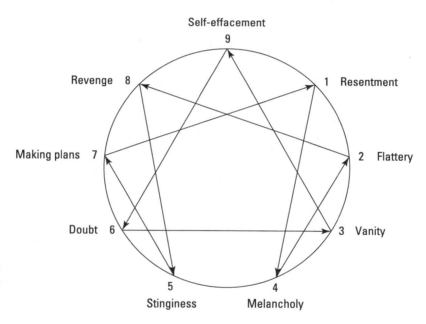

FIGURE 6-2: The unique ways in which each type reacts.

I explain each reaction in the following sections.

Your Convictions

You see reality through the prism of your unique experiences. People think that what they see is real: They see what they see! What they *don't* see is the part of reality that this prism, their filter, is shielding them from. People have become convinced that the section of reality is accurate just as they see it. From this perspective, they believe certain things and establish their convictions. In the following sections, you will find nine descriptions of feelings that people of different Enneagram types recognize in themselves. They report on their internal convictions and their mental fixations.

When you look at fixations, it relates to your head center that is on the level of your personality, the ego. It's also called the *Lower Self*. Your fixations often relate to what you yourself consider your less attractive side — your weaknesses.

These nine descriptions come from people who have developed good self-observation skills and reached a stage in their development in which they want to honestly recognize their own nature. Of course, all the types also have their strengths, but I don't consider them for now. First, let's look at the fixations of the types, which means that the descriptions can seem rather negative.

Perfectionists: Resentment

Perfectionists believe that they have to be flawless in order to be seen, appreciated, and loved. They often recall a good feeling from receiving confirmation that they were behaving perfectly or that they had delivered a perfect performance, for example. Their own, spontaneous impulses become secondary to their striving for perfection. Internally, they are convinced that someone who makes mistakes and doesn't turn out to be perfect won't be loved. That's why Type 1 people don't like to make mistakes. The mental fixation of resentment occurs when, despite all efforts and exertions, the person still can't succeed in improving something, doing it well, or being good at it. It's just as bad if the efforts are obstructed or not seen and recognized. The person or thing blocking the efforts becomes the object of resentment. This can be the Type 1 person, another person, or the situation. In the latter case, the perfectionist analyzes to determine who can be blamed for the situation.

Providers: Flattery

Providers believe that they have to earn being seen, appreciated, and loved, and that they first need to help others and compliment them. They often remember the good feeling that came from making themselves useful as children and that their efforts were seen and appreciated. Their own spontaneous will becomes secondary to serving others. Providers don't like having their help rejected, because they consider it a personal rejection. The mental fixation of flattery occurs when another person who is valuable or interesting appears and the Type 2 person desperately wants to be perceived and esteemed by them.

Achievers: Vanity

Achievers believe that they have to accomplish something in order to be seen, appreciated, and loved. They must be the absolute best in order to deserve and receive attention and applause. They often remember the good feeling from receiving applause for their achievements as children. Contact with themselves and their own feelings becomes secondary to perceiving themselves through the eyes of others, revising what the achiever must do in the eyes of others in order to be seen and appreciated. For a Type 3 person, other people must also make an effort and dedicate themselves to achieving something, just like Type 3 does. Those who fail don't deserve to be seen or appreciated. This is why failure is terrible for the people who recognize themselves as this type. The mental fixation of vanity occurs so that the person can convey a successful image to the outside world.

Individualists: Melancholy

Individualists believe that in order to feel noticed, fulfilled, and loved, they need to find that ideal represented by an intense and genuine love. They strive for this by looking for the unique special love or situation that will fulfill them completely. Because they continually compare reality with the idealized image, persons who are Type 4 create their own disappointments. They often remember how painful it was to be different as a child, to be an outsider. The mental fixation of melancholy occurs when reality (once again) doesn't correspond to the internalized and idealized image, when striving for a deep sense of connection (again) leads nowhere, and when a Type 4 person feels validated in feeling different, unique, misunderstood, or separate from others.

Observers: Stinginess

Observers believe that the people and the world around them expect everything from them and that they themselves are not given their due. They feel that they lack the energy, time, means, and strength to offer something to others. They realize that they prefer to be left alone and stay in their private sphere, where they don't have to meet other people's expectations. Observers often remember the good feeling of being left alone as a child in their own world of thoughts. Isolation from others and their own feelings become more important than relationships to others. Their principle is "live and let live." This is why people who recognize themselves in this type often see others as overwhelming, pushy, or bossy. The mental fixation of stinginess occurs when they have the sense that people expect something of them.

Loyal skeptics: Doubt

Loyal skeptics believe that people and the world around them aren't trustworthy, that dangers, risks, and secret plans are just around the corner. They often remember how unpredictable people's activities can be and how this made them feel insecure and ambushed as children. Their own, spontaneous trust becomes secondary to the alertness that is needed to protect themselves. The person (unconsciously) becomes convinced that a feeling of safety can be achieved by being constantly on guard and questioning everything, by predicting possible negative scenarios, and by eliminating or actively fighting risks. The deal with others is this: "Let's give each other the information we need to fight our insecurities. Don't you think I'm nice? Then please tell me that you think I'm nice. I would prefer that to being afraid that you might not like me." The mental fixation of doubt arises as soon as things occur that trigger alarm in Type 6. This can also occur when decisions have to be made. In this head type, the mental fixation is almost consistently active.

Optimists: Making plans

Optimists have learned that the world around them is frustrating and restrictive and causes pain. They can escape this belief by fleeing into the many beautiful possibilities that exist in their minds. Optimists mentally crave opportunities, possibilities, and joy, and interpret anything that could become unpleasant as something positive. After all, you can look at anything from two sides, especially with the mental skills that this child has developed. The deal with others is this: "Give me my freedom and I'll give you yours. If you think I'm nice, I'll think you're nice, too. Come, let's play together." The mental fixation of making plans occurs as soon as something happens that fascinates or inspires Type 7 but also something that might trigger reactions if limits are imposed. This immediately creates the need to check out, even if only mentally.

Bosses/Protectors: Revenge

Bosses/Protectors believe that the world is tough and unfair, a jungle in which you must show your strength in order to survive. People who have Type 8 believe that you can't be innocent and vulnerable; you have to protect yourself. They often recall situations in which they were vulnerable and abused, when they decided that they would never let anything like that happen again. Their own, spontaneous impulse to be innocent becomes secondary to the desire for invulnerability, strength, power, and respect. Another good strategy to keep others at a distance is to build a fortress and let only a few people inside. The deal here is, "The strongest will win. That's fair, and I happen to be that person." The mental fixation of revenge sets in as soon as Type 8 feels that something violent is inflicted on the truth or if this type is affected by a (deeply buried) sense of vulnerability or fairness. The general response of a Type 8 is to fight.

Mediators: Self-effacing

Mediators believe that they have to maintain peace and harmony in order to be seen, appreciated, and loved, and thus they can't make even tiny waves. Discord has to be avoided at all cost. They often remember how they already made themselves invisible as children and were literally overlooked. Their own, spontaneous impulse to be seen and heard becomes secondary to a striving for harmony. The strong internal energy to assert oneself becomes dormant. Mediators often don't like people who are loud and distinctive and energetically stand up for themselves. It interferes with the internal serenity, peace, and harmony. This is why people who recognize themselves in this type have a hard time becoming visible, clearly asserting themselves, and maybe even becoming angry in the process. The mental fixation of self-effacement appears as soon as Type 9 is triggered, which often occurs around others. Then people with Type 9 see themselves as being completely absorbed by another person, agreeing with their ideas and desires and forgetting themselves.

Chapter **7**

Talking about the Passions

C hapter 6 introduces the functions of the head center; in this chapter, you learn about your emotional (or heart) center. Whereas the head center has fixations, the heart center has passions. Feeling passion for something, living passionately — these are regarded positively in the Western world. People in the West generally see passions as full of energy and associate them with the heart and their love of somebody or something. From a spiritual point of view — and from the Enneagram's perspective as well — the passions involve the free movement of life energy that we all carry inside us and that we were born with. The trendy word *flow* also refers to this state. Things are in flow; they move as if on their own. This flow provides energy — in the form of inspiration, for example — but this isn't the kind of passion I'm talking about here.

The meaning of *passion* that I'm asking you to consider here at the level of the ego corresponds to how the word was used in earlier times. Back then it was synonymous with vices that had taken root and grown inside humans. Think back to the 19th century: Having a passion such as lust, and especially acting on it, was certainly not seen as a virtue at that time. Since people started exploring the human psyche thousands of years ago, vices were seen as the source of human suffering. I discuss in this chapter what this means and how vices affect people.

And How Do You Feel Today?

"I'm unhappy and it's your fault."

In psychology, this statement is known as the *transfer theory* — or at least as one part of it. What psychologists call an *external attribute* refers to people's tendency to look for explanations or causes outside of themselves. Humans believe that the cause of their unhappiness lies with someone else, and they also experience it this way. At times there is some truth to this statement, but even then that fact does little to help anyone.

After all, you can't change other people, and if someone has consciously or unconsciously done you harm, it's unlikely that they can reverse it. You have no choice but to take responsibility for your feeling of being unhappy, angry, or sad. That means you have to look for your own way to end the suffering inside you. If another person can strike a blow like this — by throwing you off balance and making you unhappy — you're vulnerable. Wouldn't it be nice to find a way to make you less prone to being unbalanced? If you want to take this path, the first step is to reveal what makes you vulnerable — what throws you off balance so easily, in other words.

REMEMBER

When you want to develop yourself, you often want to get rid of things inside you. To succeed, you should first be clear about what exactly causes your suffering. To find out what exactly you're dealing with, you need to take a closer look at yourself. Whenever you want to get rid of something, it often helps to see how you actually came to possess it. So, what is the source of *your* passions?

Getting the Passions — and Getting Rid of Them

If you want to penetrate to the source of your passions, you need to see where they come from — how they're created and how they work inside you. One strategy is to look backward in time and search for old texts that mention these passions and vices. The fact is that you're not alone on this journey of discovering how your mind works— you're actually in good company. Old documents have detailed stories about how this excavation process is done, of people who started on it hundreds of years ago. I suggest that you look at what you can learn from those who came before. You'll also encounter them in other parts of this book. And furthermore, you'll get an idea of where this topic fits in with the Enneagram. It's one aspect of the Enneagram that is already centuries old. Let's start with a mini-history and then do a bit of personal history by returning to your own childhood.

Passions create suffering

First, let's travel back in time, to the fourth century AD. Evagrius Ponticus (345–399 AD) was considered a talented monk and an outstanding intellectual. He belonged to a group of monks, now referred to as the Desert Fathers, who lived reclusively in hermitages (which is where the word *hermit* comes from) in the desert south of Alexandria and explored their own thoughts and feelings. Evagrius examined the origins of human suffering. In a nutshell, his goal was to find a way to reunite with God. Although this goal was later forgotten, and even fought against by the Catholic Church, people during early Christian times widely believed that the path to God led within oneself. In other Christian churches, this remained the starting point, or it was later rediscovered.

Emotionally charged thoughts

Evagrius (refer to the preceding section) made a serious effort to analyze what disturbed his fellow humans. His writings reveal that his experiences as a sought-after spiritual companion brought him substantial psychological insights. Evagrius detected a pattern in the information he collected: He distinguished between eight "emotionally charged thoughts" that hindered monks during their prayers and in their hermit's life. He called them *logismoi*. (They continue to be applied in the Enneagram; today they're called "the passions.") These emotionally charged thoughts bothered the monks while praying, and thus in their desired connection with God. Evagrius defined a first step toward being connected once again with God, a step he called *praktik^e* — activity focused on exercising the virtues and avoiding the vices. In the language of his time, he wrote that each vice is delivered by its own spirit, or *daimon*. This neutral term could also represent good spirits, though Evagrius used the word for the evil spirits that instilled the vices in people. He named eight of these spirits: gluttony, lust, greed, sadness, anger, despondency, vanity, and pride. You might be familiar with seven of these terms; ever since the time of Pope Gregory I (around 590 AD), Christianity has labeled them the seven deadly sins.

Vices fly to you

It's not too far-fetched to imagine evil spirits breathing the vices into humans: In Chapter 5, I present an exercise asking you to stop your thoughts for a certain period. In this process, many people find that thoughts just appear out of nowhere. Where do they come from? They aren't created by conscious thought, because you didn't even want to think. I don't know whether modern neurobiological research has been able to determine which part of the human brain produces these uninvited thoughts, but in times when medical knowledge was still limited — which was definitely the case in medieval Europe — it doesn't seem particularly farfetched to think of them as being breathed into you. But by whom? It had to be something invisible — a spirit, a *daimon*.

The philosopher and mystic Plotinus (204–270 AD) had doubts about this whole *daimon* concept and believed that evil arose mainly from a lack of the good. This is assumed in the Enneagram, an assumption that contributes to the path of your further development. Vices arise from the absence of virtues. Plotinus wrote a great deal about virtues and vices in his work *The Enneads.* He was influential, for example, on the father of the Catholic Church, St. Augustine, as well as on St. Thomas Aquinas and the 20th century psychiatrist, psychoanalyst, and thinker C.G. Jung.

Reverting to childhood

This chapter starts out by associating the word *passion* with the life energy in humans. In small children in particular, you can easily observe this freely flowing life energy. Small children don't yet understand the concept of time, place, or danger. They play happily and freely and are not yet conscious much of themselves. Neither do small children yet have much of a memory or anticipate what the future will bring — these are the head categories I mention in Chapter 5. Because small children lack a general sense of time, they live in the now. They are completely receptive but also totally innocent and vulnerable to what is coming. They have neither any memory capacity yet (directed toward the past) nor planning capacity (for the future). For them, there is only the now.

Living in a fantasy world

Small children have an enormous imagination but aren't yet capable of differentiating between reality and imagination. That's why children live in a magical world. The goblins in a book seem real because they exist in the book and thus *are* real to the child. You can also see how much a child lives in the present when they're in pain. One moment the child cries heartbreakingly — and the next moment the pain is gone, the tears suddenly stop, and the child happily continues playing. Mom and dad often need another moment to recover from the incident. If you ask an hour later, "Didn't that frighten you?" the child often just displays a blank expression. They fell down earlier, but that incident no longer matters now.

Developing a capacity for memory and anticipation

Children's nervous systems and brains continue to grow, and they eventually develop their memory capacity. Children remember what hurt, what was sad, or what was funny. Over time, they learn to anticipate, in order to avoid things that aren't funny, and to sidestep to somewhere else that *is* fun. When this capacity for remembering and anticipation is developed, it also creates a sense of place and time. Children slowly leave the here-and-now.

A second effect of maintaining a memory of what it means to be in pain or to be sad consists of children learning to plan ahead in order to avoid these emotions in the future or, if it does come to that, to suffer less from them. Children develop a protective layer; every time they feel pain, a slight tension arises against the free flow of life energy. How can you visualize this effect? Think about what most people do when their lives become suspenseful or they experience danger: They hold their breath. These are the kinds of tensions and contractions that I'm talking about here. How does it help you to hold your breath when danger is on the scene? You might think that continuing to breathe increases the chances of survival. But holding your breath helps you avoid feeling any fear in that moment. It suppresses the feeling. Humans' conscious and unconscious survival strategies definitely have a purpose.

Recognizing that everything has a price

It's often easy to see advantages in how people behave. What their behavior costs them, however, is usually outside their field of vision. For children, the price of these unconscious contractions is not at all clear. Yes, children protect themselves by briefly shielding themselves from unpleasant feelings, but they're also denying themselves access to their life energy and natural receptivity. Each time children imperceptibly and instantly feel internal tension, they block the free flow of life energy, and thus their ability to be completely receptive to the outside world comes to an end. "Not feeling" ultimately aims to temporarily prevent reception. Limiting the receptivity also encompasses the loss of direct and open contact with the higher virtues, such as innocence and lightheartedness. The hard "shell" that grows inside children doesn't just protect them — it's also an obstacle in their contact with themselves, their environment, and other people, and in their strengths and virtues. This creates space inside for the development of vices — or what the Enneagram calls "the passions." (See Figure 7-1).

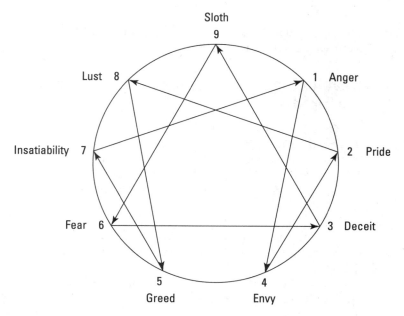

FIGURE 7-1:
The nine deadly
passions.

The Nine Deadly Vices (Reprise)

Many philosophers, theologians, mystics, authors, and poets write about human vices — such as Dante Alighieri, in his *Purgatorio*, part of his *The Divine Comedy*. These folks tend to use different names, categories, and numbers, but the general thrust is the same. The different Enneagram teachers also use different names, such as the seven deadly sins of Christianity, which Oscar Ichazo integrated into the Enneagram. Dante also described fear and deception, and Ichazo likewise added them to the corresponding personality structures. Richard Rohr stresses shamelessness, but Helen Palmer, basing herself on Dante, replaces Rohr's shamelessness with lust and excessiveness. (See Table 7-1; for a graphical representation, refer to Figure 7-1.) She did this because people who recognized themselves in Type 8 in her panels kept reporting that they were much more likely to see lust, rather than shamelessness, as the underlying passion.

REMEMBER

Many Enneagram types have preferred terms that they recognize more easily than the names used here. I keep hearing from people with Type 1 in the panel that they don't detect or experience anger, but that "annoyance" is quite common. I didn't revise the term for this book, simply because the underlying passion of people with Type 1 is still anger. People with Type 1 who have observed themselves for a while and have gotten to know themselves better also see this. Annoyance is just the form of anger that is more accepted by people with Type 1.

TABLE 7-1:　　**Comparing the Passions, 1500 Years Apart**

Evagrious (345–399 AD)	Enneagram (1970 AD)
Wrath	Anger
Arrogance	Pride
Vanity	Deception
Despondency	Envy
Greed	Greed
N/A	Fear
Gluttony	Insatiability
Fornication	Lust/excess
Listlessness	Sloth

Seeing vices or passions as cornerstones of our personalities

As you observe yourself, you'll likely recognize inside you several of the vices I mention in the previous section. In the panel interviews, I hear detailed reports from people about what they perceive inside themselves. And, I regularly hear how people experience their various vices. During the self-observation in the panels, it also becomes apparent how strongly variable is the extent to which the various vices play a role in someone's life. The passion of my type plays a major role for me. I have problems with it every day, and I find it extremely difficult to manage. I have to deal with other passions from time to time, but not as often. In the stories I hear from panel members, the passion of their particular type strikingly comes to the forefront in difficult situations, whereas that doesn't happen with one of the other eight passions. Here again, the difference lies in the extent to which someone is controlled by a passion. Letting go of my type's passion provides me with the first 80 percent of inner freedom I need in order to take up a new position in life and deal with people and things in a different way. I found out that this passion represents the greatest obstacle in my connection to myself. I even see that the other passions become truly visible in my self-observation only when I can let go of my type's particular passion.

Caution: Detour ahead

WARNING

Before I started on my path toward self-development, I felt barely any fear, if at all. As a result of my personal development I made contact with the fear inside myself and thus also became afraid. After boarding airplanes with no worries my entire life, I suddenly had a fear of flying. So, this warning about side effects is warranted. It's a beautiful but strenuous path, and you should be aware of it ahead of time. I realized that, despite the fear of flying, I kept feeling increasingly complete. Instead of just seeing red, I also got to know the other colors of the rainbow. Fear isn't a pleasant feeling, but it also taught me a few things. Of course, the fear was already somewhere inside me and influenced me, but I didn't know it, because I didn't feel it. Now I can look this beast in the eye and do something about it. The path toward development had already brought me to the point that I could let go of a passion. So, why shouldn't I apply what I learned to this new passion that was emerging?

I have a single comment on the question of whether it's true what we Enneagram practitioners claim — that the passions are the cornerstone of the personality structure and every Enneagram type therefore has its own passion. In my approach to the Enneagram, nothing human is alien to you. Yes, most people who get to know themselves discover multiple passions within themselves. But one passion is dominant — that of one's own Enneagram type. It's the key to the door that you must pass through on your internal journey of development in order to be free again.

Chapter **8**

Living with the Passions

In Chapter 7, I explain the concepts of passions and vices and describe their background. In this chapter, I discuss in greater detail the individual passions of the nine types and how they manifest themselves. The designations of the passions have a broader meaning than they do in everyday language. You'll find out that the passions are energy sources inside you that set you in motion. Nine types of passion represent nine different kinds of energy — just like some cars are powered by diesel, and others by electricity. Both are energy sources, but an electric car drives differently than a diesel vehicle.

No Motion without Energy

Vices, or ABC, are the source of all internal suffering in humans. Let's assume that you're greedy. Where is your attention focused? You hoard unconsciously, and your nature is unconsciously focused on keeping hold of what you have. Unconsciously, you see what you don't have yet but would like to have. Unconsciously, your greed comes between you and other people because getting or keeping what you have has — unconsciously — become more important to you than having a good relationship with another person. No, you prefer not to buy the next round at the bar and, yes, you have good reasons for it. But, over time, you will receive fewer and fewer invitations to come along. You don't have a grip on your passion of greed. You can't act any differently even if your behavior makes you suffer. I'd venture a guess that you'll never be happy if you continue to let this passion rule you.

Now, it's natural to associate greed with money, but the greed of the Enneagram type has many more layers to it than what is meant by the everyday use of the word *greed*. It is more about the persons themselves than it is about money. (You can find more details about this aspect of greed later in this chapter.) For every passion out there, people in panel interviews state so many examples of what's actually entailed that you could write a book about these alone. The panel members don't just express the obvious, like in the previous example. No, in a detailed and multifaceted way, they talk about how the energy of the passions are expressed inside them.

It's rare or even impossible to find stories like these in books. They come directly from the people as they observe themselves during their everyday activities.

Here's a summary of what the people themselves say about it:

Nothing moves without energy. This statement is true for cars and machines and also for you. Humans consume food and it provides energy to grow, heal, and literally to move. But you, and other humans, are set in motion not just with the energy you get from food — the passions are also seen as a source of energy that is necessary to get you moving. Just think about how powerful anger is in terms of energy; how forcefully and overwhelmingly it can surge outward; how the energy from anger can inspire people to assert themselves; how anger can become so powerful that people literally go to war without respect for, or consideration of, other people's interests. The energy of fear would rather encourage fleeing at that point.

I'm intentionally referring to types of energy here. The energy from anger is different from that of pride, fear, or lust. As a result, each of the various Enneagram types has its own coloration, or aura. As an energy source, the passions form the cornerstone of the personality structure. Being driven by pride or fear leads to different worries and different behavior, but it also leads people to project different things.

The Individual Passions

Each type has its own passion, and each passion has its own kind of energy. What kinds of behavior do the passions bring out in each type? I describe them all in this section.

Anger

Everyone is familiar with anger, in themselves or in others. Anger is the dominant passion of Type 1. This isn't about the general meaning of anger — annoyance in the way everyone experiences it when they have good reason. Here's a summary of how anger affects people with Type 1:

People with Type 1 are called perfectionists *because they tend to make a dedicated effort to improve situations. They are often idealistic people who want to create beauty in the world — and in themselves. Becoming annoyed, or even angry, isn't part of the plan. This is why perfectionists have developed the habit of suppressing their own rage. When anger arises, they experience it as an annoyance and become irritated. (Bystanders in the presence of these folks can also easily experience the annoyance or tension being carried.) Anger can arise, for example, when others don't act as responsibly as a perfectionist does. One of these people uses the Biblical story of Adam and Eve to illustrate his anger: As a child, he was always appalled whenever he heard the story of Paradise — how Adam and Eve were kicked out after behaving thoughtlessly and thus brought misfortune to all of mankind. Perfectionists always try, in effect, to restore Paradise. They believe that the world would be a great place to live — if all the thoughtless, irresponsible people wouldn't mess it all up.*

Pride

Everyone is familiar with pride, in themselves or in others. Pride is the dominant passion of Type 2. This isn't about the general meaning of the word *pride*, in the sense that everyone experiences pride when there is a reason for it. People with Type 2 have something different to report — their pride is different. Here's a summary:

People with Type 2 are called providers *because they are greatly oriented toward supporting other people and are emotionally available to others, and they sense other people's needs. When you compliment providers, they consider it justified. They think in line with an earnings model: They have given something and thus have earned appreciation. At the same time, they aren't attuned to receiving anything, not even compliments. The entire mechanism is designed so that providers are the ones who give. Pride immediately comes to the surface to ward off the compliment: "Oh, that wasn't a big deal." But deep inside, people with Type 2 think differently. Although they hide it away inside, they still secretly feel pride in their indispensability and achievements. Pride doesn't stand in the way only when it comes to receiving compliments but also when providers need help from others. The earnings model of providers is only about providers giving something; it doesn't include receiving anything without having done something for it. In summary, the pride is expressed by not accepting anything. Providers have "wounded pride" if they don't receive the appreciation they think they deserve. They are also fully aware of (and revel in) their own secret, internal pride in their strengths and achievements and believe that they know better what another person needs than that person does.*

Deception

Everyone is familiar with deception, in themselves or in others. It's a word often associated with shame, and people who recognize themselves in the mechanism of Type 3, achievers, are often shocked to hear that deception is the dominant passion of their personality structure. But this isn't deception in the general sense — it's not about cheating others and bamboozling them, usually in connection with money. This isn't the specific kind of deception that constitutes part of the personality structure of achievers. It's not what they report; for them, the deception looks different. A summary would look like this:

> The deception of people with Type 3 is a kind of self-deception or self-delusion. They are also referred to as actors because they tend to represent a nice image of themselves, their relationships, their family, and their work. For Type 3, just as for the other heart types, it's important to be seen. Literally in all kinds of ways, an actor has developed a strategy to become visible, to be successful, and to garner applause. A person with Type 3 does this in all areas — at work as well as at home — and plays different roles in the process (perhaps as the ideal in-law, partner, parent, or boss.) Actors worry that their true selves aren't good enough, and so they "perform a show" with these roles. Actors mislead themselves and others because they hide behind the facade of successful roles. The deception of Type 3 consists of identifying with accomplishments and external aspects to fulfill the image of being a successful, dynamic person so that they can be appreciated.

Envy

Everyone is familiar with envy, in themselves or in others. Envy is the dominant passion of Type 4. It's not envy in the sense of resentment, though. Here's a summary of how people with Type 4 experience envy:

> People with Type 4 often have a subliminal feeling that they lack qualities inside them and experiences in their lives, which makes them feel empty. The feeling of this lack is accompanied by a deep desire to fill the internal emptiness — a longing for depth, completion, and fulfillment. Through their prism for viewing the world, people with Type 4 see that other people have qualities they lack. It's the classic case of the grass always being greener on the other side. Type 4 doesn't really care about superficial items like stylish cars; they are far more concerned with the essential elements of life. A single person with Type 4, for example, can idealize a partnership and be envious of others who live in a seemingly ideal relationship. Conversely, someone with a Type 4 who has a partner might idealize the solitude shown by good friends. These people don't feel resentful in the sense of not wanting others to have things — they just see what others have and also want that for themselves. They want what they imagine as an ideal, though it isn't available or present.

Greed

Everyone is familiar with greed, in themselves or in others. Greed is the dominant passion of Type 5. (Just a reminder: Greed isn't related to money, so the example from earlier in this chapter isn't entirely appropriate, but I'm leaving it there because it's memorable.) When it comes to the specific greed as a part of the Type 5 personality structure, however, I'm talking about something else. Here's a summary of what greed means for people with this type:

People with Type 5 often demonstrate in panel discussions that they place great value on the precise use of language. Instead of greed, they prefer to talk about restraint. (Because the passions are about the kinds of energy related to the types, I share the opinion of Type 5 that restraint better describes their energy.) They don't necessarily restrain their money, but rather their own person. People with Type 5 perceive what happens around them from a restrained — safe — position. They have a subliminal feeling of absence; they believe they aren't good enough and don't have enough possessions. This is exactly why people with Type 5 are concerned with other people's expectations. They worry that they can't offer what is expected of them, that people always demand more whenever you meet their initial expectations: "Give them an inch and they'll take a mile" is how this type views others. They are afraid that the demands will never end and thus they act frugally with themselves, their time, their energy, and their knowledge. The object of the greed of Type 5 depends on what is important to that person. For example, some are generous with money but reserved when it comes to information about themselves, their work, or their interests.

Fear

Fear is certainly not unique to a Type 6. Although all types are familiar with fear, it's only crucial when it comes to the personality structure of Type 6. Fear is the dominant passion of this type, the loyal skeptic. Take a look at how their fear becomes apparent:

In contrast to the passions of the types I describe earlier in this chapter, the fear of the loyal skeptic is the most basic kind of fear: fear of insecurity and of living in a dangerous world. It's the primal fear that causes people to be on guard when it comes to their physical survival. Everyone has this fear, but in the loyal skeptic, it defines life to such a degree that their vigilance never wanes and is focused on all aspects of their lives. This is true even when it has nothing to do with the safety of their physical survival. People with Type 6 are almost constantly in a state of alarm — they look out for risks and security gaps, not just in certain situations but also in people and relationships. It's their habit to always be on guard.

EVERY TYPE KNOWS ALL ABOUT FEAR

WARNING

What people are afraid of, and to what extent, depends on the individual type. Here are some of the obvious examples of the individual types: Type 1 is terrified of making a mistake. Other types also occasionally have this fear, but not as often as Type 1. Type 2 is afraid of being rejected and left alone. Type 3 fears failure and not being able to tell a success story or "falling through the cracks" when it comes to getting noticed. Type 4 is also familiar with the fear of rejection, but out of shame, and with the fear of feeling inadequate and not belonging. Type 5 people are afraid of actually living their lives to the fullest and of giving too much of themselves. Type 7 is afraid of pain and suffering, of being restrained, and of no longer having options and opportunities. Type 8 knows no fear — at least that's what Type 8 people like to believe about themselves, and most people see them as fearless when it comes to things you can fear in the outer world. But people with Type 8 are afraid of their own, internal world, of the vulnerability they might find there, of the possibility of being overwhelmed by the larger, evil outer world as soon as they show that they're vulnerable. Type 9 fears nothing more than conflicts and discord between people.

Insatiability

Everyone is familiar with insatiability in one form or another. Even a Type 5 can be immoderate, for example, when it comes to acquiring knowledge. Insatiability is a predominant passion in the personality structure of Type 7. Here is a summary of what that means:

> In people with Type 7, the optimists or bon vivants, *insatiability relates to life itself. Optimists have the fundamental desire to live and experience life in all its richness, utilizing all its options and opportunities. Optimists have developed a craving for new opportunities, new experiences, and new joy. If people with Type 7 organize a business meeting, they might care about reaching the company goals, but for them personally, it's even more important that the meeting was a pleasant experience for everyone. The energy associated with insatiability comes with a desire for freedom, which is why the optimist is allergic to limitations and restrictions. The insatiability of this head type is also a mental matter; it can be lived primarily in the mind without anything having to be implemented in reality.*

Lust

Does everyone experience lust? For each passion mentioned earlier in this chapter, I claim that everyone has at least a trace of it inside, and lust is no exception. This passion appeals to most people in Enneagram training sessions and boosts the energy of the group. The passion of lust builds up energy, as is demonstrated on those occasions when it's introduced to the discussion. Lust is associated with sexuality, which arouses energy. Lust is the dominant passion of Type 8, the boss/protector.

> *When it comes to the Type 8 personality structure, the passion or energy of lust isn't only sexual. Someone with Type 8, the boss/protector, has a lust for life — a lust that comes with a lot of energy. Because this type seems to have an unlimited amount of energy, they are often thought to have a strong presence. Other people reckon with them, even when they don't do or say anything. The boss/protector has developed a strategy to become big and strong, to belong to the powerful group — the group of people that protects others, not the one needing protection. (Type 8 has awakened too much energy inside for that!) The energy of lust is a sensuality affecting all areas of life that are important to the boss/protector. It's the lust for power, for food, but also for battle, because a battle is an event by which you can measure and experience your own strength.*

Sloth

Everyone is familiar with sloth, in themselves or in others. Here as well, this isn't about the general meaning of sloth. People with Type 9 aren't lazier than others — for example, when it comes to their work. On the contrary, people with Type 9 actually work quite hard. They have an inclination to forget themselves. If they work in the garden, for example, they might forget to stop until it suddenly grows dark, their back is stiff, and they're famished. So it's by no means true that sloth refers to an unwillingness to work when it comes to the personality structure of Type 9. It is far more the following situation:

> *Slothfulness here is a spiritual slothfulness that prevents Type 9 people from doing what would be good for them — recognizing their own needs and wishes, for example. Instead, a Type 9 lets others lead them. Many spiritual movements mention that humans are "sleeping," that we live automatically when we don't decide to take the path of the "awakened ones." Type 9 is a reminder of this principle of sleeping. In their striving to maintain harmony, they have the automatic tendency to merge with others, which is easier and takes less energy than asserting themselves. People with Type 9 can forget themselves when they merge with others. They are generally easily distracted and decide on the more convenient path instead of the one that might be their true priority. This is the way in which Type 9 is lazy: Even thinking about what might be good for them takes an effort, which is why they prefer to keep putting it off.*

Chapter **9**

Examining Our Actions

I n Chapter 6, I talk about the head center. Chapters 7 and 8 talk about the heart. There I introduce you to the most important elements and technical terms that play a role in developing the personality structures, such as attentiveness, fixation, and passions. In this chapter, you find out how all this is implemented in action. You'll get to know another element of the type mechanism — the defense mechanisms. They are also expressed by your actions.

This chapter treats your third center, the instinctive gut, or body center. Here you can read how the fixation of your thoughts and the passions of your heart interact with and strengthen each other: the type mechanism. It's dynamic and reveals what happens inside you. If you can understand this mechanism, you'll find good starting points for your personal development.

The evil spirits don't know our heart; they get their knowledge from our deeds.

They learn from the spoken word and the movements of the body.

But because these signs show them what is concealed inside the heart, it gives them an opportunity to attack us.

Evagrius Ponticus

(A summary of "The Treatise on Evil Thoughts")

Thinking, Feeling, Acting

The metaphor of the chariot is familiar from various spiritual traditions. It describes a scenario like the following: A set of horses is harnessed to a chariot. The charioteer holds the reins. Together, the horses and the charioteer represent your lower self. The horses represent your heart center, your passion — always in motion, always sensitive. This energy moves the chariot forward, but it can also run away with you at any moment, if something in the area triggers that action. The charioteer symbolizes the head center. Using his mind, he tries to keep the horses — the passions — under control, to steer it and guide it in the right direction. Sometimes it works, sometimes it doesn't. The charioteer (the head) surveys the surroundings and then determines the destination of the journey and how to get there. The charioteer and the horses pull the chariot wherever they habitually go.

Now imagine that, instead of a chariot with a lone charioteer, you have a horse-and-carriage with a coachman as the driver up top and a passenger inside. The carriage's curtains are closed. The passenger inside is your internal observer. The observer is sleeping and letting the coachman and horse do their thing. When the observer awakens, opens the curtains, and looks out, she can also take over the guidance of the carriage ride. But if the observer continues to sleep, the journey's destination will be a surprise.

Defining Defense Mechanisms

The writer T.S. Eliot claimed that people can handle only a certain dose of reality. If you had no defense mechanisms, you probably couldn't bear living. So maybe these mechanisms should be called *self-protection* strategies or *emotional armor.* Sigmund Freud, the father of psychoanalysis, developed the theory of *defense mechanisms:* They're functions that the mind uses to keep certain instinctual efforts and desires — or realities that might trigger too much fear and sadness — away from consciousness. Freud, as an Austrian, used the German word *Abwehrmechanismen* to label what he had discovered. The trouble is, whereas *Abwehr* can certainly mean "defense," it can also mean "resistance." When Freud's work was translated into English, the translators went with *defense system* or *defense mechanism*, and this term is the one that entered common usage. Strictly speaking, it's better to stick with Freud's other meaning and talk about resistance mechanisms. Both terms are used synonymously in practice.

Each type has developed their own pain and worries, but each has also developed their own survival strategy, whose purpose is to prevent the pain from happening and take control of whatever is worrisome. The defense mechanisms are part of the survival strategy. They help prevent you from feeling your underlying fear and maintain your ideal self-image. In principle, everyone has access to all defense mechanisms, but each type has developed one much more strongly than the others. It is the glue, so to speak, which holds that type together.

Here's a short list of each defense mechanism (I cover the topic in more detail again when I describe the type mechanisms later in the chapter):

» **Reaction formation (Type 1, the Perfectionist):** It arises whenever an impulse or need isn't lived out but is suppressed immediately. Something else is done instead. The suppression of impulses helps prevent uncontrolled behavior, and thus mistakes. This helps Type 1 react in an acceptable and controlled manner anytime and anywhere. This reaction makes it possible to retain the ideal self-image: "I'm a good, decent person."

» **Suppression (Type 2, the Provider):** Their own will, desires, and needs are unconsciously suppressed, which can also be called repression. Their desires and needs disappear off the radar. This makes it easy to prioritize and fulfill the needs of other people, and thus be in relationship with them. Suppressing one's own needs makes it possible to maintain an ideal self-image: "I'm a giving, nice person."

» **Identification (Type 3, the Achiever):** Their own identity is suppressed; they have no contact with it. Instead, a new identification is created with a new successful role. This helps with assuming the characteristics of the desired, successful image; it feels like the person's actual identity in terms of the energy. It neutralizes the feeling of being unsuccessful and unappreciated. The ideal self-image can thus be kept alive: "I'm a successful person."

» **Introjection (Type 4, the Individualist):** Introjection consists of adopting idealized images from the outside world and grafting them onto one's own system of thoughts and feelings, experiencing them as distinctive and striving toward them. You might idealize a certain other person, for example, or an object or the expressed, assumed opinions or judgments of (valuable) others. What is acquired is experienced as the type's own and fills an internal void. It also forms a relationship with the idealized or valuable other. The ideal self-image can thus be maintained: "I'm a special, unique person."

» **Isolation (Type 5, the Observer):** The isolation of affects or feelings is a way to split them off from the type's image of themselves. It helps release one's own feelings and needs from having to be thought about and thus reduces their impact on the self. This is useful if you want to avoid mental chaos and keep calm and maintain an overview on what is happening around you. The effects that the feelings of other people may have on you are also reduced in the same way. The ideal self-image can thus be maintained: "I'm a calm, stable, and understanding person."

>> **Projection (Type 6, the Loyal Skeptic):** This includes attributing internal worries, assumed dangers, and fears to other people and external situations — for example, to assume the following from a person they don't like: "You don't like me, do you?" The benefit of the projection consists of finding explanations for their own inner fear and insecurity in the outside world, which means that their own feeling can be considered real. This makes it possible to retain their ideal self-image: "I'm a careful and realistic person."

>> **Rationalization (Type 7, the Optimist):** This one can be understood as the habit of positively reinterpreting everything that might be painful or negative. It reduces painful and negative experiences by giving them a new meaning and makes it possible to circumvent experiences like being limited or in pain. This contributes to maintaining an ideal self-image: "I'm an optimistic, positive person."

>> **Denial (Type 8, the Boss/Protector):** In this case, the denial of reality consists of not perceiving danger, fear, vulnerability, other people's feelings, their "truths," and many things that the relevant person doesn't feel comfortable with, to such an extent that they don't even exist in that person's experience. This makes it possible to retain the ideal self-image: "I'm a fair and sincere person."

>> **Numbness (Type 9, the Mediator):** Being numb feels like falling asleep and helps people with that type to forget themselves. This makes life appear consistently easy and comfortable. In this sleepy state, conflicts and confrontations can be avoided and life continues to be harmonious and peaceful. And so the ideal self-image can be retained: "I'm a peaceful, harmonious person."

You have now been introduced to all aspects of the type mechanism — the centers, the objects of attention, the fixations, the passions, the defense mechanisms. In this chapter, I tell you more about how the mechanism is composed for the individual types. The interaction between thinking and feeling sets you in motion and makes you act. You'll find out how the strategies of the individual types work. People who speak about their type mechanism in Enneagram panels often say that the strategy they "chose" as a child has to do with one or several of the Freudian principles of wanting to

>> Run away from unpleasant things

>> Move toward pleasant things

>> Be seen, heard, appreciated, loved

REMEMBER

You can find these three principles in the explanations of the type mechanisms. Now that I've presented all elements of the personality structure, I can explain the nine type mechanisms, by approaching the types in connection with their most important center: first, the head center, with the three head types; and then the gut center, with the three gut types; and finally, the heart center, with the three heart types.

The head center

The *head* is the seat of your thoughts. Head types share the inclination to think first and act later. Their preference and habit are to engage themselves with their mind. Over in Chapter 6, I talk about the four main activities of the head: remember, think, plan, and imagine (fantasize). The three types of the head center specialize in perceiving and understanding the world by way of the head. (See Figure 9-1.) Although each of these three types does this in their own way, they still share the inclination to explore things via their heads, by imagining, structuring, conceptualizing, associating, analyzing, and so on. Fear is the underlying emotion of the three head center types (Type 5, the Observer; Type 6, the Loyal Skeptic; Type 7, the Optimist).

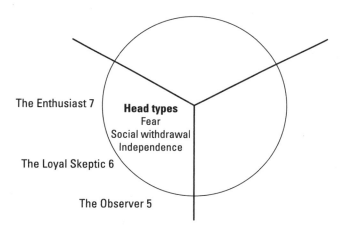

FIGURE 9-1:
Head types think
first and act later.

When it comes to survival, I know of two strategies: fight or flight. These are based on the two emotions, or passions, of anger and fear. Anger gives you the energy that makes you big and strong in order to fight, and fear ensures that you run for your life. The verifiable physical effect of both is the same: increased adrenaline levels in the blood. I also know of a third strategy: paralysis, or freezing up, can be another effect of fear. In severely traumatic situations, this effect can be so strong that people literally can't remember what happened — in this extreme form, too, fear can help with self-protection and (psychological) survival.

Let's start with the core type of the three head types, Type 6. I call it the *core* type because it's the middle one of the three head types, but also because fear most clearly and directly plays a role for Type 6. Fear is the passion of Type 6.

The Type 6 type mechanism

I have previously collected the following aspects for this type:

Type 6 is a head type. Its passion is fear, the fixation is doubt, and the defense mechanism is projection. This type is referred to as the loyal skeptic, questioner, or devil's advocate.

People with Type 6 share a subliminal feeling of fear and insecurity. They even have the deep, fundamental fear or worry that they can't survive in this dangerous world. Additionally, on the same deep level is minimal self-confidence, if any, that the person can manage this situation alone, which creates a feeling of dependency. One way in which this outlook reveals itself to be a head type is that the head center is highly developed and used to control this sense of fear. The strategy of developing a sense of security rests precisely in being alert and predicting catastrophic scenarios. People with Type 6 have a vivid imagination in this regard. The mental focus or habit to doubt everything and anyone (including themselves) gives people with this type the sense of not being surprised or overwhelmed by unforeseen events because they are constantly on guard. They keep a close eye on everything and everyone.

At first glance, however, the Loyal Skeptic designation doesn't seem to fit this image, with its passion of fear. The skepticism doesn't just refer to uncertain situations but also particularly to people who give the impression of behaving unpredictably, which makes them untrustworthy. This leads to the habit of imagining the worst and then testing people in this regard. It takes a long time to build trust. But if a person is deemed trustworthy, Type 6 stays forever loyal to that person, not only because this is a noble quality but also because people with Type 6 find it pleasant to have reliable (and predictable) people around them, especially if they are figures of authority. The projection is that people with Type 6 assume that others equally value security, predictability, and clarity and that they value feeling safe and can recognize risks. People need to give each other the information they need in order to fight insecurity. Be clear and transparent, also about what is happening inside you.

The Type 5 type mechanism

I have previously collected the following aspects for this type:

Type 5 is a head type. Its passion is greed, the fixation is stinginess, and the defense mechanism is isolation. Common designations are observer, thinker, researcher, and analyst.

Fear is the main underlying emotion of this head type. People with Type 5 may not be as afraid of the outside world as others, but they fear the emotional inner world. They don't understand much about this (in their minds), which confuses them and throws them off balance. This is true for the emotions of others as much as their own. This outlook is annoying, and the strategy of people with Type 5 for avoiding this or sweeping it under the rug is to escape inward, into their own thoughts. In their heads is an overview and insight, control, and calm. This is how the defense mechanism of isolation works: People with Type 5 isolate themselves from other people and from their own feelings. This isolation lets them live by their reason and inner peace as much as possible. As a result, people with Type 5 are focused on themselves, and they value privacy. They share the feeling that others expect more from them than they can offer. This is why they treat themselves, their time, their energy, and their knowledge frugally. That is the mental focus of stinginess: wanting to preserve themselves. Part of their strategy consists of being as independent of others as possible. If you don't have to ask others for anything, it reduces the likelihood that others want something from you. Their motto is "Live and let live. I'm giving you your space, and you should give me my space, too."

The Type 7 type mechanism

I have previously collected the following aspects for this type:

> *Type 7 is a head type. Its passion is insatiability, the fixation is making plans for the future, and the defense mechanism is rationalization. It's also called optimist, visionary, futurist, or planner.*

Just like the other two types, this one fights against fear. Though the fear of the outside makes people with Type 5 turn inward, those with Type 7 turn outward out of fear of their own inner selves. People with Type 7 are afraid of all unpleasant feelings they might experience, especially those that cause pain. They also fear being "trapped" inside, or unable to escape the bonds of their emotions. Based on the fear of their own inner pain, people with Type 7 prefer to focus on the outside world, where all options and opportunities are open. This is where Type 7 feels free and can decide on an optimistic, positive life.

The head type is reflected this way: People with Type 7 can work well in boring and less pleasant jobs, for example. People with Type 7 have to be able to decide on an optimistic, positive life, and this opportunity always exists in their minds. This is why planning is the fixation, or mental focus. The defense mechanism of rationalization functions as the glue for the type mechanism because the ability to reinterpret painful or negative experiences in a positive way actually leads to the avoidance of pain. People with Type 7 check out mentally so that they no longer have to deal with their suffering, and thus they protect themselves. The head center is strongly developed, including the strength of associative thinking. Type 7 easily combines many different things into creative new concepts and opportunities. Making plans aims for the future, just like all the Type 7's. This is where this type also gets its name: optimist, visionary, futurist, planner. The *associative* strength of Type 7, the ability to quickly arrive at a synthesis, also has a drawback: In Enneagram panels, people with Type 7 often report that their minds operate at a hectic pace.

The gut center

Your gut, or body, is the part of you that's visible to the outside world; your body performs your actions. This is where the energy is stored that you need in order to act. Gut types (see Figure 9-2) often talk about how they receive signals with their bodies — whether the atmosphere around them seems pleasant or tense, for example, or whether danger is lurking. It's their gut speaking to them.

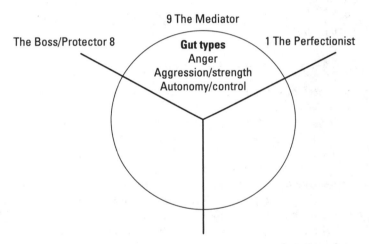

FIGURE 9-2:
Gut types have
the energy to act.

Scientists are learning more about the areas in the brain that are responsible for various functions. The drives seem to come from the reptilian brain — the basal ganglia (striatum) and brainstem that make up the most primitive part of the human brain. This fact was still completely unknown when the first spiritual traditions were developed, so the drives were assigned to the area in which they were experienced and expressed in the outside world: the lower body. The physical survival instinct and your drives are located in your lower body (although they are directed by the brain). Your instinct or drive to survive can focus on different areas: self-preservation (food, roof over your head), passing on your genes (reproduction), or preserving your group. Humans have been herd animals since prehistoric times and need the group to survive. Anger also plays an important role with regard to survival. It provides the inner energy humans need in order to assert themselves, to engage in the fight. Anger is the underlying emotion or energy shared by the three gut types.

In examining the gut types, I start with Type 9 — the core type of the three gut types. I call it the core type because it's the middle one of the three gut types (between Type 8 and Type 1) in the Enneagram circle in Figure 9-2.

The Type 9 type mechanism

I have previously collected the following aspects for this type:

> It's a gut type. Its passion is sluggishness, the fixation is self-effacement, and the defense mechanism is numbness. It is called mediator, networker, peacemaker, or negotiator.

For this gut type, anger plays a key role in the type mechanism. Among the three gut types, and as the core type, persons with Type 9 in particular have to make the most effort to conquer their anger and have the least contact with it.

The anger of Type 9 is expressed in passive/aggressive form. The defense mechanism of numbness ensures that this type's own anger is forgotten or put to sleep. It can be compared to a sleeping lion. It's no accident that this happens particularly to people with Type 9 — people for whom peace and harmony are the most important aspects of life. Then it's certainly convenient not to carry around any anger. It can also be useful in another respect. Anger has a certain function for humans: It provides the energy they need in order to stand up for themselves. Conflicts often arise when people stand up for their position. If you value peace and harmony above all else, it's therefore useful to simply forget the urge to assert yourself. Then there is a much lower risk of coming in conflict with other people. This is how the passion of sluggishness works: It's a kind of mental laziness, when you become too placid to either assert yourself or take care of yourself and do what's really good for you. Mentally, people with Type 9 are fully occupied by other people's wishes, thoughts, and actions. As a result of their patterns, this merging with the other happens automatically. They are in the habit of opening up to others and pleasing them. People with Type 9 forget themselves in the process.

When people with Type 9 are alone — at home in the evening, for example — and if there is some time and distance between them and others, they suddenly take their own center stage: They see what would have been important for them, what their position would have been, or what they would actually have wanted to do but didn't do because of the other(s). When the others are absent, the anger rises up all at once — anger that the Type 9 person had forgotten themselves or hadn't asserted themselves, and so on. The anger is directed toward the other person but also toward themselves. If others are present, in rare cases a Type 9 person can explode with rage, even when the targets of this rage happen to be loved ones. This seems strange, but only with these people do people with Type 9 feel safe enough to get angry, because the greatest fear of a Type 9 is that their anger causes them to lose a relationship. For a person striving toward peace and harmony, this is certainly the worst thing that can happen. In reality, people can be astonished when they have this kind of experience with a Type 9, especially since their rage — once unleashed — can express itself very aggressively. After all, people who rarely get angry don't have much practice in dealing with anger itself.

The Type 1 type mechanism

I have previously collected the following aspects for this type:

It's a gut type. Its passion is anger, the fixation is resentment, and the defense mechanism is reaction formation. This type is called a perfectionist, reformer, moralist, teacher, or world improver.

Type 1 is a gut type and its underlying passion is anger. Like those with Type 5, people with Type 1 are focused on the inside. Their anger is well-concealed in their gut. This gives Type 1 a certain advantage. How do perfectionists know if something is perfect? They don't know, which is why they set the bar high, just in case — preferably, as high as possible. People with Type 1 also develop standards because, with standards you can tell where you stand. This is primarily directed toward Type 1 persons themselves — their own behavior. The bar is also high here, just in case, and the standard is zero tolerance.

Someone with Type 1 has developed an interior helper for this: the superego. Every healthy person has a superego. It's your conscience that lets you distinguish between good and evil. For Type 1, however, it's an extra-superego, a strict sentinel who always monitors whether Type 1 sticks exactly to the rules. In the Enneagram, the sentinel of Type 1 is called the inner critic. This strict critic, as the inner voice, comments on everything a Type 1 does, which is rarely good enough. Even if others refuse to do what is required of them, the inner critic is still angry with Type 1 because the person should have known this beforehand.

What does this have to do with concealed anger? The standard for good behavior leaves no room for anger. The inner critic considers it the gravest kind of error. That's why it has to be suppressed. This is why the anger is expressed in the strength of the inner critic against Type 1 itself. If the anger of people with Type 1 at some point becomes truly unstoppable and comes out, it will feel good at that moment, and then these persons can completely let themselves go. Only afterward do the feelings of guilt and admonitions from the inner critic come. This is because the mental fixation of resentment insists that it's someone else's fault if Type 1 strays from the path of virtue. The resentment is often expressed to others in a scolding tone.

People with Type 1, by the way, allow themselves to get angry at others if they feel entitled to it. This might happen if an employee is often late, for example, after the person with Type 1 has already told the person several times in a friendly manner that punctuality would be appreciated. The defense mechanism of the reaction formation is that the anger, when it arises, isn't expressed quickly and severely, but rather in a moderate form of annoyance that is acceptable to Type 1. Many people recognize this annoyance more easily than their anger. The reaction formation also plays a role if the employee is late for the first time. Although Type 1 already gets angry at this point, the person doesn't think it's justified yet and won't allow themselves to show it. Instead, they present themselves as extremely patient, expressing understanding for being late and stating in a friendly way that they would be happy for the tardiness not to happen quite so often. So the reaction formation helps Type 1 show a controlled demeanor and appropriate behavior. This affects not only their anger but also every impulse that arises.

The Type 8 type mechanism

I have previously collected the following aspects for this type:

> *It's a gut type. Its passion is lust, the fixation is revenge, and the defense mechanism is denial. Its names are boss/protector, fighter, person in charge, leader, or challenger.*

Anger also plays a key role for gut Type 8. Just like Type 7 and Type 2, Type 8 is oriented outward. Though people with Type 1 suppress the energy of their anger, this energy clearly and explicitly goes outward for Type 8, toward contact with the outside world. Type 8 doesn't suppress much; the energy needed to assert oneself is easily and quickly available. People with Type 8 also use this energy to make themselves big and strong when the situation calls for it. By nature, Type 8 people have the situation, the room, and others under control. Type 8 is direct and clear and confronts easily. Compared to most other types, Type 8 doesn't even experience asserting oneself as a form of confrontation.

Above all, the Enneagram teaches how relative everything is. What is seen as a confrontation from the perspective of one type is definitely not seen the same from the perspective of another. This alone creates many misunderstandings between people: They believe that they understand the same thing by the word *confrontation* or *conflict,* but this isn't the case. When you ask people with Type 8 whether they regularly argue or get into conflicts, they usually say no. In the perception of the Type 8 person, they have only briefly spoken their mind — nothing more. People with Type 8 don't realize that other people and types need about an hour to recover from the verbal slaps they've handed out. This also has to do with the defense mechanism of denial. As just described, persons with Type 8 protect their own vulnerability by denying it. This lets them distinguish themselves as strong and powerful people in the outside world. The denial doesn't refer only to their own vulnerability but also to many other things, such as the ideas, wishes, truths, and interests of others. In combative situations in particular, people with Type 8 can be totally blind to this and thus fail despite their own power and strength. The mental fixation of revenge doesn't seem that difficult for this fighter, leader, and challenger, but it won't occur often because other people prefer to avoid Type 8. A Type 8 often doesn't know exactly what they project, can't understand such a reaction, and therefore feel unhappy.

The heart center

The heart center is the center from which humans connect with the outside world, with others. The heart types are oriented toward "matters of the heart": love, affection, their (social) environment, the people around them. (See Figure 9-3.) All three heart types share the underlying emotion of sadness. The sadness is due to the fact that they feel disconnected from their environment, but it also has to do with the question shared by all heart types: the question of identity, the "Who am I?". In its development, each child goes through an identification stage in which it becomes conscious of itself and forms its own identity. For the heart types, this has remained an open question; they see themselves through the eyes of others to find an answer for what their own identity might be. Many people like getting attention, but it isn't as big a deal for them as it is for the three heart types. Each heart type has developed its own strategy to answer the question about their identity and combat the subliminal feeling of sadness.

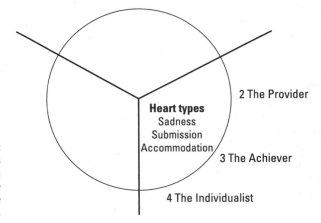

FIGURE 9-3:
Heart types concentrate on affairs of the heart in the broadest sense.

Let's start with the core type of the three heart types, Type 3. I call it the core type because it's the middle one of the three heart types (between Type 2 and Type 4 in the circle).

The Type 3 type mechanism

I have previously collected the following aspects for this type:

It's a heart type. Its passion is deception, the fixation is vanity, and the defense mechanism is identification. This type is called dynamic, successful, ambitious, performer, or striving.

From the orientation toward others, striving for attention and recognition, this child developed a strategy for getting applause for their achievements and by racking up points. People with Type 3 often talk about how great it was to be in the spotlight on stage early on in life. The answer to the question "Who am I?" was, "If I have to become anything, then make it something successful." Just like actors, people with Type 3 can play different roles, but each role they take on is that of a successful type: the ideal son-in-law, the sweetest partner, the boss who is good at motivating others, and so on. This is caused by their mental fixation of vanity. The defense mechanism of identification helps them assume the characteristics of the desired image as if they were their own. This allows people with Type 3 to deceive themselves and their environment. Type 3 persons are engaged with taking on successful roles and hide themselves behind this façade. Deep inside, they also worry that everything is empty beneath the shells of their roles — or that if anything were concealed under there, they would shy away from it. This is why they prefer to stick with their roles and go on with the show starring their successful image. In every role, people with Type 3 are constantly busy achieving their set goals, fulfilling their tasks, and keeping up a nice façade. The advantage of this constant engagement is that people with Type 3 don't feel the underlying sadness. Deep inside, they know that it exists, which means they can't sit still. Otherwise, that feeling might surface. The deception of Type 3 consists of identifying with achievements and superficial matters to satisfy their idea of success and recognition. Many report that their greatest inner fear is that someone could come around and pop this bubble.

The Type 4 type mechanism

I have previously collected the following aspects for this type:

It's a heart type. Its passion is envy, the fixation is melancholy, and the defense mechanism is introjection. This type is called an individualist, artist, or creative idealist.

Just like Type 5 and Type 1, Type 4 turns inward to answer the question "Who am I?" People with Type 4 consider themselves the center of the universe. Heart types are oriented toward others. Type 4 persons do this so that they can compare themselves. People with Type 4 come to the conclusion that they're different and unique compared to what they see around them. When Type 4 individuals see themselves through someone else's eyes, they might feel ashamed precisely because they realize how different they are, or how far apart they are. They don't belong to the group but neither do they want to belong. Nonetheless, they have the need for relationships and connection. In a certain way, Type 4 even wants to be normal, like the others. This creates a sense of melancholy. As a result, the inner lives of people with Type 4 are ruled by a constant dichotomy: attract or repel, belong or create boundaries, feel superior and then inferior again, and so on. To define the image of "Who am I?," the strategy of people with Type 4 is to internalize what is being idealized — this is how the defense mechanism of introjection works. Compare this with Type 3, who internally strives toward an image of success. People with Type 4, for example, see strengths in someone and idealize them ("it would be incredible to be just like that") and also want to have these strengths. Motivated by the passion of envy, they now start to awaken these strengths inside them and strive for them. By nature, their attention is directed toward the important and special qualities that may be lacking in their own character or their own lives. This creates a mechanism that overlooks what is positive and good in the here-and-now and attracts what is positive in the then-and-there, but is missing in the here-and-now. Because people with Type 4 are so strongly oriented toward their own inner world, their heart center is highly developed. Emotions, including sadness about being different, are increased. This allows a Type 4 to avoid, in any case, everyday boredom and mediocrity.

The Type 2 type mechanism

I have previously collected the following aspects for this type:

> *It's a heart type. Its passion is pride, the fixation is flattery, and the defense mechanism is suppression. This type is called a provider, helper, seducer, servant, or manipulator.*

As a heart type, people with Type 2 are also heavily oriented toward others and feel deep inside the subliminal sadness of the question "Who am I?" Their own identity is adapted to the outside world and other people. By being there for others and making themselves indispensable, they create an identity. The question "Who am I?" is answered with this reply: "I'm someone whom others consider helpful, who is needed by others, whom others consider nice," and so on. Just like the other heart types, people with Type 2 see themselves through the eyes of others.

The habit of being available for others, sensing other people's needs, and always giving arises from the other person's perspective, but is based on the needs of Type 2 persons themselves. They derive their identity from these habits, even a reason for their very existence — who would people with Type 2 be if no one would need them? That's why they seem selfless at first glance, but at heart, they get something quite important for their sacrifice: a reason for existing and attention from others. "I'm perceived; therefore, I am." This is why Type 2 persons are oriented so much toward others — because others give them what they themselves care about.

People with Type 2 derive their self-esteem from being indispensable. At the same time, they are too proud inside to realize that they also have requirements and are in need of others. The image of a Type 2 looks like this: "Others need me. That's how the world works, not the other way around." This is why it's terrible for Type 2 persons if their help isn't needed or is even rejected. It feels like a personal rejection that hurts their pride. The goal of the flattery of Type 2 is not only to have the other person make room for them but also to "sell" their own help and thus be valuable. Type 2 believes in an earnings model and weighs how much was already given. At some point, payday will arrive.

Because people with Type 2 feel that they give of themselves through their help, what the others give back usually isn't sufficient. They also aren't aware of when they feel it might be payday and they don't mention it to the other person. And, this is how people with Type 2 create their own disappointments — because another person, who has gotten used to them helping gladly and joyfully, doesn't know that the time has arrived to pay up. I often hear people with Type 2 talk about how disappointed they are by others and how they are always left alone when something difficult happens. Because of their strong orientation toward helping, they don't notice when others try to help *them*. A final aspect here is the role of their defense mechanism — suppression. As described earlier, Type 2 persons are there for others to such a high degree only because they suppress their own needs and desires — but such needs and such desires still exist. However, if you were to ask people with Type 2 what they want or need, they wouldn't know, indicating the depth of their suppression. In fact, Type 2 persons give others what they actually want for themselves. The unconscious deal is this: "I'll meet your needs — you'll meet mine" and "I'll help you; and you'll help me." A deal that is rarely made in the Type 2 system is this: "Help me first, and then I'll help you."

Chapter **10**

The Final Word on Types

Maybe you're still "digesting" the main course of Part 2, which presents the components of the type mechanisms to you. This chapter, the dessert, is a light and fluffy finish to this rather savory part of the book. This chapter offers you the following interesting insights about the types, which you're free to read in comfort for your very own entertainment:

» What people of a particular type generally like

» What they generally dislike

» What others find annoying about them

I close out this chapter by listing the strengths shared by people of the same type.

Taking a Look at Two Quirky Tables

Quite a few things can be derived from being different, from living with different worries and striving for things that are the focus of your attention but not the focus of others. These characteristics are often listed in the descriptions of the Enneagram types. Tables 10-1 and 10-2 show you what the types value, what they like even less than other people do, and what other people sometimes find annoying about them.

REMEMBER

Try to understand the mentioned characteristics from the perspective of the type mechanism.

TABLE 10-1: ## Type Characteristics

Type	What the Types Like	What They Find Annoying	What Others Find Annoying about a Certain Type
Type 1	Quality; responsible people; honesty	Shoddy workmanship, laxity, irresponsibility	(Unspoken) criticism, perfectionism, rigidity
Type 2	Being helpful, being emotionally there for others, friendliness	Not being recognized, rejection, unfriendliness, absent-minded behavior	Excessive helpfulness, meddling, manipulation, paternalism
Type 3	Setting the pace, success, self-confidence	Inefficiency, failure, losing face	Superficiality or insincerity, lack of integrity, profiling to gain attention
Type 4	Authenticity, depth, sensitivity	The things (qualities and/or possessions) others seemingly have, insensitivity, the banal	Moody, melancholy, having unrealistic expectations
Type 5	Intelligence, respect for others' personal space, careful use of language	Confused thinking, chaos, emotional reaction, lack of structure, excessive expectations	Distant, introverted, excessively questioning and analyzing, difficult to connect with
Type 6	Loyalty, clarity, openness	Unreliability, ambiguity, not knowing where I stand with someone	Distrust, not being believed, overly cautious and prone to second-guessing, the feeling of being tested by others
Type 7	Optimism, having a rich personality, open to new possibilities	Limits, routines, or anything else that causes pain or minimizes having fun	Self-centered, sugarcoating everything, dominating all forms of communication
Type 8	Being direct, empowerment, fairness	Lack of respect, inequity, having to toe the line	Controlling, disrespectful, unable to recognize the views and interests of others
Type 9	Harmony, stability, tranquility	Disagreement/discussion, change, tension	Procrastinating, avoiding problems or conflicts, lack of clarity

TABLE 10-2: ## The Strengths of Each Type

Type	Qualities
Type 1 **The Perfectionist**	Industrious, honest, responsible, diligent, idealistic, independent, dedicated, does the right thing, has high standards
Type 2 **The Provider**	Generous, helpful, giving, romantic, sensitive, appreciative, supportive, energetic, lively, expressive, willing
Type 3 **The Achiever**	Industrious, enthusiastic, hopeful, encouraging, solution-oriented, efficient, practical, competent; has leadership qualities and is able to articulate clear goals
Type 4 **The Individualist**	Sensitive, empathetic (compassionate), intense, romantic, passionate, idealistic; sees new and creative opportunities (from unexpected perspectives), in touch with emotions, appreciative of things that are unique and/or special
Type 5 **The Observer**	Educated and eager to learn, knowledgeable, pensive, objective (calm in a crisis), respectful, appreciative of the simple things, reliable, ascetic; can also keep a secret
Type 6 **The Loyal Skeptic**	Thoughtful, warm, protective, devoted to others, trusting (after a certain amount of time), intuitive, sensitive, full of good ideas, sharply perceptive, loyal, honest, funny
Type 7 **The Optimist**	Playful, cheerful, inventive, imaginative, energetic, optimistic, inspiring, enthusiastic; loves life and recognizes opportunities
Type 8 **Boss/Protector**	Strong, powerful, exciting, intense, decisive, courageous, assertive, protective of others, fair, friendly, sincere, honest, clear, direct, firm
Type 9 **The Mediator**	Careful, conscientious of others, empathetic, adaptable, accepting, supportive, predictable, reliable, sensitive, stable, calm, receptive, nonjudgmental

3

Working with the Information You Get

IN THIS CHAPTER

» Practicing self-management

» Taking an empathy booster

» Refining consultation techniques

» Finding out more about effective communication

» Taking a closer look at the communication characteristics of the individual types

Chapter **11**

Applying the Enneagram in the Workplace

This chapter is all about Enneagram applications in the workplace, which should prove particularly interesting to professional consultants who have to deal with people's inability to be effective employees. Many people could use a good tool to more rapidly assess the characteristics of people with whom they interact, but this applies particularly well to managers, mediators, coaches, personnel managers, (couples) therapists, pastors, organizational consultants, (management) trainers, advisers, lecturers, doctors, entrepreneurs, and others. In which profession do you not have to deal with people's ability (or lack thereof) to act effectively?

There are numerous jobs where support for a program of personal development isn't part of the standard protocol, even if the consultants would be glad to provide it for their clients. Think about the work situation of a mediator, for example: If the disputing parties at the mediator's table could be inspired to pursue self-awareness and development, it could help solve the problem — but when someone is placed in a difficult and often embarrassing or insecure position, asking for all parties to take the time to do some serious inner work seems particularly unrealistic. I'm often asked: "How are we supposed to deal with all that, in addition to the immediate issues facing us now?" This chapter gives you some answers to that question.

A Workplace Overview

I want to start this section by describing some aspects, techniques, and applications of the Enneagram that have proven of great practical use in many professions — and are also suitable for use at home.

I often offer introductory sessions for the Enneagram to special occupational groups. In these settings, the possible applications for each professional group take center stage. In most situations, the Enneagram is used because it can greatly benefit someone in their profession.

For consultation jobs, this benefit consists of

>> Self-management

>> An increased capacity for empathy

With the help of the Enneagram, it's easier to sympathize with another person, meaning that clients can be assessed quickly, thoroughly, and precisely, leading to a more effective and efficient cooperation with greater profit.

>> The refinement of professional skills

Mastering self-management

The greatest benefit of the Enneagram may consist of offering a reference point for self-management. How can you manage others if you don't have a grip on yourself? This applies to many jobs, not just managers. Developing your skills with regard to self-management will help you improve in general. You'll notice that things will keep getting easier and more pleasant, especially when it comes to the workplace. You can gain a lot through self-management, because you'll notice that it helps you perform your job more professionally. The following example shows what I'm talking about.

EXAMPLE

Margaret (Type 9) works independently as a financial consultant. She specializes in family businesses and often takes on the role of a test audience for the owner. She has a home office. Because of her work situation, she likes to receive customers at her office. However, she has to consider that she easily feels rushed. Margaret is easily excitable and has a hard time saying no. (In fact, she's already had a burnout.) At the moment, Margaret is spinning in circles: A new customer called to confirm an appointment for tomorrow — at his company. Before Margaret was really aware of it, she had already agreed. But it takes a significant amount of time to drive to the company and, when she accepted the job, she clarified that meetings would have to take place at her office — otherwise, she wouldn't be able to take on new customers. Margaret is in a tight spot tomorrow because the drive time will prevent her from attending other meetings that she had already long ago committed to. What should she do?

Wouldn't it be nice if Margaret could identify her type mechanism, which makes her say yes quickly, even if she doesn't want something? And wouldn't it be even better if she could learn self-management to avoid stepping into the same trap each time?

EXAMPLE

Mary (Type 1), an educator, is a sweetheart. She has endless patience to explain everything in detail to the children, gently and patiently, and clearly and exactly. She explains things step-by-step, with all details. If a child doesn't do what she wants, she explains the task again. With all her patience, Mary needs a lot of words because she worries that the children won't understand her otherwise. But Stan is part of her children's group. He falls asleep during all the talking. As soon as Mary starts, he has already switched off. The educator doesn't understand why Stan isn't catching on to what she wants from him. After all, she's explaining it in great detail. Stan would understand the message better if it were presented briefly and to the point. Then he can listen and understand what he has to do. His mother has already explained this preference to the educator: She should tell Stan what is asked of him in as few words as possible — preferably, with information like this: "These are the rules, and this is agreed, and this is how it's done. When I check on you in ten minutes, you'll be finished, right? So go ahead and start working." This expectation is expressed clearly. But it's so far removed from Mary's normal interaction with children that she can't get the words out.

Defining self-management

Self-management is the ability to observe, recognize, and learn to accept your thoughts, feelings, and actions in order to adapt them to what is effective in a particular situation and interaction with another person. All this happens with the knowledge that life will present new challenges to you every day. One important challenge consists of seeing these situations as development opportunities. The situations and people that you consider difficult are precisely the ones that give you an opportunity to grow.

Thinking through the various aspects of the development of self-management, the following characteristics come to the top of the list:

>> **Self-consciousness:** This involves the ability to observe yourself to develop self-awareness. Self-consciousness is when someone can perceive thoughts, feelings, and actions at the moment at which they arise.

>> **Degree of self-motivation and responsibility:** This one plays a great role when it comes to the development of self-management — the degree to

which someone is internally motivated to change, to assume responsibility for oneself and one's behavior. As long as people remain stuck in the outlook that something isn't their fault because it's someone else's responsibility, their development stagnates.

>> **Receptivity to feedback:** The willingness for, and receptivity to, feedback starts with someone's demeanor. Only if someone presents themselves as open to feedback do other people dare give it. Someone who is receptive to feedback can really listen to it, let it get close to them, and do something with it. At the same time, this person can differentiate between appropriate feedback and *prejudiced* opinion (tinged by the type).

>> **Emotional maturity:** This one is the degree to which someone assumes responsibility for themselves. Do you see yourself as a victim who depends on others? This one decides whether someone can act only reactively or observe a situation from a distance while perceiving not just their own perspective but also that of the other person. It's the degree to which you can develop an overview of the different factors and perspectives that influence the situation so that each one can be considered.

Here are some tips for your own self-management regimen:

>> **Start writing in a journal.** Take five minutes for this task each morning and evening.

>> **Write down your learning goals.** Also write the learning pitfalls that are hindering you on your path to these goals.

>> **Find out what it is that makes you fall into the same trap over and over again.** Use your knowledge of your Enneagram type to determine what's behind this habit.

>> **Always have a Plan B (and C and D):** For each pitfall, come up with three alternatives that you want to rehearse.

>> **Focus on a single resolution for the day.** You can do this in the morning, while eating breakfast or taking a shower. You can work on one of the alternatives to how you approach someone that you want to rehearse when the right situation arises.

>> **Take stock of yourself throughout the day.** You can set up a fixed time for a daily review, a moment to sense how you feel.

>> **Before going to sleep at night, evaluate how the day went.** What led to your having tried (or not tried) that one resolution you had set for yourself earlier? What stopped you? Was it difficult or much simpler than you thought? What happened inside you? What did you learn from the experience? Write down the answer and think about a resolution for the next day. Maybe try that one next?

EXAMPLE

Tim (Type 4) wants to manage himself and become more serene and positive. At work, he noticed that his tendency to talk mainly about problems at work whenever he strikes up a conversation with his colleagues has caused others to keep their distance and be reluctant to start any kind of conversation with him. His colleagues also react by increasingly pointing out the positive side of things and apparently are no longer listening to him. Tim started a journal to help him keep track of his thoughts. Mornings, he focuses on a resolution for the day, and evenings, he looks back at how it went and considers a new resolution for the next day. He notices that it works for him when he keeps everything as simple as possible and proceeds in small steps. Here's what that process looks like:

Journal

Monday

Resolution: Stop myself when I catch myself expressing my emotions negatively, and then reword them positively.

Evaluation: I caught myself three times during the team meeting. Twice, the rewording didn't work. The third time, I asked the team for a moment so that I could reword my sentence. Roy (Type 2) responded to this request amazingly well and offered his help!

Tuesday

Resolution: Ask Roy to give me a sign when I do "it" again.

Evaluation: . . .

Recognizing that what works for you doesn't always work for others

When you want to work more effectively, you need to learn to adapt your approach to match whatever is good for others. You may tell yourself that you're just different and it feels wrong for you to align your approach with the approach of someone else — in effect, offering them what works for them. That attitude will probably prevent you from actually trying this strategy, but you may be passing on a great opportunity. The only way to know for sure is to give it a try and see whether it works. By offering an approach that might fit for the other person, you grant yourself this experience, and when you see how this works, you build self-confidence and internalize this new work method. The following is an exercise you should try.

PRACTICE

You probably have someone close to you with whom you keep encountering the same problem. It might be as part of a discussion, when working together with someone, when supporting a client, or with someone at home. It doesn't have to be a big deal; issues that aren't all that serious are actually better suited for exercises. Think about how you have previously dealt with this on the basis of your settled habits as a result of your type. What could you do differently if you would adapt your behavior to fit the other person? Prepare this experiment with the following steps:

>> What is the nature of the situation?

>> What have you done previously based on your type-dependent action strategies?

>> How does this affect the other person?

>> What doesn't work?

>> What would you like to achieve instead?

>> What might work better for the other person?

Overcoming obstacles

How do you find out what works better for the other person? How can you coordinate with that person?

In the exercise in the previous section, you might have already noticed that this question creates problems for you. (That's why I suggest just asking the other person what works for them!) But you can also learn to empathize by familiarizing yourself with the concept and immersing yourself in a study of the Enneagram types. For that to work, though, you have to know which type the other person has. How can you find out?

INCREASING YOUR CAPACITY FOR EMPATHY

If you reflect deeply on yourself and engage with the other eight types, the Enneagram will help you better understand other people's feelings. What might be happening inside the other person? Which approach might function for that person, and which might not? For some employees or clients, it can be helpful to give them more space and time for a decision; for others, it would be exactly the wrong thing. The designs of the Enneagram help you develop a fast, in-depth, and precise insight into your client so that you can work for that client more effectively, more efficiently, and with a greater benefit. Working with the Enneagram can also help you coordinate your approach to what works for the other person. Based on your own type, you usually subconsciously assume that what works for you also applies to all others. This limits the alternatives for actions, usually to the approach that works best for you or that you would want for yourself. Because every person is different, however, you also should know that your own approach is likely not suitable for all others.

IF I ONLY DID [BLANK] MORE, OR LESS, OR DIFFERENTLY . . .

Suppose that you have no idea what might work better for another person or what could prevent the usual difficult situation from recurring. You think: "I really tried everything. I can't think of anything else!" People often hear this complaint in coaching sessions and meditations and the like. Ask the other person! Tell them that you tend to approach something in a certain way — that you noticed it doesn't work this way for them — and ask what would work instead. You'll be surprised by how much people enjoy being asked such a question.

When you work on yourself with the Enneagram, you gain knowledge and insights through self-observation and reflection. If it's about you, you can conveniently look directly inside yourself. When you want to use the Enneagram for others, however, you can't look inside their heads to see what happens there. Of course, it's particularly nice if the Enneagram is applied in a (work) situation and there is the possibility of working with the employee or client to explore their type. This immediately gets you talking about how their inner thought processes work. But there are many situations where such openness isn't possible. Then it isn't advisable to work explicitly with the Enneagram. Just think back to the example of Margaret, the financial consultant. What could she do with the Enneagram? Read on to find out.

Working with Hypotheses

Assume that, in your position, it isn't possible to carry out the standard type assessment interview with the relevant person. As I have stressed time and again, you can't determine the other person's Enneagram type merely on the basis of their external behavior. What's called for here is your empathy, for your intention to truly empathize with the other person. If this intention isn't genuine, it won't succeed.

My argument here is that, if you're in a situation where you're able to use all the tools of the Enneagram to assess the types of other people, all you can really do is train yourself to hear and see the other person better. By getting into the habit of not being judgmental, you can ask yourself sincerely: What might be happening inside the other person? What is their attention focused on? What do they seem to consider truly important deep inside? This explorative and empathetic attitude results in a hypothesis about which type the other person might have. You can ask this person about it: "Do I understand correctly that . . .?" This gives you the foundation of your hypothesis. Relating to another person, combined with knowledge about the Enneagram, immediately results in a deeper insight into the other person. With that insight under your belt, you can now test your hypothesis with more specific questions.

When it comes to other people, you work on the basis of hypotheses. In the best-case scenario, you make assumptions and try to empathize with the other person. By developing awareness and committing to learning, you can improve your skills. But reality checks are still necessary! You also need to be open-minded so that you always keep in mind that you might have assessed the other person incorrectly. Keep in mind that, in the final analysis, no one can know what happens in another person's mind. As soon as you think that you *do* know, your alarm bells should be going off.

Improved consultation techniques

One final professional benefit provided by the Enneagram involves the role it can play in refining general consultation techniques. Many training events take place each year in which various general consultation and management techniques are taught. The list of popular topics is long: effective communication, creating memorable presentations, giving productive feedback, influencing the decision-making process, developing assertiveness, acting more effectively. When you learn a new technique, the material tends to all look the same for each participant. You're taught to give feedback, for example, on the basis that one-size-fits-all when it comes to learning styles. At a technical level, all this does in fact apply. Of course, you know that, at a practical level, people give and receive feedback in very different ways. The participants often come up with their own analyses of their strengths and weaknesses as giver and receiver of feedback.

DIFFERENT INFORMATION (AND DIFFERENT SOURCES OF INFORMATION)

Several things help you increase your observational skills and assume an open and curious posture at the same time. Knowing that there are different sources of information and various types of information can be a great help in this regard. Here's what to look for:

- Can you characterize the general impression people make — for example, how they express themselves?

- Can you see what engages these individuals?

- Are they mainly trying to excel at something?

- Do they want to help?

- Are they impatient?

- Do they have a tendency to be overdramatic?

- Do they see the pessimistic side of things, or do they stop to analyze what might work in a situation?

- Are they frugal with words, playful and casual, or do they try to grasp the reins in each situation?

- Are they direct or even harsh?

- Do they work harmoniously with others, or do they mainly act defiantly?

These are habits that you can observe and that point toward a certain type. On the other hand, having one habit or the other in abundance means that you can clearly exclude certain other types.

You can also practice to consciously perceive these actions in others:

- **Nonverbal behavior:** Gestures, attitude, mannerisms, agility, facial expressions, eye movements, rigid stares

- **Voice signals:** Speed, volume, rhythm, tone, style

- **The energy projected by the other:** Intensity, dominance, tension (muscles), extroverted or introverted

- **Attentiveness:** Focused or chaotic; directed outward or inward; tending more toward feeling, thinking or acting; on the whole or in detail; trusting or controlling; genuine or all pretense; being present or being absent; being positive or negative; oriented toward the past, present, or future; oriented more toward oneself or more toward others; leader or supportive follower

You'll be surprised by all the things you can "read" from a person when you look more closely without judging!

Using your knowledge of human nature in a structured way and adapting and practicing the giving/receiving of feedback on that basis is, of course, far too much for basic training. All participants learn the same approach during assertiveness training, for example, but all participants are different and each has their own problems when it comes to assertiveness. Good trainers note these individual differences and give the participants appropriate tips accordingly. We humans are all different. After having learned certain techniques in general, the next step is refinement, which consists of enhancing and applying any type-specific professional learning. This includes knowing your own type and taking this knowledge into consideration. This coordination between your own type and that of the other is the ultimate refinement.

Effective communication

In this section, I want to present a certain skill in more detail as one example that can stand in for many. This is Skill 1, one that's at the heart of all areas related to effective, professional, and emotionally intelligent action — namely, effective communication. Communication is *the* key competence that plays a role in every job. The ability to communicate effectively greatly influences career opportunities and success. Everyone needs this skill and uses it continually in everyday life. People communicate from early morning to late at night: on the phone, in meetings, with customers, in emails, in the hallway, in writing, privately with another, at court, with colleagues, at the hospital, with partners, at school, or while shopping. Success at work and the maintenance of long-lasting relationships depends entirely on an individual's ability to communicate.

REMEMBER

Human communication is targeted. With its help, you want to maintain and stabilize relationships, you want to be understood correctly, you hope to achieve an effect, you want to exert an influence. But let's be honest: In reality, people don't always manage to do this. Have you ever caught yourself not listening at all when someone else is speaking? Or speaking over or interrupting someone who hasn't finished speaking yet? Or is it the other way around for you, so that others don't listen to you and they interrupt you? Have you ever been misunderstood?

Why do some people communicate more effectively than others? Just as with all aspects of activity, the level of personal development plays a definite role here. It actually has nothing to do with the respective type, but the personally preferred style and tendencies during communication, along with the development points at which one can learn to communicate better, certainly depend on the type. Each type has its own communication style with its own strengths and weaknesses. For everyone, this is compounded by body language and other nonverbal behavior that affects communication.

REMEMBER

When I talk about optimizing communication, I mean the quality of sending and receiving. You'll experience that this quality has an effect on the people with whom you communicate.

To see what I mean, check out the characteristic properties of each Enneagram type when acting as senders and recipients:

>> **Type 1**

- *Sender:* Precise, direct, careful, clear, and detailed. Attention is paid to the tasks at hand and what can be improved. Tends to work and communicate with focus and seriousness, and occasionally forgets to relax. Jokes, superficialities, and small talk that diminish focus and speed during work are lost on Type 1 or rejected. Reacts quickly and sometimes defensively.

Explains a lot, provides a lot of additional information, and tends to be defensive and look for validation. Often uses words like *must, should, may, proper, and right and wrong.*

- *Recipient:* Because Type 1 is focused on avoiding errors and thus preventing criticism, this person's receiving antennas are directed precisely toward anything that might come remotely close to criticism. Anything that does must be noticed immediately so that it can be refuted and corrected just as quickly. Because Type 1 persons can be so filled by, and convinced of, their own ideas, they don't always hear what the other person is trying to say.

›› Type 2

- *Sender:* Attentive, social, interested, warm, smiling, relaxed — in a word, *pleasant.* A person with Type 2 gives compliments, asks questions, and focuses on the other and what that person has to say. They can give people the sense that they are seen and listened to. Flattery is not unusual for Type 2. They often take the lead in a conversation, in the role of the questioner. The message they send is, "You're important to me. I want to establish a connection. Please like me." The conversation is often about people because Type 2 people are interested in people. If they're disappointed by others, they can bemoan this fact and even complain for quite some time.

- *Recipient:* Often, they precisely remember things that someone has told them previously and long forgotten again. A Type 2 person receives signals on how they're doing. If someone else interjects with an idea, a suggestion, or an offer, a Type 2 person often rejects this automatically, often even before the other person has finished speaking. The filters in the discussion are set to ensure that the other person considers Type 2 individuals to be nice, but also whether they like the other person and want to help them. In a discussion, they filter how important the other one is, and how interesting it is for Type 2 to carve out a place with this other person by making an effort (giving something).

›› Type 3

- *Sender:* Clear, efficient, charming, well-packaged, goal-oriented, quick, and not one word too many. The Type 3 person exudes self-confidence. The other types often see them as fairly superficial. As goal- and task-oriented as they are, they often appear impatient and driven, sometimes to the point that they no longer notice the other person. This is particularly true when it seems as if the individual they have to deal with can't contribute much to achieving their goals or seems incompetent. A team member who stands in the way of reaching the goal effectively and efficiently can drive this type crazy. Type 3 individuals let other persons know when their time is up. The conversation can't take too long.

- *Recipient:* With their enthusiastic, charming approach, intended to win points with the other person, a Type 3 person can initially give others the feeling of being noticed — but this can't take too long. In some people with Type 3, discussion partners notice this immediately, even if the Type 3 person wants to conceal it. They're oriented toward reaching a goal; their filter is set to receive information that can serve this goal. Actually listening and receiving isn't a strong point of this type. Additionally, Type 3 persons filter whether others and the information they provide represent an aid or a threat to their own success.

» Type 4

- *Sender:* Intense; sometimes gentle, quiet, and loving — and sometimes downright stubborn and powerful; a Type 4 person projects an urgent and insistent demeanor. These individuals often seem to be the followers in discussions, and they adapt to the other, probing the depths. The words *I, me,* and *mine* often appear in their speech. The discussion topics that interest them are feelings and the sharing of personal stories. A Type 4 person has a tendency to ask personal questions. A conversation they start is either about the beautiful things in life or about problems. Making things problematic is their natural reaction. Others sometimes feel that they have to walk on eggshells around this type and thus avoid conversations or any contact at all.

- *Recipient:* A Type 4 person is sensitive to others and their reactions. The filter through which these folks perceive the world reacts to whether the other person rejects them. They are concerned with their own shortcomings and filter the other person's message accordingly. A Type 4 person might have trouble opening up to the positive and good intentions of the other person. They're sensitive to getting another person's full attention and being well understood. They have developed their antennas to this end and can react quickly and fiercely if they don't feel sufficiently considered or (heaven forbid!) understood.

» Type 5

- *Sender:* Knows two stylistic directions: First, this minimalist says only the most essential statements in a few words — briefly, specifically, and to the point — and at the other extreme, can get be quite verbose and hold virtual lectures. The kind of sending style chosen by people with Type 5 depends on their level of expertise on the subject and on the audience. They waste their precious words only on those who are worth it. These individuals keep quiet if they don't feel competent when it comes to a topic. People with Type 5 generally have a good sense of language and choose their words carefully. They share their thoughts but only few feelings, if any.

- *Recipient:* A Type 5 person is reserved and prefers watching, listening, and questioning. They generally assume an objective, neutral, and nonjudgmental position. The filters of these persons are focused on the expectations and demands of others. The filters become active when they get the sense that they're failing — perhaps if something is demanded of them that they can't provide or if it concerns topics that they feel less than competent about, such as emotions. A Type 5 person filters for other people's feelings. When those become overwhelming, this type shields themselves.

» Type 6

- *Sender:* Warm, calm, sympathetic, and alternately questioning, doubtful, or assertive. When people with Type 6 are assertive, it's often strongly emphasized in a nonverbal way, as though they would have to convince themselves. They discuss their doubts and worries and establish what-if scenarios. People with Type 6 are familiar with the phrase "Yes, but." As vigilant as they are, they pay close attention to the other person while speaking. People with this type respond to the slightest signals from the other with the phrase, "Now, you probably believe . . ." and thus complete the other person's sentences.

- *Recipient:* A Type 6 person is on guard: Does the other person mean what they're saying? This prevents the Type 6 person from receiving what the other one really says or means. What stands most in the way of reception for this type is the habit of *projecting* — completing other people's sentences instead of really listening to them and trusting that what they say is what they actually mean. This can give their conversation partners the feeling of being tested and judged as noncredible.

» Type 7

- *Sender:* Quick, spontaneous, cheerful, optimistic, charming. A Type 7 tells compelling stories and has always experienced something worth telling. Thanks to the heavily associative reasoning of people with this type, they jump from topic to topic and the conversation is never boring. When they're finished, they move to the next discussion partner. Type 7 individuals actively move when they speak. They seem to emit an electrical charge and act like their very own transmission stations. They're more focused on themselves and their own stories than on the other person.

- *Recipient:* This is the difficult side of Type 7. As soon as someone else says something, people with this type often have difficulties controlling their associative reasoning. The pleasant part is that they usually react with enthusiasm whenever a new topic is brought up. But while the other person is still speaking, Type 7 individuals are already completely fascinated by what is going on in their own minds. It's obvious that they're no longer listening. Because people with this type are busy with their own thoughts, they sometimes interrupt others in the middle of talking, complete the other person's sentences, or move on to an entirely different topic. It's difficult for them to focus on what someone else is saying for a longer period. As a result, others often get the sense that they aren't being listened to.

» Type 8

- *Sender:* Direct, open, honest, fast, short, authoritative, rude. Controls the discussion and the situation as the sender. This doesn't mean that Type 8 people are always speaking. They can keep their mouths shut, but they always stay in control. They easily grow impatient if the conversation takes too long or goes into too much detail, or if too much thinking is required. People with Type 8 can't relate to talk that seems to them like so much nuanced, intellectual drivel. They want talk that is short and sweet. Rules are rules, and they are adhered to. This type likes one-liners like this: "I say what I think and I do what I say."

- *Recipient:* With a Type 8 person, it's possible that their own reality stands in the way when it comes to recognizing what the other person is saying. Denial is a strong mechanism in Type 8 individuals, which ensures that the other's messages or truths won't be received. The message has to be short, powerful, and clearly worded in order to be received. When people with Type 8 ask a question, it can be intimidating. If they think a topic isn't interesting, they like to make jokes, turn away from the conversation, focus on completely different topics, or run away. This may seem strange to others, but a Type 8 person isn't bothered by it.

» Type 9

- *Sender:* Relaxed, comfortable, and often a slow pace (or sluggish pace, to others). This type sometimes sends unclear signals — they say yes, for example, when they really mean no. They can provide detailed information in a logical, step-by-step sequence. People with Type 9 make an effort to be fair and analyze and consider all sides of a situation. Because of this thoroughness, they sometimes seem unclear and uninteresting to others.

- *Recipient:* Type 9 persons are oriented toward the other person and follow what the other says or wants. They are good listeners. They're receptive to signals which indicate that they aren't being taken seriously or considered, or that their polite, differentiated suggestions aren't being adopted. If people with Type 9 are asked to do something, they occasionally resist. Because they do their best to adhere to their ideas and positions, they occasionally also do something that they would consider terrible in another person: not listen. A Type 9 person can send affirmative signals and act in a rejecting manner. Often, it only seems as if Type 9 persons are really listening and open to what you're saying — in reality, this isn't always the case.

Take a moment to identify your own communication style. Let yourself be inspired by the examples. Which of these do you recognize in yourself?

Characteristics of my speaking style (think of pacing, volume, nonverbal expressions, eye contact, and directness, for example):

_____

_____

_____

Characteristics of my communication style as a sender:

_____

_____

_____

Characteristics of my communication style as a recipient:

_____

_____

_____

Checking your effectiveness

After you know the characteristics of the various types as senders and recipients and have taken a closer look at your own communication style, it's time to improve the effectiveness. How can you communicate more effectively?

Here are a few tips:

>> Become aware of your type-specific pitfalls and strengths.

>> Learn to ground yourself and be present in the here and now.

>> Become aware of the specific strengths and pitfalls of the other types.

>> Learn to appreciate the strengths of the other types, and consider which of these strengths you can still learn from.

>> Learn to be lenient in accepting the pitfalls of the other types, and keep in mind that other people have just as hard a time with your difficulties as you do with theirs.

>> Learn to come into contact with yourself and others.

>> Practice active listening, and let others know that you hear and see them.

>> Practice opening up to the thoughts and feelings of the other person and to realize that you don't have to agree with them — you just have to respect them.

Here are a few questions that are always useful here:

Do I understand this correctly? Do you mean that . . .?

Did I hear correctly that . . .?

I'm asking myself whether or not . . .

Do you like it when . . .?

REMEMBER

With these and other, similar questions, you mainly communicate that you're trying to hear as well as understand the other.

When it comes to the individual types. you can take advantage of an entire range of development opportunities and exercises. With your type in mind, check out the different ways you can increase the effectiveness of your communication:

>> **Type 1**

- Direct your attention toward others and make contact with them.

- Find more room in your schedule for relaxation, for others, and for other solutions.

- Learn to slow down your reactions by truly and completely listening to the other.

- Learn to relax while explaining, justifying, and defending your own standpoint, which means restraining yourself.

- Replace *must* wording with *may* or *can*.

>> **Type 2**

- Direct attention toward yourself and make contact with yourself.

- Make more room for your own wishes and needs, and figure out how you can gain exactly this from the other person.

- Give the other person more room in order to also ask questions and influence the content and progress of the conversation; learn how to follow.

- Slow down your reactions and thus learn to hear, consider, and appreciate the ideas, offers, suggestions, or compliments of the other.

- Don't worry so much about paying compliments or flattering the other. (Save your energy!)

- Overcome the fear of not being considered nice, and learn to ask for things for yourself. (Not having to manipulate others into liking you is another great energy-saver!)

» Type 3

- Direct attention toward the other person and make contact with them.

- Learn to restrain yourself, restrain yourself, restrain yourself!

- Give the other persons more room by truly seeing and hearing them.

- Be interested in what the others are concerned with.

- Relax during your determined courses of action and in the hunt after your image of success.

- Overcome the fear of not appearing to be successful; give yourself the chance to experience that people appreciate someone not because of their success and accolades but as a person. (It's yet another effective energy-saving measure!)

» Type 4

- Direct your attention toward others and make contact with them.

- Create more room for the experiences of others and for a rational course of action.

- Learn that the world of feelings isn't necessarily superior to that of thinking, and also make room for a balance between emotion and reason in discussions.

- Figure out how to slow down your reactions and to first ask the other person how they see things, rather than immediately let loose with your own opinion.

- Relax in adopting a rational approach to the others, receiving them without immediately making a judgment.

- Learn to take other opinions into consideration and to not immediately interpret them as a lack of understanding by others.

- In addition to thinking about the problem, deliberately make space to also see this problem from the positive side; listen when others emphasize these aspects.

» Type 5

- Direct your attention toward your own feelings and make contact with them.

- Give others more room; use reality checks to test whether others really expect or demand something from you; fear of that being the case is often unfounded.

- Avoid withdrawing automatically, and practice to stay present in your contact with other people.

- Practice coming up with more direct and spontaneous reactions, communicating without the built-in protection and interference of thinking.

- Instead of thinking, thinking, thinking first and then maybe doing or saying something, directly do or say something.

- Rather than search for ten reasons not to say something, look for the one reason to say it after all, and practice paying attention to it.

» Type 6

- Direct your attention toward the other person and make contact with them.

- Create more room for relaxation, for others, and for trust.

- Incorporate reality checks into your interactions, consciously detecting your own filters and projection mechanisms, asking the others how they see or experience it, and so on.

- Create more mental space for yourself by considering the other person's answers and accepting the fact that they might actually be true and sincere.

- Every time you have an inclination to say what-if or yes-but, first call out "Stop!" and then take a deep breath and say something that helps to overcome such emotions as fear, doubt, worry, and distrust. ("Innocent until proven guilty" is a great start.)

- Slow down your reactions with breathing techniques. A Type 6 person often breathes haltingly, even while speaking; learning fluent belly breathing helps this type relax in adverse situations.

⟫ Type 7

- Direct your attention toward others and make contact with them.

- Focus on the other person — their entire story or answer.

- Slow down your reaction when talking to others, and take a break when someone has finished speaking. Use this time for listening.

- Every time your mind threatens to tune out or your chain of associations begins so that you lose the other person completely, shout "Stop!" to yourself. Then take a deep breath and listen to the other person again.

- Give the other person more room; when they make a suggestion and your own thoughts find all kinds of ways to see how it could be different, tell yourself that it just might work like this, too — just like the other person wants or suggests — and thus learn to accept ideas from others. (Managers in particular seem to like it if their employees actually do what is asked of them every now and then.)

⟫ Type 8

- Direct your attention toward others and make contact with them.

- Create more room to really listen to the other person and recognize their ideas, interests, and questions as equally real; consider something from multiple sides, not just from your own reality.

- Slow down reactions by taking a breath now and then while speaking. (You're allowed to take a break every now and then!)

- Focus on what the other person is actually trying to say; realize that others often want to explain something when they speak to you, even if it seems long and unclear; learn to stop yourself from reacting and just be patient with the other person.

- Practice thinking first and then acting or responding later.

⟫ Type 9

- Direct your attention toward yourself and make contact with yourself; in the presence of others and during your interaction with them, practice staying aware of yourself, literally keeping in touch with yourself.

- Learn to convey your message briefly and to the point, and speak louder and more clearly in the process; a good breathing technique helps here, too.

- Repress the desire to please, and realize that others are never so quickly offended as a Type 9 person believes they are, with their fear of confrontation.

- Practice grounding yourself, be present and visible, and stay like that even when others show that they see and hear you and take you seriously—don't make yourself small and invisible again!

Select one of these options for improving yourself, and ask yourself which one is a priority for you. Focus on this item and then work on it for a longer time. As soon as the new aspect is integrated into your communication style — when it has become a new, well-integrated habit, in other words — select the next item. Although this path seems slow, it will likely lead to true improvements. Just take things one step at a time.

I want to improve this item:

Which one?

_____
_____
_____
_____

How?

_____
_____
_____
_____

List the help that I need to accomplish this (journaling or feedback from third parties, for example):

_____
_____
_____
_____

This is how I'll know that I'm on the right path:

_____
_____
_____
_____

IN THIS CHAPTER

» Fostering accurate management with the Enneagram

» Helping with interventions, feedback, and conflicts

» Taking a closer look at escalation phases

» Achieving greater success as a mediator with the Enneagram

» Managing conflicting types

Chapter **12**

Working with Specific Enneagram Applications in the Workplace

I n this chapter, I cover how you can use the Enneagram to help manage and mediate conflicts in the workplace. Let's get right to it.

The Enneagram Approach to Management

Successful management involves so many aspects that bookshelves are full of books just on this topic. It wouldn't be at all difficult to write an entire book about how the Enneagram can help you become a better manager. I, however, keep it to just one chapter, where I discuss two important skills associated with managers: interventions and feedback. Before I do that, though, I first want to introduce you to the phenomena known in psychological circles as relationship definitions.

If you're aware of the relationship definition and know how to influence it so that it fits your current situation, you have a useful and valuable tool on hand. This awareness can help managers notice when something is wrong in the relationship definition that exists between them and those who are being managed — an awareness that can do much to help resolve a problem. If issues surrounding the relationship definition aren't resolved, most of the other means available to managers to get through to a managed person may turn out to be useless.

I see myself as your boss, but do you see me the same way?

A *relationship definition* is the subconscious image humans have of their relationship to others. My idea of the nature of that relationship and how the other person views that relationship can be quite different. If that's the case, the exchange that should be happening between you and me probably won't happen, regardless of whether it involves messages, instructions, or feedback.

When it comes to tips about management, most of the emphasis is placed on the managers themselves rather than on the individuals being managed. The fact is, most of the research, training, and advanced education are designed to develop leadership qualities. That means one aspect of management receives precious less attention: namely, that effective management also requires people who are willing to be managed. The model of sender-and-recipient has already been used for a long time in the communication sciences. Nonetheless, sending usually takes center stage in communication training. The same is true of giving and receiving feedback as well as managing and letting yourself be managed.

Ensuring that the employees align themselves with the wishes of management is part of a manager's task — good managers do it well and poor managers do it poorly. The management task also includes the ability to assert authority or make their influence felt, ensuring that management directives are received by those being managed. Managers apply tools consciously or subconsciously to exert this influence. One important tool is the relationship definition.

Examining relationship definitions in practice

People subconsciously adhere to a relationship definition in each interaction they have with others. Here's an example of a definition of relationship definition in a training situation:

Trainer

See me as someone who knows their way around and can teach you something.

See yourself as someone who can still learn something in this area.

Message: We're here because we both want me to teach you something.

Assume that a participant in the group defines the relationship as follows and projects this, too:

Participant

See me as someone who has been sent here by their boss and who already knows how to do all this.

See yourself as someone who doesn't know practical applications and can still learn something from me.

Message: We're here to go through the motions.

These definitions of relationships are not at all complementary — they simply don't mesh. You probably already know how this training day will probably go — unless, of course, the trainer realizes what the participant is projecting with their particular relationship definition and can adapt to it. So in every interaction it's important to shape the relationship definition in a complementary way; otherwise, the interaction won't bear much fruit. Even small children play with these definitions, and they make them explicit more often than adults. You have probably heard a child say, "I won't listen to you — you're not my mother." At that time, the child follows this relationship definition. As an adult dealing with such a child, you can go stand on your head trying to get your message across, but if the child doesn't recognize you as someone to listen to, it's all in vain.

EXAMPLE

Let's take a look at how the Enneagram helps you create a clear image of the nature of a relationship. Here's an example involving two different relationships between a manager and an employee:

Manager Type 6:

See me as someone who pays attention to anything that could go wrong.

See yourself as someone who can carefully follow me.

Message: We're here to avoid risks and ensure that nothing goes wrong.

Employee Type 3:

See me as someone who can earn points and wants to advance quickly.

See yourself as someone who, above all, shouldn't stand in my way.

Message: We're here to be the best we can be so that I can quickly move ahead in my career.

Do these attitudes complement one another? Can it work like this? Another example:

Manager Type 7:

See me as a manager who likes to give the team creative freedom.

See yourself as someone who can have freedom here and whom I trust.

Message: We're here to have fun, and then the results will come on their own!

Employee Type 8:

See me as someone who doesn't want to be managed.

See yourself as someone who shouldn't stand in my way and definitely shouldn't tell me what to do.

Message: We're here to do whatever has been agreed on.

Are these relationship definitions complementary? Will this relationship work out? Does something here look familiar?

These stereotypical examples are meant to show the principle. They are designed to help you gain insight into an interaction with someone in your environment — one that may not have been constructive so far. You can now fill in the examples for yourself and the other person in a little more detail. Start by writing down the relationship definition that you think applies to you and your counterpart.

REMEMBER

You can know the relationship definition only if the other person knows their Enneagram type and tells it to you. Maybe you already have a hypothesis about it, based on how you perceive this person, but keep in mind that it's always dangerous to work with hypotheses — they can also turn out to be false. Consider them as a starting point to begin with the work, but always test them against the reality. Maybe it's necessary to adjust your hypothesis. Start by imagining some of your own relationships by filling in some of the following blanks:

I, Type _____, see myself as _____

Job Function (if relevant) _____see yourself as_____

*Message*_____

The other person: _____ sees me as_____

Possible type: _____ sees yourself as _____

*Message*_____

Is this complementary? Does it work? _____
_____

Looking at Interventions

Intervention is a great word for interceding in a process. A coach or therapist can make an intervention in a client's development process, a management consultant can intervene in a change process, a manager can intervene in a team process, and a mediator can intervene in a conflict process. In an intervention, the process is actually stopped, which gives it a new turn. In all these examples, a third person who is outside of the process is intervening. The advantage here is that a position from the outside makes it easier to recognize what is happening in the process, which also makes it easier to see that an intervention can help and is needed. If you aren't part of the process yourself, it's easier to intervene, because you're literally free to do so.

When it comes to intervening, it's absolutely necessary to be able to

>> Perceive processes

>> Analyze quickly — situations as well as people

>> Determine whether an intervention is needed and, if so, when

>> Know how to intervene

Knowing when and how to intervene

The most difficult part of any intervention doesn't necessarily seem to be the method itself. For most people, the most difficult part is the timing: whether to intervene and, if so, when. When is the right time? Processes keep going and tend to run between one's fingers like sand. Everyone who deals with this professionally knows that there isn't a right moment. Often, no intervention occurs, because people are waiting for the right time. An effective manager controls the processes at work as well as between people and works inside the employees' sphere of influence. By closely monitoring the processes and controlling them directly with small corrections, managers constantly keep their finger on the pulse of the action.

Which kind of intervention is called for is closely connected to the timing of the intervention and the seriousness of the matter. To explain, let me give you the example of an employee who is doing inadequate work. The company has a standard for good work, and this employee is deviating from it. They have been at the company for a year and thus have had time to familiarize and train themselves. For a while, everything seemed to be going fairly smoothly, but by now, inadequacies here and there are fairly noticeable. As a manager, you're keeping a close eye on this employee, also as part of your attempt to form a clear picture of the situation. At the organizational consulting firm where I was a partner, we worked with the model shown in Figure 12-1.

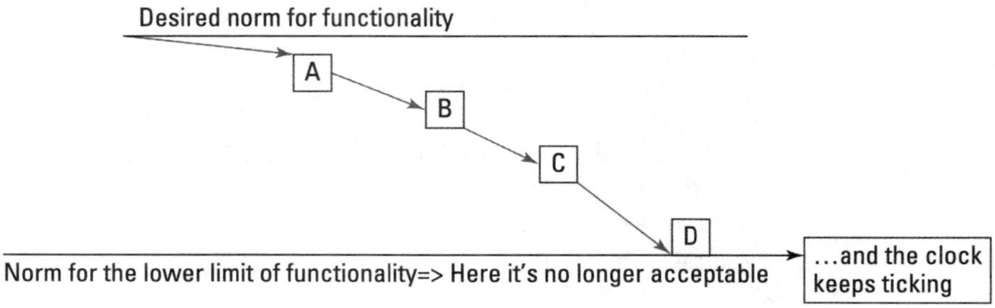

FIGURE 12-1:
The desired
standard
according
to which
an employee
should work.

Desired norm for functionality

A

B

C

D

Norm for the lower limit of functionality=> Here it's no longer acceptable

...and the clock keeps ticking

The downward line in Figure 12-1 shows how the employee's work is developing. This applies to not only the actual work performance but also the perception of the manager. Maybe it isn't really worse, but it appears so in the manager's eyes. In practice, the problem often isn't detected in time and the intervention thus comes too late, if at all. In the figure, this already brings you to Situation D: The lower limit has been reached. The employee is unaware of any fault, but the manager has determined that the lower limit has been crossed. The intervention in Situation D is already crisis management. The annual contract won't be extended. Crisis management is the most difficult form of intervention. Part of this may be that someone is removed from their position and that person's duties are handed to another employee. If the termination involved a regular, fixed-contract position, the individual's tasks or parts thereof are often redistributed across the team. How could this have been avoided?

Well, clearly, the manager could have intervened earlier:

>> **In Situation A:** By giving information (feedback)

Make sure the employee knows which standard is required, and provide feedback if this standard isn't being met.

>> **In Situation B:** By offering guidance

Guidance goes a step further, but in the best case, this phase is still just about a relatively small, correctable deviation. The issue becomes slightly more serious for the employee than the phase with feedback and advice. Now the manager is more actively involved in searching for a solution and the employee is expressly asked for diligent cooperation. The development (and any possible falling behind) are monitored together. The employee has to be more forthcoming when it comes to their work and its progress. This cooperation between employee and manager can drive any improvements, but the responsibility still lies with the employee.

» **In Situation C:** Assigning specific tasks with implied sanctions

In this situation, there is already a drastic falloff from the standard which will get completely out of hand without intervention. When the manager intervenes now, the reins will be held much tighter. This is less about cooperation; the manager simply assigns tasks. The work model currently being used by the employee must be thoroughly reorganized and the employee is informed about the consequences if improvements do not occur. This is no longer nonbinding; now sanctions are being developed — assigning certain tasks to other employees, for example.

Putting the Enneagram to good use as an aid for interventions

How all these things are handled depends on the Enneagram types involved — from detecting and acknowledging the problem and assessing the situation to the timing and choice of an appropriate intervention. The manager will have a certain prism through which to observe the situation and employee and, as I make clear throughout this book, your selective perception is tinged by your type. However, the employee's ideas and preferences as they relate to their own work are also type-specific. It's possible that the manager and employee have entirely different concepts of the situation and work performance based on their types. Here the Enneagram can be extremely helpful because it can be used to help avoid miscommunication and misunderstandings. With higher empathy, managers can give their employees much more targeted and effective feedback, support for projects, and so on.

To illustrate, here's a true story of what can happen if a manager doesn't approach a situation armed with sufficient knowledge of human nature:

EXAMPLE

Alice (Type 5) is the manager of a company being bought by a larger corporation. For a long time, she has had plans to do something else, but the new parent company wants to keep her on as a manager. Alice understands that her knowledge is in demand and doesn't mind staying. But then she and her new boss don't get along so well. The solution is obvious: a quick, clean separation. Unfortunately, it all turned out differently.

The human resources manager is asked to initiate Alice's dismissal — a costly situation because Alice has already worked as a manager at this company for 17 years. The human resources manager determines that it would be less expensive if Alice would leave of her own accord. At the executive level, it is agreed that Alice will be isolated and overlooked. She can no longer participate in the management team meetings, the other team members are asked to stop communicating with her, and the three directors ignore her. Aside from the ethical aspect (you shouldn't treat people like this), it's also a clumsy move from a business perspective. The supervisors didn't know Alice yet, but now they know her all too well.

Alice is the Enneagram Type 5. She thinks it's wonderful to be left alone to do her own thing as before. She notices things accurately and quickly understands what is going on. She calmly documents the actions taken by human resources. A year later, the management board is desperate enough and initiates a conversation to offer her a more-than-generous severance package. Some knowledge of the Enneagram wouldn't have just saved the company a lot of money but also a lot of time and frustration.

Remembering that every type handles interventions differently

For every Enneagram type, here is an example of how they deal with necessary interventions:

>> People of **Type 1** immediately notice when someone deviates from the norm. Their automatic reaction is to suppress their impulses, including the impulse to say something. Type 1 persons can only intervene when it's not just the case of a single individual, but rather a case where there's a larger pattern. Only then can they justify intervention. This often happens only after there's a need to assign tasks with sanctions tied to them or when crisis management is called for.

>> People of **Type 2** pay more attention to other people than to the work process. In addition, those with Type 2 in a management position want to come across as nice. They tend to resolve the issue for the other person, which is also a form of crisis management. Offering guidance also fits in with the natural behavior of Type 2.

>> People of **Type 3** pay attention to what results must be achieved and what tasks need to be accomplished. Although they will certainly keep an eye on the weakest player on the team as well, by their very nature they prefer not to waste time on that person. It takes the least amount of time and energy if the weakest player is taken off the field. Whenever possible, a Type 3 person quickly transitions from doing nothing to doing crisis management.

>> People of **Type 4** can recognize problems and acknowledge their significance. Fear of their own anger may keep managers with Type 4 from intervening. This is why a Type 4 person sometimes censors themselves. A Type 4 person who is less bothered by their anger-management issues will intervene directly.

>> People with **Type 5,** following the motto "Live and let live," tend not to intervene and, as result, end up giving the other person space. They acknowledge the problems but take the time to consider everything and find a solution. Taking action is a big step. This is why managers with Type 5 sometimes let their employees drift.

>> People with **Type 6** see problems by nature and detect where something goes wrong. However, they have a tough time with authority, even if they themselves are in a position of authority. People with Type 6 doubt themselves and their observations. They also see the risks that accompany an intervention. Because of their natural inclination to avoid risks, a Type 6 person often delays the intervention.

People with **Type 7** see managers and employees as equals and can't admit that hierarchies exist at the job. Given this level of equality, they simply can't find room for intervention. Interventions are also no fun, which is why Type 7 managers avoid it when possible.

>> People with **Type 8** quickly and directly intervene by nature. As managers, those with this type are naturally inclined to move within their employees' sphere of influence. A manager with Type 8 might be prevented from intervening by getting the necessary information from their employees too late (if at all) to recognize the problem in time to act on it, or by their inclination toward denial.

People with **Type 9** tend to recognize problems and their significance too late. Acknowledging a problem means noticing that they have to do something and potentially risk a confrontation, which causes resistance in those with Type 9. They promote a culture of non-interference by clinging to their model of harmony.

Giving Feedback

The art of giving and receiving feedback is communicated in many training courses and seminars each year, yet hardly anything from this major training effort is noticeable at work. How often do you experience feedback being provided according to the rules for good feedback at your company? How often do you give and get feedback yourself? Based on my experience as an organizational consult‐ ant and coach, I assume that it doesn't happen too often. Apparently, it's not enough for people to learn the techniques. Something else seems to be in the way, because good feedback still happens so rarely. This can be related to the toxic culture of an organization or department, to an inefficient management style, and to a general lack of a sense of personal security dominant in the workplace.

In Enneagram panels, representatives of all types indicate what prevents them from doing something — for example, why they specifically have difficulties giving or receiving feedback and why it's hard for them in general to give or receive. People won't give more feedback as long as something inside them prevents this. Recognizing why and when and even for whom this internal resistance arises can help you overcome it. This makes it easier for you to deal with feedback in either direction. This too is self-management: developing in this particular area and stepping beyond your internal boundaries.

Recognizing and overcoming obstacles in the giving and receiving of feedback (also in team-building situations) helps ensure that people do it more often. As an example, let me give you a more detailed description of how individuals of Type 1 naturally deal with feedback — in the giving as well as the receiving of it — and how you can handle it as a manager. This is followed by a short summary of tips that should be considered for the individual types:

Type 1

People with Type 1 react sensitively to feedback because they tend to set the bar high and also have a powerful internal critic who makes sure that this bar isn't torn down. The type mechanism consists of doing something so well that criticism (feedback) becomes unnecessary. When they receive feedback, this is a signal that the type mechanism has failed. All alarm bells go off. The type is triggered and becomes *reactive,* meaning that the type goes into a defensive position. The ego appears. For Type 1, this is the passion of anger. People with this type who haven't evolved in this area will justify themselves, explain to the other person why they're getting it wrong, and make that person feel responsible. (There is always a way to put the ball back in someone's court.) Getting feedback for a Type 1 person is a serious problem because of their quick reactivity. The same mechanism also prevents people with Type 1 from giving feedback, because they consider feedback and criticism to be the same thing and projection always plays a role. People with Type 1 know their own difficulties with feedback and the anger that arises when they get feedback, and they assume that other people are the same way. The obstacle for those with Type 1 is the fear of drawing the other person's anger onto themselves. In contrast, people with Type 1 who have developed themselves in this regard can offer feedback in a diplomatic, careful, and also cordial way.

TIP

Here's some advice for managers who want to provide feedback to the various types. Some of these tips work well for everyone, but if you want your feedback to hit home and be accepted constructively by others, it's particularly helpful to consider the points that are listed under the individual types:

A **Type 1** person likes honesty, clarity, and diligence in communication and interactions. A Type 1 person accepts feedback more easily when it is provided warmly and the message clearly indicates that the feedback concerns one aspect of the activity, not the activity as a whole. The feedback must be precise and accurate — otherwise, it faces resistance. A Type 1 person becomes particularly sensitive about signals related to feedback: It's dangerous to use the word *but*, for example. Often, this disqualifies everything that was said earlier: "You're doing all this very well, but . . ." A Type 1 person likes a learning environment that provides room for error and corrections. It helps this type if the feedback is offered in this context, which makes it much easier to accept.

>> **Type 2:** Make sure that there is enough privacy when giving feedback, be personal, and try to make a friendly and optimistic impression. Ask how the Type 2 feels in this situation. Go into less detail and emphasize the significance of positive relationships.

>> **Type 3:** Ask for the best time to have a talk. Make sure it won't take too long. Emphasize that the feedback is meant to work even more effectively and successfully. Give clear examples, preferably with names. Acknowledge good intentions. You can also appeal to the competitive instinct of a Type 3 person.

>> **Type 4:** Pay particular attention to establishing contact with the other individual. Show empathy. Use personal words like *I, we,* and so on. Avoid speaking in an accusatory or scolding tone. (This never works particularly well with anyone, but it's especially problematic for a Type 4 person, who immediately shuts down). Ask how this type feels, and listen until they have stopped speaking. Take some time for the conversation to run its course.

>> **Type 5:** Ask whether it's a good time. Say that it will be a short talk, specify how long it will take (20 minutes, for example), and clarify the topic of the discussion. Be specific and stick with the facts. Give the other person time to think about what you said. Avoid demanding an immediate reaction, but arrange an appointment shortly after the talk to address it.

>> **Type 6:** State directly what the talk is all about. Provide your assessment of the scope of the problem and note the facts. (Otherwise, it will immediately grow to a catastrophic extent in the mind of the Type 6 person and set off alarm bells.) Create a personal, friendly, compassionate atmosphere so that the employee feels safe. Explicitly say that you will support the other person. Don't make any promises you can't keep. Offer alternatives from which the person can choose. It's possible that the information has to be repeated or systematically summarized.

>> **Type 7:** Alternate between positive and critical comments. Give a Type 7 person an opportunity to present ideas early in the conversation. Keep in mind that this type is positive and (at times) self-centered and that it can thus

be difficult for your (more negative) perception to be heard. Show patience and always return to the topic in a friendly manner if a Type 7 person tries to move away or ignore anything that strikes them as negative-sounding. Provide your feedback in such a way that the Type 7 person notices your intention to help them improve. Clarify where the boundaries are and give this type the freedom to find solutions on their own within these boundaries.

>> **Type 8:** Communicate in the same style as with a Type 8 person: briefly, directly, clearly. Focus on the subject, and get to the heart of the matter. Avoid being vague. Give this type the opportunity to bring the situation under control, also during the discussion. Make clear arrangements. A Type 8 person follows the motto "Agreed is agreed." Avoid being pulled into a discussion or even an argument. With that done, be clear on what your rules are for work. For example, when you want to have something done a certain way, it's not an invitation to a discussion. Instead, make it clear that these directives are meant to be followed. Do what you say you will do and a Type 8 will respect you as the boss and stick to the arrangement.

>> **Type 9:** Take some time. Be sure to make contact. Ask personal questions, and show warmth and empathy. React in a way that's as differentiated and nonjudgmental as possible. Ask what the Type 9 person thinks about the matter. Give the person room to think about it and also come up with their own suggestions. ("Take your time, and think about it at your leisure."). Discuss possible ideas and activities together. Support the Type 9 person in the decision-making process. Discuss what else this type needs to do to tackle the matter.

Mediating When There's a Conflict

I consider conflict mediation an application area for the Enneagram for these three reasons:

>> **Conflicts are at the top of the list of what people suffer from in relationships.** This is true in their personal life and at work, what unsettles them and makes their work inferior, and what literally makes them sick.

>> **To a large degree, conflicts arise when people don't understand each other.** All the types speak their own language — just like when the Tower of Babel was destroyed in the Bible and the peoples of mankind were scattered over all the earth. People don't understand each other because they consider different areas to be important and they have different fears and worries. The Enneagram is particularly effective and valuable here because it helps people understand each other better.

CREATING YOUR VERY OWN TOWER OF BABEL SITUATION

In meetings, I periodically hear long discussions in which Mr. A repeats what he has already said, Ms. B emphasizes her position again, and Mr. A yet again states his point of view. Does this sound familiar? When you listen to the content, Mr. A and Ms. B often say almost exactly the same thing. It's usually not about the content, but rather about a tiny difference in what the two consider important. They both think that the other person doesn't understand them, because they notice that precisely the aspect they value most isn't being picked up by the other. If Mr. A and Ms. B could "hear" each other, they would quickly find a solution. But filtered through their type, they don't want to hear, or can't hear, each other. A linguistic babble isn't about one person speaking French and another speaking German. In my opinion, it's about the participants not understanding each other on a human level.

REMEMBER

>> **The value of the Enneagram comes to the fore when people are suffering.** This painful stage is a strong starting point for change and growth. Therapists know that people are willing to take care of themselves and decide on their personal development only when their distress has become great enough.

However, people who mediate conflicts professionally more often have a background as a lawyer than as a therapist. Far too often, the goal is merely to mediate the existing conflict, to end it; it's not therapy, and it's definitely not personal development. Mediators already know that the mediation process can be facilitated and sped up when you pay attention to the human aspect. For mediators and lawyers without psychological training, the Enneagram is a useful tool.

I myself am trained as a mediator and would recommend this important tool to other mediators!

To see how best to use the Enneagram as a mediation tool, let's first take a look at what's involved with mediation and what mediation is really hoping to achieve:

>> **Damage:** Unresolved conflicts are damaging to all affected parties, and when this damage isn't repaired, it continues to cause pain. Sometimes the pain recedes and the wound heals but a scar remains. In other cases, particularly in family situations, it's difficult to heal these wounds. It takes only a single event, such as a funeral or wedding, and suddenly the pain returns. Conflicts in or between organizations aren't just damaging to the affected individuals but also to the organization(s) themselves: They take time and energy away

from more productive tasks, create negative energies, and slow down internal processes, progress, and development. The result is that people are more concerned with the conflicts (in the best case, with their solution) rather than with their actual tasks; the other work gets neglected.

» **Conflicts and mediation:** Before I explain the application of the Enneagram in cases of conflict, you need to first learn something about different aspects of conflicts and mediation. Conflicts have a content-specific or objective aspect (what it's about), a personal aspect (the emotional side, the experience), and sometimes an ideological aspect (principal points of view based on culture, politics, or religion). In this section, I examine some aspects of the human side of conflicts.

The Lime Tree, an educational institute for mediators in the Netherlands, suggests that conflicts tend to run their natural courses in the same way. They distinguish between what they call three *escalation* phases:

- *Rational:* The parties, despite their disagreements, remain objective and are focused on the facts. There may be tensions and irritations, but discussions are still possible, and both sides are highly motivated to reach a win-win situation.

- *Emotional:* Personal oppositions have gained the upper hand over the factual contents. This has resulted in mistrust and a distorted image of the other party. A process consultant is needed to move ahead. There is a competitive argument, and the goal is a win-lose situation.

- *Dispute:* The parties feel that they no longer have anything to lose. Talks are no longer possible, and the counterpart is no longer being seen as a human. Each effort is destructive. An authoritative third party is needed to break up the conflict. The goal is lose-lose. ("If I can't have it, the other party shouldn't have it, either.")

Fortunately, there *are* mediators. This distribution of the escalation phases shows how quickly the personal, emotional aspect gains the upper hand in a conflict. The good thing about the efforts of mediation is that the human side is increasingly drawing attention when it comes to communicating about conflicts. If a judge arrives at a verdict regarding a conflict, the content of the conflict might be resolved, but not the pain of the involved parties — only for the "winner," if at all, and the loser's pain might even be increased. When attorneys who expressly represent their clients become involved, the dispute often escalates even further. This can be useful when it comes to resolving the underlying matter itself, but is it always good for the people and their relationship?

» **The disadvantage that comes along with an advantage:** Although no one really likes conflicts, it's helpful to recognize and accept that conflicts are part of life. It might sound strange, but this acceptance can help you deal constructively with conflicts. In fact, it would be even more helpful to learn how conflicts might ultimately even play a positive role in your life.

» **A bit more about the human aspects of conflicts:** Where do conflicts come from? What is the role of the chronic language confusion that so often occurs and which other human aspects contribute to this? In this section, you can read more about the human aspects that allow conflicts to grow and flourish.

» **You don't understand me:** The logical consequence of not being connected to each other is that humans don't want to, or can't, understand each other. When they don't want to or can't see how they are rooted in their own habits, that they don't hear the other, and that they don't recognize the other person's interests, conflicts develop. Then the message in the relationship definition is often this: "I feel bad and it's because of you." This statement is frequently (subconsciously) followed by this one: ". . . and when I feel bad, I want you to feel just as bad."

In conversations that range from being merely tedious to those that occur in conflict situations, it often happens that one or more parties actually seems to make an effort not to hear the other one and to misunderstand them. A lot of what people communicate can be perceived positively as well as negatively. This can be indicated when one or more parties lament that it seems to make no difference what they say or do because everything is misunderstood anyway. No one likes to be misunderstood. In coaching or mediation, I often ask one party how they assess the intentions of the others. If positive intentions are attributed to the other individuals, this insight can help interpret what the others are saying or doing positively. When things turn out unfavorably, this often concerns the inadvertent and unwanted effects of positive intentions. If you learn to recognize this, you can help people in conflict situations build a bridge.

» **Not my fault:** Many conflicts aren't as much about the subject as they are about the relationship. When that's the case, the relationship definitions are no longer complementary. In such a situation, people notice that they aren't being seen, heard, acknowledged, or appreciated by the other party and this hurts their feelings. A constantly active source of conflict at the relationship level is that people start with their own sedimented habits as well as with an idealized self-image.

Such idealized self-images include, for example:

- **Type 9:** I'm a peace-loving person (so conflicts aren't my fault).
- **Type 8:** I'm a fair person (so conflicts aren't my fault).
- **Type 7:** I'm a positive person (so conflicts aren't my fault).
- **Type 6:** I'm a reliable person (so conflicts aren't my fault).

- **Type 5:** I'm a calm person (so conflicts aren't my fault).
- **Type 4:** I'm a sensitive person (so conflicts aren't my fault).
- **Type 3:** I'm a constructive, reassuring person (so conflicts aren't my fault).
- **Type 2:** I'm a helpful, nice person (so conflicts aren't my fault).
- **Type 1:** I'm a good person (so conflicts aren't my fault).

Conflicts are created precisely because humans tend to see what they contribute in terms of good and positive things and that somehow the other party is at fault for this and contributes a negative aspect: "How could they do that?" It turns out that, to the extent that people are blind about themselves, they are equally incredibly clear-sighted when it comes to seeing the faults of others. Try to turn this situation around and ask yourself these two questions:

» "What am I contributing to this?"

» "What are the other person's positive intentions?"

In a conflict situation, it's often difficult to answer these questions honestly, even if you're the one asking them.

THE VALUE OF MEDIATORS WITH ENNEAGRAM TRAINING

In the training of mediators, the focus is on resolving conflicts on a personal and relationship level. It's important that people are taken seriously when it comes to their points of view — that they are acknowledged. Like no other model, the Enneagram clarifies what is important for the individual types. Miscommunication and misunderstandings often arise from the fact that everyone starts off with their own habits, believes that these also apply to others, and thus fail to hear that different things are important to the other party. In many cases, even just the recognition that one thing matters to one person and another to their counterpart already opens up space for creative solutions in a conflict. When this is examined in more detail, it may be possible that the parties actually agree much more than they initially saw or believed.

A mediator with Enneagram training recognizes the differences between the involved parties more quickly and sees what is most important to each of the two sides. A mediator with Enneagram training can help the parties develop a better understanding of themselves and of others. There is a good reason that the Enneagram plays a role in the training and advanced education of the various trade associations for mediation.

Engaging the Enneagram Types in Conflict Situations

Before turning to more detailed descriptions of each Enneagram type in a conflict situation, I want to highlight a few more relevant aspects of the individual types. When you work on a conflict, you assess the situation; you decide how you want to react, and you make assumptions about how the other person will react. Knowledge of the Enneagram types is a valuable source of information, especially in the latter case. Keep in mind that many people don't proceed as well as they normally would when they're in conflict situations. In those cases, it commonly happens that people display the behavior of their stress type more strongly. (For more on this topic, see Chapter 14.) In the assessment of how people handle conflict, the level of their personal development (and thus their stability) plays a greater role than their type.

Here are examples for each type:

>> **Type 1:** When they are labeled as being the source of the conflict about themselves, people with Type 1 tend to withdraw by nature. Then they react more by passively submitting rather than by active cooperation. (The stressor here would be a Type 4.) If it's about something that people with Type 1 are committed to (and for which the bar has been set high), they can also take over leadership and assert their will.

>> **Type 2:** People with Type 2 are very much relationship-oriented and tend to lead by nature. Their natural style is to seek cooperation and to leave conflict behind them. If persons with Type 2 become stressed, they can also assert their will and act decisively. (The stressor here would be a Type 8.)

>> **Type 3:** In conflicts, people with Type 3 appear energetic, competitive, and not relationship-oriented; they like taking the lead. Under stress, they're more likely to follow and adapt. (The stressor type would be a Type 9.)

>> **Type 4:** People with Type 4 tend to withdraw by nature. Then they react more by passively submitting rather than by active cooperation. Under stress, they become increasingly relationship-oriented and adapt more. (The stressor here would be a Type 2.)

>> **Type 5:** People with Type 5 tend to withdraw by nature. Under stress, people with Type 5 can take over the lead and formulate possible solutions for the conflict and cooperate effectively. (The stressor here would be a Type 7.)

>> **Type 6:** People with Type 6 like to avoid risks and thus tend to adapt, because they are very much relationship-oriented and like to follow. Under stress, people with Type 6 can unexpectedly take over the lead and cooperate effectively. (The stressor here would be a Type 3.)

>> **Type 7:** People with Type 7 tend to withdraw from a conflict by nature because they like to follow. A developed Type 7 person or a Type 7 person under stress (the stressor here would be a Type 1) will take over the lead and assert their will.

>> **Type 8:** People with Type 8 tend to take over the lead, make decisions, and assert their will. Under great (emotional) stress, people with Type 8 tend to withdraw (the stressor here would be Type 5), but this happens only after the opposition is out of sight and the battle has been fought to the bitter end.

>> **Type 9:** People with Type 9 are very much relationship-oriented and like to follow. This is why they tend to adapt. Under stress, people with Type 9 can suddenly take over the lead and assert their own will and perspective. (The stressor here would be a Type 6.)

IN THIS CHAPTER

» Working as a consultant with a client

» Explaining the six A's of a conversation

» Evaluating tips for therapists

» Examining the types in therapy

» Taking a look at positive psychology

Chapter **13**

Developing the Personal Abilities of Others and Ensuring Their Well-Being

I n this chapter, I cover what is probably the most often used application of the Enneagram in the consulting professions: leading individuals by the hand as they take on the hard work of personality development and guiding them on the path to their well-being.

In this chapter, I address those professions where a consultant works closely with a client — jobs like therapist, coach, consultant, pastor, and supervisor as well as career adviser, (company) social worker, and the like. I also include coaches who offer team coaching as well as therapists offering sessions for couples or groups. In these professions, consultants typically support their clients as they develop on a personal level or gain awareness in one way or another. The Enneagram is especially suitable, beneficial, and valuable in this regard.

Part 4 of this book covers the development path of each Enneagram type as well as the role the Enneagram can play in the development process — in other words, the content of the inner work being carried out. As such, this chapter emphasizes the benefit of the Enneagram in professional practice by highlighting those aspects that account for the value and applicability of the Enneagram. My takes here are intended to act as signposts and suggestions for the road ahead.

REMEMBER

For better readability, I use the word *coach*, though I could just as well say *consultant* or *therapist* or another term for the professions I just mentioned.

REMEMBER

If you spend any time with the Enneagram, at some point you become frustrated by the strict division into nine types. I personally find it rather boring to keep describing how a certain subject is expressed specifically in each of the nine types. The thing is, I know I can't limit myself to writing about just one or another type. Inevitably, this strategy results in my leaving out exactly the Enneagram type that interests you the most, and of course I can't do that. So, if you do come across yet another one of these lists where each of the nine items appears, it's always just a summary of what can be said on the topic. If you like lists, you can find a summary of each type in the appendix.

Accompanying a Client on Their Career Path

What I keep noticing about people in the consulting professions is how diligently they continue to educate themselves in their areas of specialization. They deepen their knowledge, continue to develop, and also create a toolkit for themselves. It's no wonder that many people in these professions welcome the Enneagram. In this section, you get detailed information on how to work with the Enneagram and in which situations.

REMEMBER

Knowing the Enneagram and the nine types can help coaches when formulating advice for individual clients; it lets them do this more effectively and more efficiently, and it helps them better relate to their clients.

Seeing the benefits

When you know a person's Enneagram type, you can more quickly picture the problems this person is struggling with — and thus better understand them. As a coach, therapist, or pastor, you can rapidly form a complete picture of what someone considers important deep inside and what this person's greatest fears or wishes consist of. Armed with the theory of a type's development path, you can also create a customized plan with the client in a relatively short period.

The Enneagram is also a method of self-development. You can assist your clients in assuming their own responsibility for their development process and development steps. Once this process has started, your role is primarily that of a knowledgeable guide, listener, and mirror.

REMEMBER

By using the Enneagram, consultants are in a position to not only offer support to their clients but also to access a superior method for their own, personal development — as professionals as well as individuals. The quality of the work and support offered to others increases if the consultants continually develop themselves. With the right tool — one that combines an itinerary with a method — you can stride ahead as though you were wearing seven-league boots. The Enneagram speeds up the process. It's fascinating to keep seeing this in people.

Listing the phases when it comes to offering guidance with the Enneagram

Whether with or without the Enneagram, each guidance process consists of several distinct phases: carrying out an introductory discussion (meeting, first orientation, clarification of the request for help, and the like), defining the guidance plan, executing the plan, and evaluating the results. The following phases are Enneagram-specific and are added to those I mention above:

>> **Defining the client's type:** In Chapter 4, I describe in detail how you can assess which type someone might have. In my opinion, it's always best and most sensible if the coach can perform a type assessment interview. It encourages the clients to develop their skills of self-observation and reflection (or at least start this process). The interview is thus the first step in the process.

>> **Exploring the client's type mechanism:** This involves a thorough examination of how the type mechanism works for this client. It's an intensive and fast method — a pressure-cooker method — to gain self-awareness.

>> **Transitioning from the intensification of the self-awareness to the client's unique problem.** The connection between the explored type mechanism and the unique problems experienced by the clients reveal themselves on their own. During this phase, while working on the client's concern, it's possible that the client will learn new (and necessary) skills. I tell you more about this topic in Part 4.

>> **Leveraging the results.** When the problem has been worked through, I regularly find that a new world has opened up for the clients and that they want more — more self-awareness, more self-management, more ways to relax in life, and more pleasure and less suffering. The clients discover a need for further professionalization and greater meaningfulness.

TIP

Make an appointment with the client to have another discussion two or three months after the initial sessions. I realize that getting to know the Enneagram usually has a far-ranging and intense effect on the client's life and work and that questions may arise again after some time has passed. During this follow-up discussion, clients usually ask for advice about how to deal with the people around them and for tips on how to use the Enneagram. For example: "My partner discovered that he has Type X, and maybe this is why we often get into difficult situations. We realize this now, but how can we deal with it?"

Dealing with common concerns in a therapeutic context

Some situations consistently arise in therapeutic situations. The next few sections spell out what can happen and how the Enneagram can help minimize the damage.

TECHNICAL STUFF

In this section, I describe a couple of concepts from Freud's view of the psycho-analytic process: transference and countertransference. Whenever you work with individual clients, keep an eye on the mechanisms of transference and counter-transference while interacting with your client. If the client and consultant are unaware of these processes, this may lead to the development of an interaction pattern that obstructs the success of the process as a whole. I explain these terms with a few examples.

Transference: "The coach isn't your father"

Margaret, Type 9, has made a few appointments for coaching sessions. She wants to suffer less from her feeling that others hardly pay attention to her. During the coaching sessions, Margaret discovers that the pain originates mainly from her father. To this day, she feels that he doesn't see her and doesn't know what *she* cares about, what *she's* interested in, and whether *she's* doing well — everything seems to revolve around him instead. During the coaching, Margaret learns that her father probably has Type 3. At first glance, it looks as though Margaret is gaining some insight into her interior life, but soon some things start happening during the coaching sessions that give her the sense that her coach, Tina, doesn't see her, either. Now and then she has to repeat things she has already mentioned. Margaret ran into Tina while shopping, and Tina didn't say hello to her. On a few occasions, Margaret was already speaking when Tina interrupted her in a way that made Margaret feel as if Tina didn't have the time for her — the mirror image of how Margaret felt when she was with her father. But the whole point of this coaching, in Margaret's eyes, was for Tina to see her and give her the time and attention she's been craving.

REMEMBER

The transference process in this situation consists of Margaret subconsciously attributing (distinctly negative) feelings toward a person important to her in the past to this new relationship in the present — her coach. This probably doesn't happen to her only with the coach. It's a form of projection where the characteristics of an important person from one's own life are fictitiously attributed to other people in different situations. It's also a form of identification. In this case, Margaret identifies the coach with someone from her life. Of course, everything that Margaret observes might be true — I tell you more about this possibility later in this chapter — but Margaret's conclusion that the coach pays as little attention to her as her father, giving rise to anger at the coach, certainly doesn't have to apply. The facts on the ground can probably be explained in quite a different way as well.

Countertransference: "The client isn't your little sister"

Tina, Type 3, has a client named Margaret in her coaching practice. Margaret seems to pose a challenge for Tina because Tina likes to work purposefully and efficiently and in a straight line, whereas Margaret is sometimes long-winded and takes many twists and turns. Tina is proud of the way she listens to Margaret with the patience of a saint. Margaret makes Tina think of her younger sister — Margaret always needed a lot of patience for her, too. Tina really liked her sister, which is why she is also patient with Margaret now. She feels the same care and warmth for her. She doesn't always manage to keep her mind focused on the story, but it doesn't matter. It feels good.

REMEMBER

Countertransference happens when the client triggers something in the consultant, who then reacts to it. In the previous example, Tina's countertransference is related to her own feelings of transference. Tina subconsciously transferred her positive feelings for a person important to her in the past to a person in the present, for whom she is responsible as a coach. The consultant may also have to deal with a countertransference that isn't related to their own transference. In other words, the client triggers something in you and you then feel and know that it doesn't belong to you at all. You might notice, for example, that you're handling a client cautiously and with little confrontation because the client triggers that in you, even though your natural work style is completely different.

Interaction patterns and reactivity

Tina and Margaret, coach and client, Type 3 and Type 9, pose challenges for each other. Margaret is fairly languid and values harmony and subtlety. Tina is fast and likes to work purposefully, efficiently, and in a straightforward manner. Though Tina considers herself to be extremely patient, Margaret senses her impatience. Tina's patience is certainly put to the test. Margaret speaks elaborately, repeats a lot, searches for precisely the right expressions, and considers a lot of what she says from various angles. Tina subconsciously reacts to this by searching for ways to interrupt Margaret's story to summarize it and steer her attention back to the study goal of the session. In her own opinion, Tina is doing good work; summarizing is quite a useful technique. So Tina does really see Margaret and listen to her — particularly to what she thinks is relevant for a goal-oriented solution. Nonetheless, Margaret feels she isn't being paid attention to, because Tina apparently isn't interested in everything she says, with all its subtleties. Sometimes Margaret seems irritated when Tina asks a question and Margaret replies that she already talked about this subject during the first session. But Tina is aware that this is also related to Margaret's problems — she started the coaching because she didn't feel noticed.

REMEMBER

As soon as two (or more) people deal with each other, an interaction pattern is created. Tina reacts to Margaret, and Margaret reacts to Tina. They differ with respect to their preferred pace, rhythm, timing, and focus. The more Tina speeds ahead, the more persistently Margaret steps on the brakes, tries to delay, and demands attention to the subtleties that she considers important. She's the client, after all. It's astonishing how many conflicts are caused by mostly subconscious factors such as rhythm, pace, and timing.

TECHNICAL STUFF

I refer to reactivity when people are *triggered* in their type, causing them to be fixed more firmly in their type mechanism and showing strong type-specific reactions.

Trigger points are the points that act on you like the famous red cape does on a bull — things that drive you up the wall, in other words. For Tina, this red cape of sorts is sluggishness, though for Margaret it's anything giving her the impression that no one is listening to her.

WARNING

Interaction patterns and reactivity aren't exclusively reserved for the relationship and interaction between consultants and clients. They appear during any interpersonal contact. You can also experience an interaction pattern at the farmer's market, for example, if it isn't clear who is next in line. This is also a good place to occasionally observe the reactivity of the different types.

The Six A's of a Conversation

My Enneagram colleague Hannah Nathans introduced the six A's in her guide to the consulting professions. She presents them as six important factors for organizational consultants, but these aspects apply, in my opinion, to any professional discussion. Some of them seem quite obvious at first glance, but I know — mainly from the years I spent as an organizational consultant — that out in the real world what seems obvious in theory is never quite so obvious in practice. These are the six A's of a conversation:

>> Attending to the discussion partner

>> Attending to your own signals

>> Attuning

>> Adding

>> Assertiveness (respect for yourself and others)

>> Alternatives

Attending to the discussion partner

Be unconditionally attentive. To do this, you temporarily have to set aside your own ideas and convictions. Avoid using your discussion partner's story as a hook to append your own narrative. Listening doesn't consist of waiting for the other person to catch their breath in order to immediately burst out with your own story. The Enneagram practice teaches you to stay more in the here and now, to be grounded and present. This makes it easier to listen actively and completely to the other person!

You communicate and show your attention by listening actively. Follow these tips:

>> **Give nonverbal signals.** They indicate that you're listening and following along.

>> **Ask open-ended questions.** These let the other person tell their story and give them the sense that they have enough space and time to say what they want.

>> **Follow up.** Delve deeper, but also let the client see your attentiveness and interest.

>> **Summarize.** Ensure that you understand everything correctly; but again, this is a signal that you're working with the information you're getting.

Attending to your own signals

Self-awareness and self-observation are important skills. Learn to listen to your intuition and observe your physical reactions. Your emotions or your intuition will occasionally let you know that you're seeing and hearing more than is obvious.

Sometimes you know that something will happen or you react with a sensation (such as tension). These signals can have meaning. It's important to control whether what you're experiencing is noticeable to the other person. Learn to not just send signals but also talk about what you feel, if that aspect is important for the conversation. When I began my coaching sessions, I already noticed that I often ask myself seemingly strange questions. At first, they seemed too crazy to express. But one day I referred to the feeling in front of my client: "A strange question is occurring to me. I'll just pass it on to you. Let's see if this means anything to you." This often turned out to be like touching a raw nerve, resulting in a breakthrough in the process. I've heard about similar experiences from other coaches.

Attuning

TECHNICAL STUFF

The word *attune* is a general term that refers to everything a consultant does to be on the same wavelength as the client. It contributes to having a constructive discussion. Even external factors such as clothes, posture, use of language, eye contact, and the mode of expression can help. The consultant also coordinates with the learning-and-work style of the other person. In neurolinguistic programming (NLP), this process is also called *rapport*; other methods talk of *establishing contact* or *professionally reflecting*. All the terms mean more or less the same thing.

With the Enneagram, you know an even more subtle way of attuning — attuning to another person's personality and energy. When you know the Enneagram type, you already have a lot of information you can attune to. You have an idea of what is important for the individual types and can address it specifically. Every Enneagram type has its own, energetic aura. It can't be sensed or measured, but with the right training, you can learn to notice it. It's related to the fact that each type has its own pace, its own rhythm, and its own intensity. The problem already became apparent in the earlier example of coach Tina and client Margaret. Some types want to get ahead as quickly as possible, and others, such as Ian (Type 6) put on the brakes, so to speak, particularly in such moments, and resist it. If you don't attune as a consultant, this is like sand in a gearbox — it will gum up the works considerably, bringing things to a standstill. Attuning is an important requirement to really get in contact with the other person and feel connected. It doesn't require knowledge about the Enneagram. However, it helps to know the types in order to perceive them more easily and quickly.

Examining how rapport works

Attuning starts with *grounding* yourself, where you first connect with yourself in the here and now. You empty your mind and no longer think about today's concerns or the ones you must not forget tomorrow. You turn your attention inside yourself and place your feet firmly on the ground.

When you're grounded, you're in the best state of balance — and it's difficult to dislodge you from it. You're also particularly present and alert. In this starting position, you let go of your type in the background while your internal observer moves to the forefront. Also from this starting position, you connect with others. Imagine that you want to dock a boat: If you don't attach the rope in two places to the dock, the boat drifts. When you're grounded, however, you can often sense a kind of delay inside yourself, which makes it easier to truly see and hear the other person. In this condition, you can also easily perceive the other's pace, rhythm, intensity, and other characteristics and can attune to them, which means you take on the same characteristics. This *energetic attuning* is the highest form of rapport.

Benefiting from the fact that people are herd animals

When it's relevant for a client's particular situation, you can use attuning as a tool to influence the other's pace. In neurolinguistic programming, this is taught as a technique with designations such as *pacing* or *leading.* As herd animals, we humans have the tendency to subconsciously go along with others. If the other person speaks more loudly, we also raise our voice; if the other one is slouching in a chair, it feels like a subconscious invitation to sit similarly. When the other person is carrying around a lot of tension and not taking an issue in stride, many people unconsciously adopt this stance and acquire a similar tension. They even mimic how other people breathe. During exciting meetings or difficult conversations, some people almost stop breathing or just breathe at the top of their chests. If someone then consciously takes a deep breath, many others do the same and the situation is briefly relaxing again. In such a difficult conversation, you as a consultant can also ask everyone to inhale deeply. This literally brings fresh air into the group. When you're attuned to the other person, you can use this principle to take that person along in a direction that is useful for the guidance. (For more on NLP's methods, check out Kate Burton's *Neuro-linguistic Programming For Dummies* as well as her *Coaching with NLP For Dummies,* both published by Wiley.)

Adding

TECHNICAL STUFF

Adding — or filling in the gaps, to use another common term — refers to content and happens in two ways. First, as a consultant, you can literally "fill in" the other person by adding to the conversation. We often tend to do this by nature. When clients talk, you see what they see but also what they don't see — where there's a gap or blind spot, in other words. Then you add to their understanding of themselves by asking questions so that the clients reach the insight on their own. (Or you can simply tell them about it.)

The second way adding works is at the level of strengths. When you have clients who take a long time to think something over, you can fill in the gap by suggesting that they cut through the (impossibly tangled) Gordian knot more quickly. You can do that by conveying to your client, as part of your consulting work, their true strengths. Everyone has a predominant strength, which nearly always appears in connection with facing a challenge. As someone with Type 8, Stan integrates his strengths in leadership, taking initiative and setting a direction in his team. For the team performance as a whole and as a challenge for Stan, it's important for him to learn to also give other people on the team some space for their strengths and to also follow sometimes, when necessary. If you try to limit Stan's strength right at the beginning of the team coaching, by telling him that he simply has to follow more, you'll trigger a level of high resistance on his part — the limitation is something he seems allergic to. So the sequence is this: Coordinate first (relationship/acceptance), and then add (content). You can add on the basis of your expertise as well as on your Enneagram type or other strengths.

Assertiveness

The term *assertiveness* often makes one think of the admonition "Be assertive and stand up for yourself!" It's a little different within the context of the six A's for consultations, however. To expand on the term a little, I introduce a few aspects of the Rose of Leary, a model describing personal interaction proposed by the famed psychologist Timothy Leary. (See Figure 13-1.) The Rose of Leary uses two axes to show which position people can occupy in a relationship or in communication in relationship to one other.

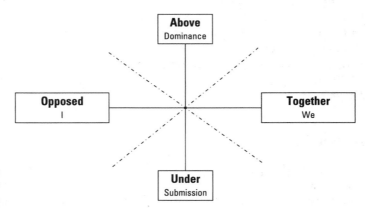

FIGURE 13-1:
The Rose
of Leary.

The call to be assertive and stand up for yourself doesn't apply to everyone. Some people tend to naturally assume the Above position (refer to Figure 13-1) in relation to other people. They lead, take the initiative, and appear dominant. This is likely true for Mary (Type 1), Roy (Type 2), Tina (Type 3), and Stan (Type 8). Some people, however, tend to naturally assume the Below position. So they position themselves "beneath" the other person in the interaction, tending to follow and wait. This probably applies to some degree to Margaret (Type 9), Ian (Type 6), and Alice (Type 5). If they're following and waiting, that doesn't necessarily mean that they're cooperating, however. Even if it may look like cooperation, these types might resist internally — saying yes but acting out no, for example. By nature, Tim (Type 4) tends to be on the Opposed side, whereas Louise (Type 7) is on the Together side because being there is fun!

One excellent way to practice assertiveness is to assert yourself and respect the other person. Then aggressiveness becomes asserting yourself without respecting the other, and non-assertiveness becomes not asserting yourself. The people who tend to assume the Below position in the Rose of Leary are likely non-assertive: They don't noticeably or sufficiently assert themselves. People who tend to be in the Above position are also likely to inhabit that space with some aggressiveness. Here, *aggressive* refers not to the use of (verbal) violence but rather to asserting yourself without respecting the other person — for example, by not recognizing or considering the other's will, ideas, or interests.

The non-assertive and aggressive positions aren't functional in a discussion. The interests of one party aren't being considered enough, which sooner or later will cause problems. Then the people in the Below position will move increasingly toward the Opposed side, and it will be difficult for the conversation or relationship to lead to constructive results. The call to assertiveness can therefore be understood to encourage recognition, respect, and consideration of the interest of both parties. For some Enneagram types, this means that they have to become more assertive by prevailing; for others, it can mean that they become more assertive by giving others more space and respect.

Alternatives

When you, as a consultant, suggest a solution and it means nothing to the client, you may encounter an impasse. You have done your best as a consultant and can certainly relate to the solution, but the client won't understand or accept that it's a good one. It's more effective to look for alternatives together, especially if the client is certainly capable of coming up with their own solutions by now. If someone comes up with an idea, it doesn't have to be pushed through against that person's will.

REMEMBER

In the consulting process, it isn't wrong for the client to show resistance in certain places. The resistance can be an indication of an issue that is still well concealed beneath surface for the client. This can provide an idea of where to look for the source of the pain or for what the client truly considers important. In addition, the protest (saying "This won't work," for example) offers a starting point for searching for alternatives ("Then what will work, and in which conditions?").

Recognizing the Need for a Healthy Foundation

The philosopher and mystic G.I. Gurdjieff claims that only those people who are familiar with all possible internal mechanisms are in a position to work effectively with others. He thinks that someone who tinkers with an individual part without knowing the whole thing can actually cause harm, especially when the work is being done on other levels of consciousness. (See Part 4.) You have to know what you're doing, even if it's about a concept as seemingly harmless as meditation and attention training. During an Internet search, I recently came across a report about mindfulness work with someone who had experienced severe trauma (from the hands of a psychologist, no less). It caused fairly severe consequences, and some serious damage. I think that a healthy foundation is needed before working with these advanced growth techniques.

TIP

In case of doubt, just let it be! The consultant as well as the client must have a healthy basis for working with people in the area of growth and development.

Keep in mind that consultants also have an Enneagram type. This means that each of them also has a type bias that influences the way they work. It's where the strengths in their work originate, along with the pitfalls; the type bias sets the patterns according to which they filter their perception. This filter determines what consultants actually see and don't see. As a Type 6 person, Ian strives for security and wants to avoid risks — this filters his perception. He definitely sees possible dangers but can miss opportunities for success.

Given that consultants each have their own type, I want to present an outline of the pitfalls and development points for coaches, therapists, and pastors according to their individual types. The next few sections present a brief impression of what can be said on this subject, a kind of indicator of where the dangers of counter-transference lurk for the individual types.

Recognizing when you're in a position to work with others

In addition to the usual prerequisites in terms of knowledge and skills that are needed to assist people in a consulting profession are further guidelines for the Enneagram. Responsible Enneagram training focuses on a single principle: Do no harm. It's possible to cause damage, so you can't be careful enough when you guide other people. For that reason, I describe a few development stages that every responsible consultant should complete. These guidelines should give consultants an idea of where they are and in which direction their development is heading.

>> **In working with the Enneagram, the consultant's personal development level is an important factor — it's easy to measure.** People who still identify strongly with their type generally aren't far enough along yet to work with others. Identification with your own type means that there's little or no awareness of the internal observer. This is the only way to observe yourself, in effect, from the outside and practice some self-management. One characteristic of identifying with your own type, for example, is that someone is still heavily triggered by type-specific factors and becomes reactive in a type-specific way. This means that either an internal on–off switch hasn't been found yet or the person is — still — unable to operate the switch as needed. The good news: It can be practiced. Anyone who wants to do so can learn how to do it.

One basic criterion of the Enneagram is that consultants who work with people recognize these mechanisms as soon as they appear. It's initially about recognition, therefore, not yet about working with them.

>> **The following stage is about self-management.** At a certain level of consciousness, the internal observer is alert. The internal on–off switch has been discovered, and the consultant being trained is learning to operate it freely. At a distance, the coach can observe what happens in the interaction and process with the client. When a transference occurs, coaches see that it comes from the other person, and they have enough of a handle on their emotions that they don't react to it in a type-specific fashion. The coach's self-management consists of letting go of their own type and avoiding their own reactivity.

In the earlier example, Tina demonstrates that she is troubled by her impatience. As a result, she doesn't always listen well and often has the urge to pick up the pace. She doesn't notice that this situation won't work well for Margaret. When Margaret gets angry, Tina attempts to explain it by pointing to a situation or issue outside of herself — she doesn't think that the reason might lie in some dissatisfaction with the coaching. Tina isn't yet able to observe from a distance what happens in the interaction between her and Margaret, and she doesn't yet have the self-management to let go of her type. Apparently, Tina still strongly identifies with her type. Although she notices her own impatience, she suppresses it rather than lets go of it.

>> **The next level goes a step further.** The coaches don't just master self-management; they don't even see the client's transference as annoying or inconvenient — they don't take it personally, in other words. The coaches are familiar with these mechanisms; they can see through them and maintain their personal distance. They recognize that the characteristics being projected onto them don't actually relate to them. It's never pleasant when something that doesn't relate to you is attributed to you, but this often happens in the consulting professions. For the consultant, however, the focus is always on the therapeutic goal. In consideration of this goal, the coaches determine whether they're working with the client's transference.

EVEN THE BEST CONSULTANTS MAKE THE OCCASIONAL MISTAKE

Usually things go well, but once in a while you make a mistake. There's always some small detail that is overlooked. The most important advice is not to rule out mistakes, but rather to develop awareness for things that might happen. As a consultant, you therefore also have to become aware of what hasn't gone so well. With that knowledge, you have an opportunity for evaluation and reflection, which lets you learn from your own mistakes. The Enneagram makes it easier for consultants to discover their own trigger points, reactivity, and transference — and, above all, to notice them the moment they occur. This is also the most difficult task. Practice makes perfect, you know!

Recognizing when therapy can help — and when you need to send a person on to a specialist

Working with the Enneagram as a personal development method is intended for people who act in an average and healthy manner — people who want to continue developing and growing, in other words. But then there's the matter of determining what is healthy. How can you determine it? Sometimes the boundary between being healthy and becoming ill can be a thin and blurry line. And this line isn't fixed — everyone experiences phases in life in which they feel healthy or less healthy.

Many professional groups offer support designed to improve personal interactions, growth, and well-being. What the various professional groups offer in this area often overlap, with the same models, methods, and techniques often being used. The boundary between services offered by a coach or a therapist isn't always immediately clear. A client chooses the consultant that they believe can help. As a result, a client might ask a coach to help out with a workplace issue but then allow a concealed trauma to surface during the coaching process. This client probably has developed sophisticated survival mechanisms that allow them to behave in a way that seems healthy from the outside, though you can see, after a closer look inside, that painful, open wounds still exist and must be healed. What will the consultant do then? How much support can that person offer the client, and when do they pass the client on to someone else?

Knowing what to pay attention to in an emotional crisis

Clients have to be supported in line with the current state of their health. In some cases, this might mean that they need to be sent to a psychotherapist. Most professional consultants aren't trained to work with people who have mental disorders, and the difficult part is that these disorders are often not easy to identify. And, unless you're a trained therapist, neither have you learned to recognize when it might be advisable to recommend a therapist or another consultant. Educational institutes offer training, for good reason, on topics such as psychopathology for coaches. This isn't about learning treatment methods but rather about recognizing signs indicating that the client should be sent to a therapist.

A good training program for consultants who want to work with the Enneagram should pay particular attention to indications that another kind of support might be more appropriate. To start a process of personal development and internal growth, a healthy ego and healthy internal structure are particularly crucial — it's the foundation you need to build on. If your psychic core is unhealthy or in bad condition, you can't grow — you first have to heal. That's why being on the path of personal development is a particularly suitable time to encounter and deal with unprocessed issues from the past.

Recognizing that consultants are also biased because of their type

Good training is of course essential, but it's also important that consultants recognize how their Enneagram type can introduce a certain bias in their dealings with clients. The following list summarizes the biases I associate with each type of consultant:

>> **Type 1:** Runs the risk of taking over the client's responsibility for the process and their own development. There's a danger that the client will be treated like a small child who can't take responsibility for their own learning process. Consultants who have this type tend to work diligently themselves, with the good intention of doing something for the other person as well as possible. They are sincere and highly responsible, which poses the risk that the clients feel pampered and do less work on their own while the consultants work ever more diligently. The development task for consultants who have this type consists of teaching clients to take on responsibility for their own development while the consultants lean back and relax. In addition, consultants of this type like to lecture and explain everything in great detail. The task here is to ask more questions and let their clients discover more awareness on their own.

>> **Type 2:** Must avoid the trap of subconsciously striving for the honor they might gain with the helpful knowledge and skills they offer. Dangerously, their main motto is, "Look how good I am at helping you" — and they want, above all, to be considered nice. Consultants of this type generously pay compliments and aim to make the other person feel good. The strategy behind this approach is, "When

you leave me and feel good, thanks to my help, then I also feel good about myself." Consultants of this type want to please everyone. The risk is that their clients won't be encouraged to do their own work or be inspired to carry out a program of self-help or simply be able to learn sufficiently. The consultant's thought process here is, "If the clients can help themselves, I ultimately become superfluous, which wasn't my intention." Such consultants feel valued only when the other person needs them. The development tasks for consultants of this type are to make themselves superfluous and put the clients in a position to help themselves. If it's necessary and helps the learning process, the consultants also have to learn to pay fewer compliments and confront the clients more frequently and clearly with their weaknesses and with the learning tasks needed to help them improve. (You can't necessarily help clients who have Type 7 if you make them feel even better.)

>> **Type 3:** Runs the risk of working too rapidly and being too goal-oriented. People who have Type 3 want to see *results*. They're more likely to start out at their own (fast) pace than to coordinate with the client's pace. Similar to how people with Type 3 don't take time for themselves or get in touch with their feelings, the consultants might also neglect their client's emotions when guiding them on their personal development journey. It can be helpful for a Type 3 consultant to spend some time and attention on this area, but people with Type 3 don't consider themselves experts in this area. Feelings make them insecure; they don't really know what to do with them. This is why they prefer to ignore them whenever possible — a strategy that they feel also saves time. Coaches who have Type 3 are ambitious and want to be the best coaches in the world. This is why the clients' paths have to become success stories and garner praise — from the clients' employers, for example. When faced with clients who demonstrate only slight or slow progress — those with little chance for success, in other words — these coaches give up. The development task for coaches with this type is easy to guess: Learn to slow down, take time to experience their own feelings, and develop patience with slower and less successful clients.

>> **Type 4:** Runs the risk of potentially aiming toward a connection with the client, maybe even experiencing a personal relationship instead of a professional one. There's a danger that Type 4 consultants, as true emotional junkies, may get stuck in this position and analyze the realm of feelings in increasing detail, even if a different strategy would be more helpful for the client's development. A client might have sufficiently worked through an issue but their Type 4 consultant hasn't had their fill of it yet. Type 4 consultants are so strongly oriented toward feelings that they consider it shallow and dull to appeal to the head center and continue their guidance at a cognitive level, even if this becomes necessary. The development task for consultants of this type

consists of finding more balance between being involved and (professionally) distant, as well as between attentiveness toward feelings and toward thinking.

>> **Type 5:** Runs the risk that they prefer to focus exclusively on the rational aspect of their clients' problems. They aim for a rational analysis and an appropriate rational solution. In addition, consultants who have this type tend to come up with the solution themselves, not least because they think that the clients expect this of them. This is why not much space or time remains for the emotional side of the problem and the client — the exact opposite of the situation with Type 4 consultants. You would have to add them both and then divide them in two to create a balanced mix of skills, time, and attentiveness when it comes to the head and heart centers. The development task for Type 5 consultants consists of

- Engaging also with the emotional side of the problems being faced by their clients as well as the emotions of the clients themselves

- Developing patience when it comes to letting them find solutions on their own

>> **Type 6:** Runs the risk of seeing danger lurking behind everything, warding everything off, approaching topics negatively and pessimistically, doubting explanations, and projecting their own ideas and worries onto the client. "Yes, but" and "You will probably" are phrases often used by Type 6 consultants. The lack of self-confidence and authority in this type also poses a risk. The worry of making a mistake as a consultant creates a strong orientation toward the things that could go wrong. The development task for this type consists of generating confidence that what the clients are saying is also what they mean and want to say. Additionally, the consultants have to learn to trust that things can also go well and that the client doesn't automatically share their worries and fears. This means they also have to learn to believe their clients when they say that they aren't afraid.

>> **Type 7:** Runs the risk of focusing on those aspects of the clients and their problems that interest and fascinate the consultants themselves. It's not productive for the client if the experience of the discussion and the learning process is more important for the consultant than the result. In addition, Type 7 consultants prefer to avoid problems. They're talented at explaining negative issues with a positive spin and are more focused on interesting possibilities for the future. When it comes to working with the client on problems in the here and now, it turns out that Type 7 consultants just don't have the patience. That can lead to a situation where the clients feel they're not being listened to or that their problems aren't being taken seriously. It may well happen that a consultant's optimism rubs off on the client and they leave the session with a sense of relief, cheerfully going on along their way with a positive attitude. That mood rarely lasts for long, however — precisely because the actual problem wasn't adequately resolved. For these

consultants, the development task consists of avoiding running away when painful topics are being covered and addressing them more profoundly if it's relevant to the learning process and to solving the underlying problem. Type 7 consultants have the challenge to stay focused on the client; they need to concentrate on the desired result and resist pushing themselves to the forefront of the discussion.

>> **Type 8:** Can compare their pitfall to that of Type 1 — namely, the risk of taking over the client's problems. Type 1 consultants tend to assume their client's responsibilities, whereas those with Type 8 assume leadership and make the problem their own. It's a small distinction, but it leads to different results. Type 8 consultants run the risk that because they want to protect their clients, they may instead deprive them of (perhaps painful) learning opportunities. On the other hand, they also tend to think that their clients have been stuck in the victim's role for too long. As a result, the consultants quickly lose their patience. When that happens, they feel compelled to say something like this: "We've already discussed this once, and I told you what you have to do. We've even discussed it a second time. If you still don't accept it the third time around, we're finished." The development task for consultants of this type consists of recognizing that other people are different from them and developing the patience to deal with it. Type 8 consultants also have to learn that their own way of dealing with problems isn't necessarily the way others deal with them. The consultants have to see themselves as standing next to their clients rather than looking down on them from above. That means leaving the leadership of the learning process to the clients and having the respect and patience necessary to surrender this leadership role.

>> **Type 9:** Runs the risk of becoming so immersed in their clients' stories that they no longer maintain enough distance to work toward change. The consultants thus live alongside the clients instead of controlling the process and directing it. These consultants may have so much understanding of the clients' stories that they may not see the other side — what the clients themselves aren't mentioning and may not be seeing, in other words. As a result, the consultants can't function much beyond being a mirror. The development task for this type consists of controlling the process, keeping their emotional distance, and avoiding becoming too immersed in the clients' stories.

Extras for therapists (and others)

In this section, I look beyond consultants and describe the special professional benefit that the Enneagram holds for therapists — such as how the various Enneagram types present themselves in therapy and which processes work (and which don't) for each individual type. I base my discussion in part on Carolyn

Bartlett's book *The Enneagram Field Guide: Notes on Using the Enneagram in Counseling, Therapy and Personal Growth* (Nine Gates Publishing). In that book, she not only interviewed numerous therapists but also analyzed people who participated in therapy, to inquire about what helped them (and what didn't). A strategy that turns out to be useful for one person doesn't necessarily work for someone else. Bartlett asked questions such as "What should the therapist know/understand about your type?"

The method that works and the one that doesn't work is always type-specific. Carolyn Bartlett writes that the Enneagram is a shortcut to a diagnosis to quickly get to know the client better and to get oneself and the therapy attuned to the client at an early stage.

For finding out more about the links between the Enneagram and traditional psychology, Carolyn Bartlett's book *The Enneagram Field Guide* is a treasure trove. The author truly builds a bridge between the Enneagram and mainstream psychology that seamlessly transitions from what we communicate to consultants to what psychotherapists need to hear about the Enneagram, which is why I like to present her work. With his background as psychiatrist and gestalt therapist, the cofounder of the modern Enneagram, Claudio Naranjo, MD, has also written several books on the topic, including *Character and Neurosis: An Integrative View* (Gateways Books & Tapes).

Seeing the Enneagram's professional benefit for therapists

The Enneagram isn't a form of therapy, but it does offer benefits, as described in this list:

>> Establish contact and trust between the therapist and client more quickly and accurately

>> Help a therapist quickly recognize the true nature of the client — for example, their underlying patterns and problems, motivations, survival strategies, defense mechanisms, and challenges/problems in relationships

>> Help the therapist recognize their own countertransference and reactivity more precisely and thoroughly

>> Aid in communicating in a more coordinated fashion with the client as well as coming up with a more purposeful choice of therapy and treatment strategy

>> Provide clearer insights into the methods that can be used (or not used) for individual clients

>> Ensure that the choice of therapy is based less on one's own preferences but rather on the best methods for the client

REMEMBER

The Enneagram is fundamentally democratic: The therapist can present the outline to the client and work to involve the client more intensely in the development process. The Enneagram can contribute to a client's learning to accept themselves with the insight that everyone has a specific personality structure and that each type is equally furnished with talents and problems, and strengths and weaknesses. Finally, the Enneagram can lead to the insight that the clients aren't alone with their problems. This acceptance creates room for development and increases the client's confidence that changes are possible and can even be pleasant and exciting.

Seeing how each type behaves in therapy as a client

As is the case with the consultant/client relationship, each Enneagram type reacts differently in a therapeutic situation:

>> **Type 1:** A Type 1 client is critical toward themselves and can bad-mouth themselves (in Enneagram terms, they have a strong internal critic or an overdeveloped superego). These compulsive tendencies make such clients prone to being workaholics (including at home, in the garden, and elsewhere) and to succumbing to burnout. Personal stories can revolve (resentfully) around the client's feeling neglected and being compared with others. In this instance, they can appear to be almost too fair and honest. They avoid taking a closer look at their own feelings and tend to analyze them instead of feeling them. Type 1 clients are also inclined toward depression, obsessive thoughts, and intrusive "bad" thoughts.

>> **Type 2:** A Type 2 client tends to establish a friendly, empathetic relationship to the therapist, dressing attractively for this purpose and maintaining eye contact. This person tends to flatter and put on a seductive air (also to distract the therapist from subjects that the Type 2 doesn't want to address deep inside). They seem completely focused on relationships, on others, on people. Type 2 clients are barely aware of their own needs and wishes and can be endlessly giving-giving-giving. This in turn can lead to having panicky reactions and anger and then violating their own high standards because they feel trapped in their sense of being needed. Type 2 clients can appear emotional, proud, theatrical, and dramatic.

>> **Type 3:** A Type 3 client can easily reel off all the slogans and clichés of positive thinking. They go into therapy when their self-image is damaged — after a failed relationship or a problem at work, for example. They may be in a bad physical state or burnt out. They avoid introspection but react enthusiastically to suggestions and tasks. The social support from outside can be weak and limited, even if the type likes to claim the opposite. One major source of stress for a Type 3 client is the fear that when they're preoccupied with their feelings

and turn toward the inside, they might not find a pattern of success. Then the Type 3 client worries that they won't be able to maintain this successful image to the outside. They avoid the healthy step of slowing down, fearing that they will lose energy and lose their successful self-image.

» **Type 4:** A Type 4 client likes to present themselves as outsiders. Sometimes they show a broad range of moods — from moody and dramatic to angry and provocative, from artistic and expressive to introspective and reserved. A Type 4 tends to get depressed, exhibit their old wounds, and potentially experience low self-esteem or feel something lacking in themselves. Or, in contrast to this, they feel superior because of their being unique and different. They might have trouble structuring their everyday life as they devote their energies to looking for profundity and authenticity. At the same time, they avoid ordinary situations and superficial routine. A Type 4 client can also have an incorrect or distorted image of their body and may have an eating disorder.

» **Type 5:** A Type 5 client can appear shy, somewhat shallow, careful, moderate, and reserved. Their verbal responses are either quite brief or characterized by an intellectual verboseness. They answer questions overly intellectually, thus showing their superiority. Loneliness and isolation are often the reasons for their therapy; but it could also be a partner who wants more contact and communication. A Type 5 client also visits a therapist so that they can find out how their own emotional and social systems function. They might worry about revealing themselves too much and fear an invasion of their privacy, their inner life, and their thoughts.

» **Type 6:** Clients of the phobic Type 6 clearly display the tension they're under with their alert posture, their restless glances around their surroundings, their wide-open eyes, and their disjointed speech. Those with the counterphobic Type 6 can appear quite direct, confrontational, and even aggressive (like Type 8). Both can appear questioning and testing limits, saying "Yes, but," contradicting the therapist, and often making contradictory statements of their own as a way to conceal their true problems. They seem to distrust the therapist or at least the therapist's authority — a strong trigger of reactivity for many therapists. A Type 6 client can say a lot about all the things that can go wrong and often see themselves as less strong than others, more as an underdog and a victim.

» **Type 7:** A Type 7 client can appear curious and interested and have a relaxed demeanor ("I may be here, but we both know that I don't really need this — it's just an interesting diversion!") and they tend to present their suffering and problems on a smaller scale than is reality. They're charming, they like to see their own role in a problematic situation in a positive light, and they're self-centered. (The other people in the difficult situation remain unmentioned.) They use highly exaggerated words but can also become critical and confrontational if they feel cornered. A Type 7 client tends to mentally work on problems and, when they understand them in their own minds, feel that they are done with counseling!

>> **Type 8:** A Type 8 client makes a grand entrance, with a lot of authority, energy, and intensity. They are often straightforward and direct and can be confrontational and demanding. A Type 8 client can easily start to complain and become angry. They're self-centered, and they focus on their own truths and interests. It's difficult for a Type 8 client to imagine that others may also have truths and interests. Those who have Type 8 can appear controlling and dominant in relationships and leave little room for others. In conflicts, Type 8 clients generally don't seem to remember anything when it comes to their behavior and participation.

>> **Type 9:** A Type 9 client can be unproblematic, pleasant, passive, slightly lethargic, and vague. Many need time to find their true feelings and thoughts, and if they don't find the necessary time and space, they fall back on more vagueness and superficialities — substitutes for the real thing. When searching for the true answer, a Type 9 client can linger on unimportant aspects and details. This expands their narrative without giving much content. They're also often detached. Their attention and energy often stay fuzzy, which means that they react and answer with some delay. Because they have trouble finding their own needs, wishes, and emotions, they like to identify with others, including with the therapist ("I don't know what I want — you tell me.").

Seeing what works and what doesn't work for each type

Having an effective strategy in place for the therapeutic process is crucial for its success. The following observations concerning each type can help you come up with the appropriate strategy:

>> **Type 1:** People with Type 1 report that they shut down internally when therapists challenge them too quickly or too fiercely or address a Type 1's internal critic. Neither does it help if the therapist goes along with the (often convincing) narrative that a Type 1 comes up with in order to prove how right they were all along. One indicator of this shutting down can be a clear declaration from the Type 1 client that they feel they're being treated unfairly. If however, the therapist is less goal-oriented and works to prioritize the value of the process for the client, you can expect good results. It also helps when the therapist assists the client in interpreting and expressing feelings, exhibits patience, and is able to help the client show self-compassion.

>> **Type 2:** A Type 2 client will probably use refined techniques of flattering the therapist in order to establish the sense that they're wonderful and special.

Don't let them succeed! As a therapist working with a Type 2 client, you should be particularly on the lookout for countertransference. Adhering to professional boundaries in the client-therapist relationship is important. It does work well to ask how a Type 2 client feels, even when they claim that everything is okay. A good idea is to encourage homework between sessions that makes a Type 2 client aware of what they feel, or to ask directly about other areas of life that they aren't mentioning on their own. During the therapeutic process, you can also ask Type 2 clients themselves for assistance, thus utilizing their natural inclination to help while also teaching them to help themselves the way they always help others.

>> **Type 3:** As a therapist, it won't work to adapt to the Type 3's tendency toward superficiality, nor will it work to accept the pattern of success that Type 3 clients want to maintain, even in therapy. Therapists should recognize that Type 3 clients tend to need emotional security more than confirmation. They should also notice in time that Type 3 clients, used to the habit of always maintaining a false self, will perform the role of the best client while preserving the defense mechanism of identifying with success. The therapeutic process can work well when the therapist can offer sufficient emotional security. That allows a Type 3 client to be brave enough to discard their mask and become vulnerable if the therapist keeps asking whether something is an illusion or a reality — as long as the therapist is patient and willing to work through one psychic layer after another.

>> **Type 4:** Type 4 clients talk of two inappropriate treatment strategies by therapists that occur fairly often:

- *Therapists offer interpretations too quickly, in the form of summarizations or the like.* This makes a Type 4 client feel as though they aren't being seen or understood. (A Type 4 client feels that they inwardly experience so much complexity and inconsistency that no one, not even a therapist, can easily or quickly understand what is going on inside them.)

- *Therapists relish the introspection, depth, and suffering of their Type 4 clients because this is what's exciting to many of them.* (I can also add therapists who walk on eggshells when dealing with Type 4 clients because these clients display the full intensity and sensitivity of their emotions.) A good strategy here is for the therapist to show a lot of patience and then establish a relationship in which a Type 4 client can feel safe and noticed. These clients must be able to recognize the emotional health and stability of the therapist as well as the therapist's emotional transparency and availability, along with the willingness to admit potential mistakes — mistakes that a Type 4 client will insist are inevitable.

>> **Type 5:** It won't work for the therapist to share in the client's intellectual performance, mainly because the client's poker face and minimal nonverbal information gives no clue to what is actually going on. Nor will it help if the

therapist becomes overwhelmed by the sparse communication of a Type 5 client, causing the therapist to speak most of the time. And it's not a good idea for too much dependency to enter into the client-therapist relationship, making a Type 5 client feel vulnerable. A successful strategy here calls for the therapist to be reliable and to demonstrate their knowledge and broad experience without too much drama. The therapist should feel comfortable to create gaps in the conversation, which Type 5 clients can fill with their own observations or, even better, just feel. It also works when the therapist emphasizes their own authority and independence within the boundaries of the relationship. In addition, it helps if the therapist patiently guides their Type 5 clients away from the intellectual level and explains that this isn't the place where changes happen.

>> **Type 6:** For Type 6 clients, it won't work if the therapist can be drawn into discussions and tries to disprove the client's negative perspective and disaster scenarios (for example, if therapists use their authority to convince them that it won't actually be so bad). It also won't work if the client or therapist lands in the Opposed areas on the Rose of Leary because the process is too intellectual and cognitive. (For more on the Rose of Leary, see the earlier section "Assertiveness.") It does work well if the therapist is aware that a high priority for this type is to create a secure environment and establish a relationship. Therapists should prove that they can be trusted (for example by sending congruent messages),but they also need to ask questions. They should take the client's disaster scenarios seriously and not contradict them; they should offer a context for the process. If the clients feel that the therapists are on their side ("Together" on the Rose of Leary), this will also have a positive effect.

>> **Type 7:** The therapeutic process won't work if the therapist falls into the charming trap laid by an awakened client where the therapist accepts as fact the client's narrative that it's simply a case of everybody else just being so terribly negative rather than penetrating to the real pain underneath. Nor should the therapist believe that the Type 7 client's optimistic perspective is actually more realistic or go along with this positive narrative, thus subconsciously avoiding giving the client more realistic (and decidedly more negative) feedback. A good strategy here is for the therapist to cut through the fog and give the Type 7 client a choice: If they don't truly want to be in therapy, they can leave; and if they sincerely want help, they can stay. Abandoning the (false) positive narrative requires true dedication. It works if the therapist offers reality checks and thereby prevents the Type 7 clients from straying too far from the truth. Type 7 clients are sensitive when it comes to relationship definitions; the therapeutic process works when the therapist creates a relationship based on equivalency. All humans have the same value as people, which is how a Type 7 person acts in relationships.

>> **Type 8:** If the therapist tries to outweigh the power of a Type 8 client, they will fail. With their eye for natural power, a Type 8 client immediately sees through

this; not only will they not take it seriously, but they'll also lose respect for the therapist. However, it works well if the therapist sticks closely to being authentic and grounded. Therapists can help when they calmly prevent a Type 8 client from stepping on them and won't let them get away with obvious, short, overly intellectual answers (and jokes). Type 8 clients need to have respect for the therapist, to have someone who is on their side and isn't too sensitive — a therapist who understands that beneath the brash exterior, a Type 8 client really wants to get help.

>> **Type 9:** The therapeutic process won't work if the therapist has no experience of not only how people with Type 9 can deflect and avoid the issue but also how they can forget important emotional parts of an experience. This deflection can also consist of a smile, a joke, an endearing lack of courage — anything that draws attention away from the subject at hand that the therapist is threatening to dive into. Type 9 clients report that it won't work if the therapist adapts to their behavior and becomes too helpful, offers too much room to swerve aside, or fails to challenge or dig deep enough. What does work well is the therapist asking about what strategies haven't worked in the past. It's often easier for Type 9 clients to answer a question about something that *isn't* the case. This is also why it works if the therapist offers examples of possible answers or encourages brainstorming together to move a Type 9 client to action.

In addition to subjects of a more general nature — those related to the selected therapy method or those raised by the client — each type has specific issues that should be on the agenda. These are topics that aren't always addressed by the client but that are important and should be approached regardless of the specific request for help. They can become the key to the actual development process. Here are the specific issues linked to each type:

>> **Type 1:** The internal critic; compassion and forgiveness, contact with one's own impulses, reaction formation

>> **Type 2:** Pride; suppressing one's own feelings, establishing contact with one's own will

>> **Type 3:** Honesty and truth, success and failure, identification

>> **Type 4:** Grounding the self; rejection and desire; shame, melancholy, and depression; introjection

>> **Type 5:** Exploring one's internal emotional life as another form of knowledge; isolation

>> **Type 6:** Grounding the body, breathing, understanding fear, working with anger; projection

>> **Type 7:** Understanding fear and quieting the chatter of what Buddhists call the monkey mind (the annoying inner critic that can't shut up), dealing with negative and painful feelings, rationalizing, empathizing

>> **Type 8:** Vulnerability and protection; revenge, denial

>> **Type 9:** Learning to feel sadness, recognize and express anger, and overcome numbness

POSITIVE PSYCHOLOGY

Psychotherapists are trained to work with pathological models, meaning psychological science has a medical orientation. In other words, it's focused on analyzing disorders and then diagnosing and treating them. They have focused on where there was (and still is) the greatest need.

A space is opening up for recognizing that people are more than their disorders — that even average, healthy persons suffer from the effects of their personality structures. These people need development, growth, sense, and meaning in their lives as well. Everyone is becoming increasingly aware that they're spiritual beings in one way or another and that they have the need to serve a higher goal (for example, by dedicating themselves to the community or to other people). This aspect is attracting more attention with the rise of spiritual psychology and positive psychology — a psychology that calls for a study of what makes life most worth living. At a certain point, the dividing line between therapy and spirituality starts to blur. The Enneagram supports this by offering an insight into the spiritual strengths of the types and helps discover their true natures.

4

I Know My Type — Now What?

Chapter **14**

Developmental Aspects of the Enneagram

Your goal in life is twofold: Continue developing and growing, and gather the tools you need to better conquer the problems that are sure to come your way. But how does this work? In earlier chapters, I thoroughly explore the foundations of the Enneagram. Here in Part 4, I want to proceed methodically, outlining the developmental process as a whole. In this chapter, I describe the various levels tied to learning, consciousness, and development. On each level, you work to develop different aspects of yourself. These levels aren't part of any hierarchy, where one level is better than another. All topics and levels have to be addressed in order to achieve a harmonious development. You have to know what you're concerned with — where you stand in your development, in other words. Knowing that info is the starting point for any method of personal development. These aspects form a framework you can then use to shape your own learning and development.

Levels of Learning, Acting, Developing, and Awareness

By engaging with the various learning levels, you can see where your aspirations for personal development are heading. When you know where you stand and have a learning goal in mind, your learning path becomes clear.

Level 1: Broadening your experience, step-by-step

Incremental means doing things step-by-step. The factors that are already in place are enhanced and improved. So the first level is all about improvement, including, among other things, what you learn in life by falling down and picking yourself up again. You reach your limits and think that it might be better to try to do more of something or less of something or to try something completely different. The starting point is always your own personality type and your own basic assumptions and automatic strategies for action. What you often learn on this level are new, *compensating* skills, where you reach the limits of your type and learn to compensate for them. Learning about the strength of other Enneagram types is also part of this level. You don't need a lot of theory or time to recognize and implement clear, type-specific instructions to improve yourself and your relationships. It quickly leads to results, it's meaningful, and it's valuable, but keep in mind that the type mechanism won't change or release its hold on you at this level. The type still has control.

This first level is the learning level described in books about the Enneagram as being linked to the notion of personal development. It's also the level linked to the possible applications listed in Part 3 of this book: increasing your communicative effectiveness, giving feedback, and mediating in conflicts, for example.

REMEMBER

Development is necessary and valuable on all levels. This first level means more than acquiring valuable skills and strengths — it's also about expanding the repertoire of your behavior so that you have greater freedom to not only choose a course of action but also act more effectively and congenially, especially in relationships. It's about developing on a psychological level. A healthy ego structure is necessary to develop any of the more advanced levels of consciousness.

REMEMBER

No single type is better than another: Each one has different strengths. You can learn from the strengths of the other types by recognizing and acknowledging them as strengths. Then you can learn the way you did as a child: by watching and copying. For example:

>> A Type 9 person can learn to be more direct, clear, and assertive from someone with Type 8.

>> A Type 1 person can learn to present and promote themselves from someone with Type 3.

>> A Type 5 person can learn social skills from someone with Type 2.

All nine types can learn something from each of the other eight types. What would you like to learn from all the other types?

Level 2: Self-reflection and breaking new ground

Reconstruction refers to a change in behavior, in which the objective is to discard certain habits and replace them with ones that are more desirable or more effective. This means a transition from the old to the new. Suppose that you hear someone say, "I used to do it that way, but I don't anymore." This level is also known as *second-order learning*, which requires you to become conscious of yourself and your type mechanism. You have to learn self-observation so that you can consciously perceive your thoughts, feelings, and impressions. An interior dialogue — the *self-reflective* act — starts at this level, where you evaluate your type mechanism and start questioning your basic assumptions. You learn to recognize the limitations of your type, including how your type constrains you, and you learn to let go of your type mechanism. To do this, you have to make an effort and make some clear decisions. In fact, as a result of the reevaluation of yourself and what you previously considered to be real, you face answering a *lot* of questions, such as "Do I still want this?" and "Now that I don't want it to be this way anymore, how can I change it?" The old type still applies, but now you have the freedom to choose; you no longer have to automatically react on the basis of the type. You're free to choose actions on the level of the internal observer. Now the type mechanism has an on–off switch and you can operate it with the help of your internal observer.

You can learn from the other types on this level as well. Here are some examples:

>> A Type 5 person can learn from Type 2 how to move more freely among other people.

>> A Type 2 person can learn from Type 5 how to be more independent and to stand on their own feet.

>> A Type 4 person can learn from Type 7 how to see the bright side of life more often.

>> A Type 7 person can learn from Type 4 how to also accept the darker side of life.

At first glance, you might not see a big difference between the examples in this list and the two examples for learning on the first level. Having Type 5 learn social skills from Type 2 is different from the earlier example of Type 5 learning from Type 2 how to move more freely among people. The latter isn't a skill but rather focuses on becoming more social from the inside out. To achieve this, a Type 5 person must be able to observe themselves, let go of their own type mechanism, and thereby create space and freedom from within in order to become more social. This doesn't just change something on the action level; instead, the new internal state causes the type mechanism to relax so that it doesn't obstruct the path as much, if at all. What do you want to learn from the individual other types on this level?

Level 3: Transformational learning

A *transformation* is a true change: Something new has been created in place of the old. Achieving this change requires shining a light on one's own basic principles — and letting go of some of them. Such basic principles have been developed over time, powered by your core convictions, survival strategies, and attention style. To let some of them go requires jumping into the deep end of the swimming pool, into the unknown. You're tossing out your old shoes, so to speak, even though you have no new ones yet, and going barefoot seems like a tricky proposition. The new goal you're seeking is unclear because it's unknown and the process is hard to control. This level of learning and change requires devotion and receptivity to whatever comes next. You need courage, wisdom, and love. At this level, you step beyond your type and let go of the prevailing focus of your attention. You're free in the sense that you're no longer dominated by the automatic thoughts, feelings, and sensations of your type. This state of consciousness goes further than simple reflection — it's called being awake or being *mindful.* Learning to control this level of knowledge is a lifelong task. Transformational learning requires the willingness to learn from a perspective that isn't based on fixation or identity. It requires an open, receptive position. Starting from this position, your intellectual curiosity and emotional openness make it possible for you to experience life without the distortions or prejudices of your type.

Examining Action and Developmental Levels

To develop a better idea of the action and developmental levels associated with the different kinds of learning, it helps to have a scale in mind to gauge the intensity of each level, so I've assigned these action levels:

>> **91 to 100** (the highest action level): You have extremely good social behavior; you can deal with your problems in life before they get out of hand; you're appreciated by others because of your numerous strengths; and you have no symptomatic behavior.

>> **51 to 60** (middle action level): You see moderate symptoms or moderate problems with social behavior at work or in school.

>> **11 to 20** (second-lowest functional level): You face the danger of hurting yourself or others, your personal hygiene is occasionally neglected, and communication is reduced significantly.

In introductory training sessions for the Enneagram, I like to use a simple bar graph to illustrate what's going on. (See Figure 14-1.) The majority of people have developed a more or less healthy interior structure. You can behave in a relatively healthy way and also participate in society. In the diagram shown in Figure 14-1, this is the middle position.

Sometimes people aren't comfortable in their skin and they feel a little left of center. At other times, they feel great and everything is then much easier: They're more cheerful, and the people around them are nicer. When that's the case, everything succeeds much more easily as well. In Figure 14-1, you would then be a little to the right of the center. When you're engaged with personal development, the goal is to not only take greater control of your life but also ensure that you're to the right of center more often and for longer periods.

The rightmost point in this diagram is the highest development level: enlightenment. Examples of people at this level are Buddha and Jesus. The leftmost point in this diagram designates pathology. It refers to people whose internal structure hasn't been developed in a healthy way — someone who has a disorder or can no longer act independently in society because of their mental state, for example. Such a person can also think of himself as being on the same level as Jesus, but usually that isn't a good sign.

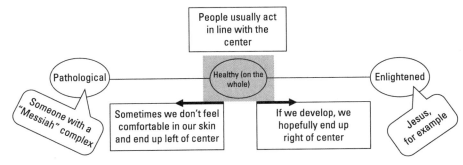

FIGURE 14-1:
The various developmental levels.

In her book *The Enneagram at Work: Towards Personal Mastery and Social Intelligence*, Hannah Nathans sets the bar to a more realistic height and calls the highest level *developed* rather than *enlightened*. She describes the various development levels this way:

>> **Developed:** Individuals at this level are constantly aware of the tendencies of their type mechanism and feel no need to interpret them positively. They can generally interrupt their type mechanism, and they can consciously choose between different levels of awareness.

>> **Average:** Individuals at this level experience the strengths as well as the pitfalls of their type. They can perceive the automatic character of their type and reflect on it. Occasionally, they're in a position to interrupt the type mechanism, and they can decide on a different course of action and implement that course.

>> **Pathological:** Individuals at this level mainly experience the negative excesses of their type, but generally attribute them to others. They aren't capable of (or ready for) self-observation and reflection, so they can't check their perception. They continue to be trapped in their delusional system. Someone who remains mainly at this level needs professional help.

REMEMBER

Don't regard the three states described in Figure 14-1 (and by Hannah Nathans) as three separate and distinct states, but rather as part of a continuum.

Nathans provides an example of the three levels for a specific type: Type 1 individuals. At the pathological stage, they are demanding, intolerant, rigid, moralizing, and angry, and they can't free themselves of these characteristics. A Type 1 individual at a developed stage shows wisdom and is idealistic, but combines them with a high level of reality; they are tolerant and genuine teachers. Nevertheless, these individuals can also have days — when highly stressed, for example — where they are still angry, demanding, and intolerant. They probably can't distance themselves from their anger and intolerance at such a time, but later they can certainly reflect on it and consider the same situation with some wisdom. They therefore occupy two different positions in the diagram at different times.

In general, people tend to wander to the negative side of the diagram under stress and move toward the developed side under ideal circumstances. The first process is called *regression,* and the second one is called *development.* Although most people want to move to the right in this continuum, it's not always so easy. Sometimes, everything works wonderfully, but at other times it's a hard row to hoe. Sometimes, when you convince yourself that you've made the move to the right, you let your good angels slumber until reality wakes you up again.

Looking at Unhealthy Personality Structures

It's all well and good to talk about enlightened individuals like Jesus and the Buddha, but at some point you have to return to earthly reality, where the enlightened state is far from common. Freud has shown that it may be much less painful, and thus easier, to retain a neurotic habit — even if it's annoying — than to confront the deeper pain of the unsolved dilemma lying beneath it. According to Freud, the concealed benefit keeps behind a veil the secret wish to change a disappointing or painful situation one has hidden from others. This veil is created by the efforts of your type — efforts that make it clear that you would rather retain a neurotic habit than look the painful reality in the eye.

The unveiling of this secret wish is at the center of the Enneagram practice: learning to see through your veil so that you can recognize and accept reality as it is. Noted psychiatrist and Enneagram educator Claudio Naranjo assumes that people are neurotic even when they're engaging in average and healthy behavior. Even flashing an automatic smile that you use to show people that you're a nice person can be seen as neurotic behavior. This is in line with G.I. Gurdjieff's insight that people spend their lives as automatons who are sleeping, living unconsciously, and behaving unconsciously — unwilling to be conscious of themselves.

Seeing how the type structures describe your neuroses

As a psychiatrist, Claudio Naranjo must have found it easy to see how the personality structures of the Enneagram resemble personality disorders that have already been diagnosed and described. Even if you're neurotic in your type according to Naranjo, though, you're still an average, healthy person. For things to reach the level of a true personality disorder, you have to have advanced far beyond the healthy level. At first glance, the object of attention, the driving forces, and the internal mechanisms may be the same, but the individuals under consideration aren't equally healthy. Decades ago, Naranjo already compared the descriptions of the Enneagram types to the descriptions of psychological disorders in the *Diagnostic and Statistical Manual of Mental Disorders (DSM)*. Of course, everyone would prefer to focus on onward development and enlightenment, but this part of reality also exists.

To illustrate the ties between personality disorders and Enneagram types, Table 14-1 lists the pathological names that Naranjo came up with for each type. Column 2 shows the personality disorders described in the *DSM* that correspond to each type.

TABLE 14-1   # Linking Personality Disorders to Enneagram Types

Naranjo's Term	Terms from the DSM That Match the Enneagram Types
Type 1: Perfectionism	Obsessive-compulsive disorder with a focus on compulsive thoughts
Type 2: Histrionic (theatrical)	Histrionic as well as dependent personality
Type 3: Marketing orientation (doing whatever you can to sell yourself)	A pathology of (self-) deception that (strangely enough) doesn't appear in the *DSM*
Type 4: Depressive/masochistic	Borderline or emotionally unstable personality disorder
Type 5: Pathological reclusiveness	Schizoid
Type 6: Paranoid	Paranoid
Type 7: Narcissistic	Narcissistic
Type 8: Sadistic	Antisocial personality
Type 9: Overadapted	Obsessive-compulsive disorder with a focus on compulsive behavior but also an avoidant and dependent personality

WARNING

You might well recognize aspects of yourself in the personality disorders I describe here, which can potentially indicate that the internal mechanism of your type is comparable with a disorder — but that certainly doesn't mean you *have* the disorder. For a medical diagnosis, you need to see a doctor, and for personality disorders, you need to see a psychiatrist. Each description lists a healthy and an unhealthy version. Before something is called a disorder, different criteria for the person's state have to be examined. Diagnostic criteria don't just include recognizing a description; the *DSM* also lists other factors for a person's state and functioning.

Before a diagnosis can be made, you need to check whether the following applies:

>> Evidence of a lasting pattern of internal experiences and modes of behavior that significantly deviate from expectations within the person's culture

>> Evidence of a lasting pattern of behavior that causes significant suffering or limitations during social or professional activities or actions in other important areas

>> Evidence of a pattern that has been stable over a long period and whose beginnings can be traced back at least to adolescence or early adulthood

>> Evidence of a lasting pattern that isn't more likely to be considered the expression or consequence of another mental disorder

>> Evidence of a lasting pattern that isn't a result of the direct physiological effect of a substance (such as drugs, medicine) or a somatic ailment (such as skull trauma)

The next several sections look in greater detail at the disorders listed in Table 14-1.

Obsessive-compulsive disorder (Type 1)

Obsessive-compulsive disorder (OCD) is characterized by a general inflexibility; the strict following of rules and processes; perfectionism; and the need for excessive order. People with obsessive-compulsive disorder are often frugal, keep their home perfectly neat, and avoid delegating tasks because they believe that the work won't be done correctly otherwise. They have few, if any, gray areas when it comes to morals or ethics: Deeds and intentions are entirely good or entirely bad. Their personal relationships are laborious because they demand far too much of their friends, partners, and children. Patients with obsessive-compulsive disorder primarily strive for perfection and feel tense if certain things aren't correct or in order.

Histrionic personality disorder (Type 2)

A *histrionic* personality disorder is characterized by exaggerated emotional expressions and a desire for attention. At first glance, the affected individuals seem lively, vivacious, enthusiastic, and charming. They like to flirt and use (sexual) seduction to attract attention. But if someone responds directly to their advances, they can react insecurely. Their emotional expressions are often stronger than would be expected in a given context. They become restless, vindictive, or depressed if they think they aren't receiving enough attention. They often think that their personal relationships are deeper than they really are, which makes them susceptible to depression. This disorder is diagnosed more often in women than in men.

Borderline personality disorder (Type 4)

A *borderline* personality disorder is characterized by a pattern of unstable interpersonal relationships, an unstable self-image, unstable emotions, and a high level of impulsiveness. Affected persons often have low self-esteem and a strong tendency to make extreme judgments. Relationships with friends and/or partners often take place on an all-or-nothing basis — often everything at first and then suddenly nothing. An individual's low self-esteem occasionally leads to self-injuries (automutilation, such as deliberately cutting and burning yourself). Some patients try to cover their insecurity with provocative behavior. Sometimes dissociation may occur: People with a borderline disorder can briefly "go away" so that they're no longer present in reality for a certain period. Then they feel like they're watching themselves "act," as if in a movie. This usually happens if they are feeling excessive stress.

Many people with borderline disorders live with the fear of being abandoned (even if this fear has no basis in reality). They may even feel lonely in groups.

No two borderline disorders are the same — they have different increments, from bearable to severe. (The American Psychiatric Association, the institution responsible for the *DSM*, also uses the term *emotionally unstable personality disorder.*)

Schizoid personality disorder (Type 5)

A *schizoid* personality disorder is characterized by detachment when it comes to social contacts and a limited range of emotional expressions. Affected persons barely have the need for close relationships and generally look for activities that they can do alone. They find little joy in doing things with others, have hardly any close friends, seem indifferent to praise and criticism, and react coolly and distant in social situations. Whether this disorder is truly a disorder is still being discussed because the affected persons and their environment don't necessarily suffer as a result. There are (symptomatic) congruities between a schizoid personality disorder and Asperger's syndrome, but the schizoid personality disorder isn't considered part of the autism spectrum.

Paranoid personality disorder (Type 6)

The term *paranoid* refers to prolonged and unsubstantiated distrust of people, which causes someone to handle friends, acquaintances, and colleagues with detachment. Contacts are allowed to get closer only when it turns out that they have no bad intentions, though an affected person often stays on guard and occasionally reacts fiercely to a small offense (such as a joke), which they consider a personal attack. If this person is in reality treated badly or betrayed, the resulting anger can last for years and possibly lead to a desire for revenge.

Paranoid personalities often distrust their life partners as well. For that reason, they watch the partner's activities more closely than normal, and the affected person sometimes appears strict or dictatorial. In certain cases, the distrust is directed against population groups, organizations, or authorities, which can lead to prejudices or protracted conflicts — conflicts that seem like only minor issues to other people. (This is why *paranoia* is also often referred to as *querulous paranoia.*)

Narcissistic personality disorder (Types 3 and 7)

A *narcissistic* personality disorder is characterized by an exaggerated sense of self-worth, a strong desire for admiration, and a low level of empathy. At first glance, narcissistic patients may appear charming and interesting, but if a relationship lasts for a longer period, the egocentrism often turns out to be a serious obstacle. They often demand special treatment and, when that doesn't happen, they easily feel insulted or underappreciated, which makes them susceptible to depressive symptoms. On the other hand, their vulnerability can also lead to temper tantrums. The life of someone with a narcissistic personality disorder is often difficult and strongly affects the people around them.

Just like an addict needs heroin, someone with a narcissistic personality disorder is dependent on attention. This attention keeps these persons' fragile self-image intact and is therefore vital to them. To garner the necessary attention, affected persons use the people in their direct surroundings, such as their partners or children. A narcissistic personality disorder can be considered a defense mechanism that is based on feelings of inferiority.

Antisocial or asocial personality disorder (Type 8)

An *antisocial* personality disorder is characterized by antisocial as well as impulsive behavior. (It used to be referred to as a *psychopathic* or *sociopathic* personality disorder.) Because many more men than women suffer from this disorder, it's also often casually referred to as the borderline personality disorder for men. Affected persons often come in contact with the police and legal system because they disregard the standards and values of society as well as the rights of others. Some believe that people who have made unusually great achievements in society show characteristics of an antisocial personality disorder because it's easier for them to make difficult decisions.

Affected persons can be quite engaging and charming but also quickly cause conflict from their impulsiveness and lack of empathy. They often lie to their advantage and have no fear, which might explain why they fail to see the consequences of their actions. Those affected rarely, if ever, feel remorse, empathy, or guilt.

Dependent personality disorder (Type 9)

A *dependent* personality disorder is characterized by lasting psychological dependency on others. Because affected persons have a strong need for affirmation and recognition, they make a great effort to please others. They can react with frustration because they either feel forced to do things they don't actually want to do or they can't express their feelings. Their overly dependent behavior can lead to difficult and unstable relationships.

When a relationship ends, affected persons often despair and can no longer care for themselves properly. They often have low self-esteem and are susceptible to other mental disorders, especially depression and anxiety disorders. The *DSM* defines the dependent personality disorder as a lasting and excessive need to be cared for, which leads to self-submission, exaggerated dependent behavior, and the fear of being abandoned. This disorder often manifests itself in different situations in young adults.

Earlier versions of the *DSM* listed a passive-aggressive personality disorder alongside the dependent personality disorder. The current *DSM* excludes passive-aggressive personality disorder because it isn't clear that it's a stand-alone personality disorder. The passive-aggressive personality disorder fits even better with the description of Type 9 on a less developed or pathological level.

THE NINE LEVELS OF DEVELOPMENT, ACCORDING TO RISO/HUDSON

Don Richard Riso and Russ Hudson (you can find more on them in Chapter 19) have come up with a model depicting nine vertical levels of awareness for personal and spiritual growth. They have described which characteristics apply to each type for each level. Some people swear by these development levels and experience great benefits from working with them — and can therefore work well with them. Others don't see themselves reflected in these levels quite as much because they believe that the psychological foundations are too weak or that the many details create the illusion of a precision that is neither reflected by reality nor supported by research results. They also see the whole thing as the result of an intellectual finger exercise, not as the result of observations and reports from the people themselves.

I don't work with the Riso/Hudson model, for other reasons. The most important one is that I work with a division of the various levels of consciousness, which you can learn more about later in this chapter. I see this model as effective and inspiring, however. For me, it represents the connection between development on a psychological level and development on a spiritual level. These things are quite personal: One person might swear by PCs, and another by Macs. Though both are computers, they have different technologies and different designs. Only a few people work with both platforms simultaneously; most choose one or the other. This is also how it works with these divisions: Ultimately, you're given a choice and you have to discover on your own what works best for you.

Exploring the Different Levels of Consciousness: Internal States

The various spiritual traditions have long described the different states of being that people find within. Meditation helped me gain knowledge about these different states of being. Now, if you're worried that I'm getting too wooly and touchy-feely here, please be reassured: I'm not talking about a topic that's way out there on the astral plane. You're surely quite familiar with some of these conditions. For example, every night when you close your eyes and fall asleep, you enter a world that isn't accessible to normal consciousness. That means sleep is a kind of internal state where your consciousness is completely relaxed.

These internal states can also be seen as levels, known in familiar terms as

>> **Lower Self:** Synonymous with your activities being driven by the type mechanism or ego; your type has taken over control in this area and directs your thinking, feeling, and action.

>> **Higher Self:** Can become active when the internal observer steps into the foreground, thus shifting the type mechanism into the background. One characteristic is that the internal observer then assumes control and directs your thinking, feeling, and action accordingly. You can feel this yourself because the freedom to choose and act is a consequence of this process.

The various states of being are also referred to as *internal states* or *states of consciousness.* In the following overview, I have parceled out these states of consciousness to several different levels that, together, form a description of your consciousness. The overview is meant to help you picture what the various levels of consciousness are like. (The way I have divided them corresponds with the anatomy of consciousness in the mystical teachings of the Kabbalah, taught in this form by my colleague Hannah Nathans in her study *Kabbala and the Enneagram.*)

REMEMBER

The Kabbalah, which originated in Jewish mysticism, is also referred to as the *tree of life.* In the Kabbalah's conceptual world, the origin of each soul is rooted in another aspect of the divine.

I wasn't raised in a spiritual tradition, and the spiritual expressions are often difficult for me, which is why I translate the terms into more pedestrian language in order to make everything comprehensible to me. I therefore consider myself a translator, so to speak, from the "old" language into a new, more easily understandable one. In this overview, you're taking a first step toward the spiritual dimension of the Enneagram.

The consciousness level of your body and of your type is present to you. (See Figure 14-2.) It's easily perceptible — you're dealing with it the moment you wake up. The state of consciousness above the body and the type — the level of the internal observer, in other words — is the first important level you have to develop. Everyone can learn how to do this — you can train the internal observer. It's just mental fitness, pure and simple.

You train your brain all your life, but in the Western world, you mainly develop your head center — and the head centers of your children — in a cognitive way. In other regions of the world, it's customary to develop the head center in other ways, also starting in childhood — for example, meditation and attention training. The level of the internal observer is the level you enter when you become aware of your automatisms — and awaken to yourself. When you mature to the point where you start to sense the suffering that exists around you, you become receptive to deeper realities. Why does suffering exist? Maybe because, otherwise, you wouldn't awaken at all. (Not many people plunge into internal work when they're happy and healthy.)

The Body Breathing Sensations Energy	We are able to perceive our own bodies. That is easy, because our bodies consist of matter. Each is its own entity: "You are you and I am I."
Type Ego/Superego Thinking, Feeling, Acting Passions/Fixations Defense mechanisms Veils, Judgements	When we are caught up in our type, it is present but we cannot see it. Our type makes us blind to its existence. We therefore consist of our thoughts, our feelings, our sensations. There is no distance; only complete and utter identification.
Inner Observer strictly neutral, No judgement is made from a distance Predisposed to the here and now **Registering or witnessing consciousness**	In this state of consciousness, we can perceive reality the way it truly is – as well as perceiving ourselves and others.
Transpersonal Feelings of unconditional love, Selflessness, Bound to higher universal values, A higher self Committed to the collective, not the individual	In this state of consciousness, we can receive the feelings and values of another order – higher virtues and ideas (see Chapter 16).
Oneness The feeling of being one with everything, Nondualism: "You and I are one" Your suffering is my suffering. Your God is my God. There are no differences.	In this state of consciousness we experience oneness. There is only oneness — no dualities.

FIGURE 14-2:
The different
levels of
consciousness.

THE TRANSPERSONAL OR
TRANSCENDENT SELF

The transpersonal, or transcendent, self is an awareness that goes beyond the individual, surpassing space and time. It's unaware of any personal problems, tensions, or
fears — admittedly, a state that's difficult to imagine. It's possible that you'll give this
notion of the transcendent self a hard pass, but maybe you'll find it worth taking a closer
look. The transcendent self is what the Swiss psychoanalyst C.G. Jung referred to as the
collective unconscious. He has passed down a great deal of knowledge that has enabled
people to become more conscious, making it possible for them to recognize, acquire,
and use the forces that are present in the collective unconscious. Jung explained the
deeper meaning of the language and images found in mythology in ways that mirrored
the way that many native people experience them. With the help of this language and
imagery, you can open yourself to an expanded — even unlimited — idea of the world,
your reality, and your universe.

Falling Down and Getting Back Up Again

Even without a model or a method like the Enneagram, humans learn in the course of life by actually living — which often means falling down and getting back up again. Many people struggle with themselves between the ages of 20 and 30, a decade where a type's personality structure has been fully developed and is still active internally, with little self-management and without restraint. Young people at this age are standing on their own two feet: They study, work, marry, bear children — four distinct areas, each of which poses a considerable challenge and where all individuals end up confronting themselves. When people talk about this period, they often discuss how they learned and developed on their own accord, by moving on from failure — by falling down and getting back up again, in other words. In the Enneagram, this process of moving on from failure takes two paths: the wing path and the stress/relaxed path, as described next.

You have wings, and you can fly

In those areas that give you the most difficulties, you first tend to work yourself into shape on your own. In my case, while I was studying and working on group teamwork projects, I discovered that by my very nature, I could see only one possible correct solution to a certain problem. I therefore dedicated myself with great enthusiasm to the task of persuading others that my solution alone was the reasonable one. (You can likely imagine what these scenarios looked like.) After encountering stiff resistance on the part of my fellow students, I realized that I would need to approach group work differently. I learned to see everything from multiple sides, I listened to my fellow students to find out their perspectives, and I realized that several solutions are often possible — and that there's no such thing as the one true path. The strengths I subconsciously developed on my own greatly resemble the strengths of an Enneagram next to mine in the circle — namely, Type 9, the mediator. Apparently, in order to balance out my type, I managed to develop strengths from my wings — the types to the right and left of me in the Enneagram circle.

In the Enneagram, the strengths to your right and left are your *wings*. Everyone has two wings they can use to bring into balance their interactions with the outside world. Please note that there's no empirical evidence for these wings and their impact on your apparent development, yet purely as a matter of observation, they do seem to exist and function as I describe them. This phenomenon gives you insight into the learning path that you have already completed on your own — and maybe you'll also find a source of inspiration here. If you don't recognize much from the types next to you in the circle, take a look at which strengths they have that you also benefit from. Learning like this is *first-level* learning: expanding your strengths and seeking out alternative behaviors.

Table 14-2 lists an example of balancing for each type and its two wings.

TABLE 14-2

Enneagram Types and Their Wings

Wing/Type/Wing	Attributes
9 **1** 2	The 9-wing ensures that Type 1 also sees nuances and has empathy for others. The 2-wing ensures that Type 1 people are less focused on themselves and care more for others.
1 **2** 3	The 1-wing ensures that Type 2 is more likely to discover and do what they want, becoming more willing to look out for themselves. The 3-wing ensures that a Type 2 person stays less in the background and wants to take center stage more often.
2 **3** 4	The 2-wing ensures that Type 3 people are less focused on themselves and care more for others. The 4-wing ensures that Type 3 gets more in touch with their emotions and learns to appreciate profundity.
3 **4** 5	The 3-wing ensures that Type 4 indulges less in emotions and engages more with the outside world. The 5-wing ensures that a Type 4 person uses their reasoning more often and listens less to their emotions.
4 **5** 6	The 4-wing ensures that Type 5 gets more in touch with their emotions and those of others. The 6-wing ensures that a Type 5 person becomes more open about themselves and shares more information with others.
5 **6** 7	The 5-wing ensures that Type 6 is more focused on their internal world and on rock-solid information. The 7-wing ensures that a Type 6 person focuses more positively on opportunities and on the things that can go well.
6 **7** 8	The 6-wing ensures that Type 7 becomes more realistic and also sees what can go wrong. The 8-wing ensures that a Type 7 person becomes more stable and grounded and doesn't mentally check out as often.
7 **8** 9	The 7-wing ensures that Type 8 makes more contact with the thinking process and can balance out actions. The 9-wing ensures that a Type 8 person can open up more and develop an eye for the interests and ideas of other people.
8 **9** 1	The 8-wing ensures that Type 9 people stand up for themselves more clearly and become less dependent. The 1-wing ensures that Type 9 people come in closer contact with their own ideas, even in the presence of others.

Take a look at what is to the left and right of your type on the Enneagram circle. What insights come to mind?

My type is _____

My wings are _____

Strengths I've already learned from the wing to my left:

_____

Strengths I've already learned from the wing to my right:

_____

What should you learn from your neighbors in the Enneagram circle?

Strengths I want to learn from the wing to my left:

_____

Strengths I want to learn from the wing to my right:

_____

To everything, a season

In times of long-lasting stress or relaxation, each person behaves differently than in normal life. The same statement applies here as for the wings: People report a fixed pattern, according to which they act differently in times of stress or relaxation. Just as you develop yourself by falling down and getting back up again, acquiring the strengths of the types next to them in the Enneagram circle, you also take on the characteristics of your relaxation or comfort points when you're relaxed and the characteristics of the stress points when you're under stress. This doesn't give you a different type, and neither is it a question of conscious development. In certain situations, people just take over the characteristics of certain types — not only the positive ones but also the ones that are less favorable. Apparently, people have easy access to the characteristics of their stress and relaxation types, which is why you naturally acquire them more quickly than the other types in the circle. Again, there is no real explanation: Many people simply say that that's how it seems to work for them.

The stress and comfort points for each type apparently aren't distributed arbitrarily; they're based on a certain pattern. The Enneagram has two lines, as shown in Figure 14-3:

>> The first line is formed by the triangle between the Types 3, 6, and 9.

>> The second connects the other types, from Type 1 to Types 4, 2, 8, 5, and 7 and back to Type 1.

The type follows the arrow along elements that the person with the type associates with stress. In the opposite direction, against the arrow, the type moves through what they consider comfort and safety.

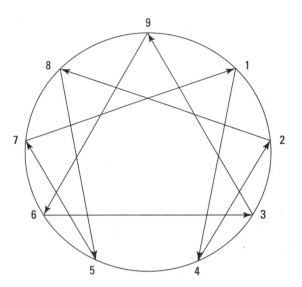

FIGURE 14-3:
The stress
types and the
relaxation types.

Table 14-3 lists four examples per type: one positive and one negative characteristic for each stress and comfort point.

ALL TALK, NO ACTION

Whenever I talk about wings or stress points or relaxation points, I always issue a strict
warning. When it comes to the Enneagram world, don't fall into this trap: "All talk but no
action." People love to talk about how the Enneagram reveals aspects of their character,
telling everybody how fascinating the concept is. The thing is, people don't use the
Enneagram as an aid to improve themselves — they just use themselves as proof of
how explanatory the Enneagram is. They might say, for example: "I see that I'm doing
this-or-that, and it makes sense because this is my 1-wing," or "I have problems with
this-or-that, and it makes sense because I'm under stress and this is my stress point."
The material offered in the Enneagram is there to help you observe yourself, yes, but
the idea is to then let go of what you see. The goal of the type identification is not for
you to cling to this identification or to identify even more strongly with your type: "Oh,
yes — now I'm doing that again, so it's good that I can watch myself doing it" (and so the
Enneagram is correct). The goal is not to stay trapped in your type, but rather to free
yourself. You *have* a type, but you are not your type — and therefore you don't have to
stay in your rut. It would be a shame if the only result is all talk and no action. That won't
help you get any further. I wrote this book in the hope that it will help you advance in
your personal development, not for you to acquire another great topic of conversation.

TABLE 14-3   Examples of Stress and Relaxation Types

Type	Stress Type / Relaxation Type	Characteristics
Type 9	6/3	**Positive:** Alert, active, and analytical; thinks clearly **Negative:** Distrustful, blames others, panicky **Positive:** Energetic, motivated, ensures that the person is seen **Negative:** Increased concern for what others think, fear of failure
Type 6	3/9	**Positive:** Result- and task-oriented, energetic, visible **Negative:** Increased concern about what others think, fear of failure **Positive:** Less distrustful, more relaxed and open to others **Negative:** Falls into passivity and indecisiveness, loss of motivation
Type 3	9/6	**Positive:** Takes their time; relaxed, open, and considerate of others **Negative:** Falls into passivity and indecisiveness, loss of motivation **Positive:** Putting one's feelings in the foreground, loyalty **Negative:** Self-doubt, feeling of insecurity, fear of image loss
Type 1	4/7	**Positive:** In touch with one's own feelings, artistic **Negative:** Self-pity, depression, feelings of inferiority **Positive:** Recognizes opportunities, experiences joy and lightness **Negative:** Irresponsible, immoderate
Type 4	2/1	**Positive:** Oriented more toward others, seeks a social environment **Negative:** Loses contact with one's own feelings and needs **Positive:** Systematic and organized, few mood swings, stable **Negative:** Too critical, nothing is good enough, intolerance (impatience)
Type 2	8/4	**Positive:** In touch with one's own will/needs, leadership qualities, self is visible **Negative:** Impulsively vindictive, controlling, forceful, never lets up **Positive:** More attention to their own feelings and has an aesthetic sense **Negative:** Self-pity, depression, feelings of inferiority
Type 8	5/2	**Positive:** Able to take a step back; moderate, reflective, objective **Negative:** Self-isolating, pulling back or dropping out, no initiative **Positive:** Has an eye for the needs or feelings of others and is committed to fulfilling those needs **Negative:** Willing to stoop to manipulation to assert one's own will, controlling of others
Type 5	7/8	**Positive:** Recognizes opportunities, experiences joy and lightness **Negative:** Puts a positive spin on difficult situations in order to avoid dealing with them, unable to decide **Positive:** Energetic and active, has leadership qualities, authoritative, visible **Negative:** Impulsively vindictive, controlling, forceful, never lets up
Type 7	1/5	**Positive:** Able to focus, brings things to a successful conclusion, has an eye for detail, realistic planner **Negative:** Too critical, too detail-oriented, "my way or the highway" **Positive:** Able to take a step back; moderate, reflective, objective **Negative:** Self-isolating, pulls back or drops out, no initiative

Chapter **15**

There Is a Path You Can Take

Let me tell you about my attempts to get fit at the gym. My fitness method — where my ten-session coupon always expires after half a year with three or four sessions left — isn't working. I really should make up my mind: Either do it right or don't do it at all. And yet, once a month doesn't do much for me.

The same is true for mental fitness. In this chapter, I show you what you can do to further advance your personal development. I give you an idea of which exercises may work, but then it's up to you to test which ones are effective for you, what you can seriously plan to do, and what you'll be able to finish.

Looking at Psychospiritual Integration

Psychospiritual integration, a personal development method advocated by the noted Enneagram specialist Helen Palmer, includes working with various levels of learning and consciousness in correlation with each other. The Enneagram offers a precise guide for the first learning level — for personal development within the type, for enhancing one's personal skills set, and for charting possible future courses of action. The first learning level also means developing on a psychological level so that you can live a healthier lifestyle and interact more harmoniously in your social environment. The Enneagram also shows a clear path for the second learning level — the level concerned with developing higher states of consciousness. This chapter focuses on the second learning level, together with the development of the internal observer.

Who is the best monk?

Psychospiritual integration consists of combining two worlds that are usually separate: You're tasked with addressing your psychological side as well as creating a connection to your spiritual side. The fact is, treating these elements as two separate sides perpetuates an illusion: There is no separation, for these two sides are intimately connected to one another. Taking the spiritual path requires letting go of your (psychological) type mechanism. For that to happen, you first have to recognize and accept it. When people set out on a spiritual journey without taking the psychological side into account, it often means that their type continues to lead them around by the nose in their spiritual work as well. How does that affect one's personal development?

Picture nine monks and nuns, all of whom are dedicated to their spiritual search. Sister Mary searches for the perfect path; Brother Peter mainly helps his fellow brothers and sisters on their paths; Sister Tina spends a lot of energy on becoming the best nun ever and has decided on a convincing role model from the get-go; Brother Tim is unique; Sister Alice leads a reclusive, ascetic life that is solely dedicated to her studies; Brother Ian lives in the safety of the monastery; and so on.

This is where many gurus sooner or later take the wrong path: If they don't let go of the ego, the spiritual path gives that ego new nourishment, and whatever is nourished will grow. An example here is the Catholic Church as an institution (a men's institution) of power. Wherever the ego is active, power, dominance, and control (PDC) will reign, along with a desire for them. When that happens, the lessons that were initially presented with love become dogmas. (The psychiatrist David Daniels characterizes PDC as the opposite of love and benevolence, or what Buddhists call compassion or goodwill. To be able to act on this higher level of love and benevolence is an important requirement for letting go of the ego.)

Doing a cost-benefit analysis

You can always just limit yourself to the first development level. By doing that, there is less — or hardly anything — that can go wrong. You can quickly gain a great deal of benefits, but the drawback here is that you will continue to feel the suffering caused by your type, and you won't gain the inner freedom and serenity that you could achieve. Nonetheless, development on the first level offers a good opportunity for you to improve your personal relationships and your interactions with the larger society as a whole. Just as in any other investment, it ultimately comes down to a cost-benefit analysis. What do you have in terms of time, energy, effort, and money to invest in taking a more spiritual path? What is your assessment of its benefit? Whether it's worth the effort is something you alone can decide!

I don't want to surrender to the gods!

In line with the Jewish-Christian tradition, people tend to associate spirituality with the belief in a god. As an atheist and a humanist, I wrestled with this idea for a long time. The Buddhist approach, as a spiritual path with no belief in gods, offered me a good starting point. It can be compared to the spiritual path of the Enneagram, in which spirituality doesn't stand for a belief, a religion, or a god.

Spiritual practice can free you from suffering — as in Buddhism. On the other hand, religious people can easily integrate the path of the Enneagram into their own, personal religious experience. It can even offer them an intensification and provide additional meaning. During my Enneagram training with Helen Palmer in San Francisco, I participated in a group that included a Buddhist monk from Thailand, a Catholic priest from the Philippines, a Brazilian shaman, and others. In the Enneagram community, there is a great variety of religious and spiritual backgrounds, and this variety is respected, tolerated, and appreciated. To me, the spiritual path means the path of true inner freedom, willpower, serenity, compassion, and, above all, love.

Evolution doesn't stand still

From time immemorial, the path of knowledge leading to personal development has been shared through stories, myths, symbols, and rituals. Think about Greek mythology, for example. I always thought that these stories were wonderful, but they didn't mean much to me. That should come as no surprise, because I am a child of this era and I speak the language of the time. As a product of Western civilization, I need to be able to grasp, understand, and comprehend what is happening in the here and now and what I do to live as part of my culture. That means I have to see myself as the result of 2,000 years of collective history, where the development of the head center has been a top priority. Evolution doesn't stand still, however. The Swiss psychiatrist C.G. Jung posited that the next step in human development must be the development of the heart center. When you look at the increasing interest in spirituality worldwide, you can see that humans may be in the process of collectively developing their heart center. That's the most important task of our time.

FOUR CONDITIONS FOR GOOD PERSONAL DEVELOPMENT

It's good and proper to work on fulfilling the following four conditions on your development path — if you notice at some point that your further development is stagnating, you're probably neglecting one of these four areas (the sequence is arbitrary):

- Self-awareness (by way of self-observation and reflection)

- Self-acceptance and appreciation

- Practice

- Support (internal and external)

Becoming Your Own Guru

It used to be customary — and it still is, in other regions of the world — to apprentice yourself to an instructor or guru. After having decided on a particular development path, you then follow that guru for the rest of your life. This tradition has also evolved as time has passed. The Enneagram fits into the more modern tradition, where you're encouraged to be independent of personal teachers.

Of course, you also need people willing to help you on your path — people capable of passing along their knowledge, skills, insights, and wisdom to you. But in the West, as soon as you can stand on your own two feet, you're expected to take your own path. After that, you can then help others on their journey. Today, someone who makes students responsible for their own learning process and teaches them to build up their internal authority is seen as a good instructor. After all, dependency is the opposite of the internal freedom that the development path should lead to. On this topic, G.I. Gurdjieff said: "Evaluate everything from the perspective of common sense, learn to trust your own comprehension, and don't accept anything rashly on command."

How many steps are on this path?

Different spiritual traditions describe their development paths differently. Some talk of 6 steps, and others 7, 9, or 12 steps. Some have different numbers altogether. The number itself isn't necessarily important. Once someone has decided to take this journey — *the* biggest step for many people on their development path, in my opinion — they have at least two more steps to look forward to:

1. Gain knowledge and (self-) awareness, freeing yourself from the ego and, in terms of thinking, feeling and acting, preparing yourself for a receptive state, for the task that awaits you.

2. Regain a connection with your own virtues, which have always been present inside you. Integrate what you're learning on your development path into your daily life. Live in connection with your own self and with others.

The development path starts with your becoming conscious of your inner autopilot — your type mechanism. You'll need help with this first step when you get started, because everyone has blind spots that they can't uncover themselves; they are inevitable and occur automatically. The development of a good internal observer is the next step. You need it so that you can keep your inner awareness in a high state of alertness. Use this observer's assistance to keep an eye on yourself. The next development step is noticing judgments you make about yourself and letting go of them, which is about recognizing who you are and accepting and acknowledging where you are right now. No one can make it further along the development path without this acknowledgment.

Being aware of your inner autopilot leads to the realization that you always have a choice: Do you follow the autopilot, or do you choose an alternative that better fits the current situation and has the optimal effect for yourself and your environment? This is the phase of testing and experimentation, in which you try to find new ways of dealing with the issues that arise in your life. Mental support is important in this process — feedback from others who witness your work, recognize and acknowledge your power and strengths, and appreciate and support you in your developmental work, for example. At the same time, they have to be honest with you and be able to assist you when you encounter difficulties. This is why I place a high value on working in groups, such as in the form of seminars. Developing an internal support system is just as important.

Training your attention: Letting go of your fixation

Let a single thought rise up inside you, and follow this thought with your attentiveness. It can be anything — a thought about your work, about your activities on your planned vacation, or one that you don't want to tell anyone yet. Then decide that you no longer want to follow this thought. Let it go. Pay attention to what this process is like, what is happening inside you, and how easy or difficult it is to let go of the thought.

If it's hard for you to stop paying attention to the thought, it may help you to characterize it for what it is: just a thought. It also helps if you turn your attention to something different — something in your surroundings; something you're seeing, reading or hearing; or something else inside you, such as another thought or your breath. Does this help make the first thought disappear?

This exercise is important because it shows you how your head center works. It's a simple exercise, but in daily practice, your suffering is often caused by your attention automatically directing itself to a particular thought — usually, one that isn't helpful. When it's about something major — when it hurts you or makes you angry — it draws your attention toward it even more intensely. The mechanism reinforces itself. The more solidly you adhere to a nonhelpful thought, the more frequently and greater the negative feelings that arise, the more firmly your attention adheres to it, and so on.

The path back to a connection with human virtues starts with letting go of the thoughts that don't help you — the ones that don't make you happier and that might be obstacles in your personal relationships or your connection with others. Before you can learn to let go of something, you have to take another step — namely, learning to recognize where your thoughts automatically wander off to and where they adhere. If you know your Enneagram type, it's easier for you to find these points.

Practice, Practice, Practice

Practice is one of the four conditions of any personal development. This concept isn't about the goal-oriented practice of an activity with the goal of becoming good at it, such as in yoga. It's about the value of the practice itself — the fact that you have something you practice, something that becomes an integral part of your life. It can be anything. Part of your journey of discovery consists of finding out what works for you and what helps you develop.

Balancing and developing the centers

When it comes to developing and balancing your center, a great deal of knowledge about the various practice methods already exists in the various spiritual traditions. I list some of these traditions and then take a look at a few practical, modern translations of these traditions, because old wine in new bottles may be more appealing to you.

Three practice methods are named in the Kabbalah of Jewish mysticism:

>> The path of studying (head)

>> The path of devotion (heart)

>> The path of daily practice (gut)

G.I. Gurdjieff places the accents a little differently. Here are his terms:

>> The path of the yogi (the battle with the spirit)

>> The path of the monk (the battle with the feelings)

>> The path of the fakir (the battle with the body)

The fakir strive to develop their physical will and attain power over the body: mind over body. Their path consists of performing difficult physical exercises, similar to the ascetic path, in which monks deny themselves all physical indulgences and have only a minimal diet. According to Gurdjieff, the fakir can reach their spiritual goal on this path as long as they don't get sick or die. But even if they reach that goal, their feelings and their mind will still be underdeveloped. They will have attained a perfect physical will but will have nothing they can use it for.

The path of the monk is the path of faith, of religious feeling, and of religious sacrifice. The path of the monk is also long and arduous. They fight their own feelings to gain control over them. By subjugating all feelings to faith, the monk develops inner peace and unity. As with the fakir, they can reach this state, but the other functions of the body and mind will be underdeveloped.

The yogi takes the path of battling with the spirit — the path of knowledge, in other words. It's the path of studying. Again, they can develop thinking skills, but the other functions for the body and feelings will be underdeveloped.

Just like the fakir and the monk, the yogi cannot harvest the fruits of their labor. They know everything, but it won't do them much good. The advantage of this path compared to the fakir and the monk is that the yogi knows where they stand and what else they still have to do. However, most people tend to stop at this point and enjoy what they have gained so far rather than continue to fight and bring in the full harvest.

As an alternative, Gurdjieff names a fourth path, one that makes it possible to take the full path of development. You don't just develop one of the three centers on this path; instead, you address the head, heart, and gut centers equally. The goal is to balance them out and integrate them.

This path doesn't require you to retreat into the desert or give up everything you live for. On the contrary, this path is the one of normal life. In this respect, setting out on the fourth path is also particularly easy. It doesn't have a fixed form, however, and you have to discover your personal path yourself. The fourth path is about expanding and developing awareness. Awareness is collected in the head, heart, and gut center. Jewish mysticism also knows about this fourth path of development and of spiritual growth in daily life.

Center practices — exercises for the centers

When working with psychospiritual integration methods, you find out about exercises for the head center as well as for the heart center and gut center. These exercises are known as *center practices.* Others refer to it as physical work, but that's not exactly accurate because it's not about the body alone. It's much more about experiencing all centers, learning to feel them, coming in contact with them, and gaining awareness.

In the Western tradition, people tend to work mainly with the head center, wanting to understand everything and thus gain knowledge. This is a practical approach, but it's not enough if nothing else is added. This is why it's necessary to practice with the three centers alternately. You learn to notice the perceptions of your body and explore the feelings of the heart center, which also helps you to relax, dissolve mental blockages, and create space within.

Getting out of your comfort zone

Whatever you choose as an exercise doesn't always have to be something that you consider pleasant and like to do. An unappealing exercise can be good for you too, even one that at first rubs you the wrong way.

Picture something that you know, deep down, would be good for you but that you don't feel like doing — at all. That's the kind of exercise that gets you out of your comfort zone. This book demonstrates that your type gives you a one-dimensional orientation, one that throws you off your internal balance. All the examples of things you can learn from the other types are all about giving you a better balance in some way, shape, or form. A rough guideline would be to do something that better balances your centers. This is how the first and greatest imbalance starts. Here are some examples of exercises that probably won't have much effect:

>> A (head) Type 5 who reads countless books in order to learn more about themselves

>> A (gut) Type 8 who takes up assertiveness or martial arts training in order to grow even bigger and stronger

>> A (heart) Type 4 who visits one workshop after another so that they can get more in touch with their feelings

The heart type here can be especially unhealthy because people with Type 4 already highly exaggerate their feelings by nature. Practicing composure is one way that might help a Type 4 person find greater balance. You can see that, for this to work, it's important to know what you're doing and where you stand — what will help you and what won't.

Attention training

Enneagram work focuses on consciously directing your attention. You've probably taken the chance to learn what your attention automatically steers toward according to your type. You've likely also learned to observe this movement because your energy follows your attention. You are now aware of how this works and that catching that moment when your attention is being steered is an important place to start. This gives you the chance to direct your attention to another goal.

When you turn your attention away from the object of fixation, you don't lose any more energy as a result. But the (negative) feelings that usually arise in such cases are also absent. Putting some distance between yourself and the object of your fixation shows you that you always have a choice between different ways to act (or not) and that you don't always have to follow an automatic pattern. Using your internal observer is a powerful tool in the process of personal development. These attention exercises are also used as a tool to empathize with the worlds of the various Enneagram types, to feel what motivates them and to recognize their automatic patterns. This gives you a greater understanding of how other people tick; you'll also see that their topics are universal and also apply to you.

Attention training means developing a state of judgment-free acceptance. The goal is to direct your attention toward what happens from one moment to the next without judging it. If you notice during an exercise that you're thinking of something else, for example, simply make a note of that fact without blaming yourself. Always return your attention to the present and direct it wherever you want it to go. Your breathing is a good point of reference because it's present at every moment. When your attention continues to slip away from the here and now, from the goal you want to direct it toward, just accept that this is a natural movement. Always try to perceive which sensations, feelings, and thoughts are inside you and accept them without judgment. Openness and acceptance will improve your learning to be attentive to what is happening inside you as well as in others.

Attention training in everyday life

When you start with your self-observations, you'll be able to recognize certain negative behaviors only later, when they occur again. You'll find yourself saying the somewhat annoying phrase, "Oh, no — I did it *again*" — it's annoying because you keep seeing how you're acting a certain way, in more and more situations, but you see it only after the fact. Not only does this prevent you from changing it, but recognizing it actually makes it seem even worse. No worries — it's just a phase.

Do not condemn yourself. Be lenient — it's just your type that is pushing itself into the foreground. In the following phase, when your internal observer already has better training, you'll see yourself act the moment it happens: "Oh, no — now I'm doing it. I'll do it in a moment." You'll see how you're doing this, you'll lose yourself at this moment, and you won't be able to restrain yourself. Not yet, anyway — that's the next step. Now your internal observer is so well-trained that you recognize the signals for how a certain situation prompts a certain reaction. You'll be able to predict it more and more often. This situation and this moment will certainly return, but you will gradually notice it and you'll be well prepared. This gives you the freedom to choose to act differently at that moment. But what are your choices? When that moment comes, you'll need a technique that keeps you from making your automatic response, and you'll also need alternative ways to act. These alternatives can consist of the skills and the set of behaviors from the first learning level.

Mindfulness is attention training

Just like the attention training you know of from the Enneagram, mindfulness is based on Buddhism. Jon Kabat-Zinn, the founder and former director of the Stress Reduction Clinic at the Health Center of the University of Massachusetts, uses mindfulness to teach people how to handle illness and stress and their accompanying pain and fear. He has taught his program of Mindfulness-Based Stress Reduction (MBSR) since 1979.

I'm introducing Kabat-Zinn's approach here because its outlines are the same as those of the Enneagram practice that I explain in this book. Kabat-Zinn also found automatic patterns of thinking in his research. With his course on mindfulness-based stress reduction, Kabat-Zinn wanted to teach his patients a different way of dealing with their concerns. Thanks to the foundation he laid, more and more doctors and psychotherapists in the United States and Europe have turned to mindfulness practice for their patients. Kabat-Zinn is now one of the heads of the Mind and Life Institute. This institute promotes the dialogue between the Dalai Lama and Western scientists with the goal of gaining more insights about the various forms of knowledge, the nature of the mind, the nature of reality, and human emotions.

Meditation

Meditation is by far the number-one practice I recommend for a practical approach to letting go of your type mechanism. People practice infinite forms of meditation around the world. (If you want to know more about meditative practices, I recommend *Meditation For Dummies*, written by Stephan Bodian and published by Wiley.) You should know the following characteristics of meditation:

>> Meditating isn't sleeping, nor is it just a nice way to relax and drift off.

>> Meditation is a method of experiencing yourself — in silence.

>> Meditation is a learning method, a way of exploring yourself. During meditation, you will encounter yourself, your type.

>> Meditation is all about focusing, about concentration training, but without exertion.

>> The more you try to reach something, to do something, the less you reach the state of inner peace and emptiness.

>> No bad or failed meditation exists — it's about the experience.

>> You learn from every experience.

David Fontana wrote several books about meditation in which he distinguished between various forms of meditation. I list a few examples here, including some from various spiritual traditions — this list gives you an idea in which direction you can search if you want to learn more about the topic:

>> **Silent meditation:** Vipassana, hatha yoga, tai chi, kundalini

>> **Flowing meditation:** Internal voice, shamanism, Christian mysticism

>> **Subjective meditation:** Zazen, koan, shikantaza

>> **Objective meditation:** Kabbala, mystery religions, bhakti yoga, jnana yoga

>> **Visualization**: In flowing as well as objective meditation

WARNING

Meditation may seem harmless at first glance, but the sentence "If it doesn't work, it won't do any harm" doesn't always apply in this case. Meditating too deeply can be risky for mentally susceptible or unstable persons. The same is true for attention training. I strongly recommend that consultants working with individuals abstain from performing attention training or meditation with people who have pathological characteristics. In those cases, it's better to recommend physical and practical changes — things that clients can benefit from directly in everyday life and where they can immediately notice improvements or feel relief. Put them directly in contact with the here and now.

REMEMBER

If you're on a developmental path, find a good teacher, but also listen to your instincts. Does what you're doing feel good? Be aware of your natural limits. Take them seriously and protect them. Stop or do something else that feels good or fulfills a need. You're responsible for yourself. If you want to become active in this area, find a good teacher and a good school and explore what works for you.

Center practices for the gut and heart center

A development path outline for the individual types occasionally indicates that you should come in closer contact with your feelings and the sensations in your body — developing the gut and heart centers, in other words. This is easier said than done, though. These terms might be new to you, so how do you deal with them?

When you develop awareness of your body, it isn't necessarily about movement but rather about observing what you experience when you move — and then come to rest again. So you don't necessarily have to do particular exercises. During your normal routine, you can also keep asking yourself, "What am I experiencing right now? What am I perceiving? What do I feel?" This keeps you in close contact with yourself. It also helps some people become aware of their limits. For one person, this might mean ensuring that others don't overstep their boundaries; for others, it might mean that they stay within their own boundaries and avoid intruding on others.

Tips for center practices

Enneagram training centers on the skill of grounding yourself. The internal observer can step into the foreground from this position when they're grounded, present, and aware. Being grounded or centered plays a role in all kinds of physical work. Various orientations also work with breathing, such as various kinds of yoga, tai chi, and other martial arts, such as wushu, kung fu, aikido, and taekwondo.

Some people find that it helps them to their bones to play sports that clear the mind. This is also beneficial for the body, even if it isn't (directly) about gathering awareness. But even that can help you let go of the type mechanism and fixations. Here are a few things to try:

>> Running, biking, skating, and other related activities

>> Dancing

>> Pilates

>> Bikram yoga

Methods that appeal to multiple centers simultaneously are generally most effective because they automatically ensure balance and integrate the centers. This is why I often work with music and silence — depending on the music, it has a more direct impact on the heart and/or body center. It's also why dancing is so effective for many people: They leave the mind behind, retreat into their bodies, and feel the life energy flow freely. Making music is also a strong combination, because it appeals to the head, heart, and gut center, all at one time.

Breathing helps

Breath work is a particularly important part of the center practices. Your type mechanism has established itself not just in the mind but also in the entire body — the nervous system, the muscles (muscle tension), and even in your breathing. Just think about those moments when you've been startled or are in suspense. What are you doing at those times? Holding your breath. It's a reflex, a contraction. Anything you often do subconsciously becomes engraved in your system. The word *character* originates from the Greek: χαράσσω means engraving or imprinting. Your type is engraved in you — that's why you have to relax your entire system if you want to let go of your type.

The knowledge that G.I. Gurdjieff discovered in Eastern traditions also includes the notion that humans need different kinds of nourishment. You need not just food to keep your physical body in shape but also inspiration to nourish your mind, for example. Air is considered nourishment for the soul. The connection between air and soul can still be traced in various languages.

The Latin word *amina* means soul and breath, which is also true of the Arabic *ruh* and the Hebrew *roch*. Gurdjieff's student J.G. Bennett reports that nomads in Central Asia brought knowledge with them from the Atlantic Ocean to the Pacific. They worshiped the air and breath as a power of the spirit that is considered the source of life and wisdom. Mastering various breathing techniques is seen as an important part of the transformation path in their tradition — a path toward freedom and wisdom.

In the end, it's still good to know that breathing plays an important role in grounding yourself so that you can let go of your type and bring the internal observer to the forefront. Your breathing is an important pillar for getting your reactivity under control, because your breathing helps you hold off. With reactivity, people react quickly. Holding off gives you time to make a choice.

Lessons in breathing?

If you want to continue working in this area, keep in mind that breath work is an important part of the Buddhist Vipassana meditation practices. Singing is also a healing form of the center practices. When you sing, you concentrate on the here and now, and when you take good singing lessons, you learn to pay attention to your breath. You can also take spiritual or therapeutic vocal lessons in which singing and breathing help you discover and resolve internal blockages. Singing helps to connect the internal world with the external.

REMEMBER

You can learn a lot from books, of course. (And I hope that this book is helpful to you.) But reading is different from acting. I try to explain the nature of our exercises in this book, but this is still different from doing and experiencing them. To take the step toward doing and experiencing, find a format that suits you so that you can practice this work with other people.

You're allowed to laugh, and preferably with others. You can't do this alone, after all. I've already mentioned that a condition for real growth and development is support. You can also learn from others, maybe differently, more intensely, or even better than from books. (When I studied, I took big leaps forward in group work — during Enneagram seminars, to be precise.) Meeting people who are working on the same task I am gives me support and inspiration and the feeling of togetherness, along with corrections and feedback regarding my blind spots. Why shouldn't you benefit from support or help if it's available, or from the joy of doing something together? When people set out on the path of being honest with themselves (and considering their uniqueness), it creates a lot of room for humor. Of all the seminars and workshops I have led, the most intense Enneagram seminars are the ones with the most laughter.

Humor: A special kind of center practice

Meditation, grounding, breathing, and bodywork are different kinds of center practices. Each in their own way supports you during your development as you release your type. I'm convinced, however, that humor has a particular healing effect. With laughter comes relaxation. I can imagine few things that are more relaxing than a real fit of laughter. At the same time, you often need to make room inside yourself and release the tension in your type to be able to laugh at all.

Humor can arise when you can observe the absurdity of certain situations along with your own absurdity. Especially in difficult situations, people tend to become more serious and take things harder. This is exactly what keeps most people locked inside their types or forces them into the type in the first place. Humor requires a certain amount of relativization, space, and distance. If you manage to achieve this within yourself and allow for humor, your type can relax and let go. At the same time, humor creates this relativization and the required space and distance. You have to breathe, but humor helps even more — it lets your life energy flow. It creates order and sweeps things clean. Humor brings air, humor brings light. As with money, you can spend your attention and energy only one time, so pay attention to what you use it for.

Chapter **16**

Jumpstarting Further Development

Become who you were before you came to be,
preserve your memory of that state of being
and gain an understanding of
how you have become what you are.

Sufi proverb

I n order to develop yourself, you have to gain compassion for yourself, as the opening Sufi proverb reminds you. If you can't see, recognize, and accept yourself in your type mechanism, you can hardly take any steps forward. It's absolutely necessary to honestly see who you really are — to gain true self-awareness — if you want to take the first step. At the same time, the type mechanism that has carried you through your life so well to this point should be viewed in an affectionate light. Translated into the language of the Enneagram, it sounds like this:

Become as you were before your type mechanism existed,
preserve your memory of it, and gain an understanding
of the type mechanism you have developed.

Claudio Naranjo says that "the truth about ourselves can free us, for once you have truly understood something about ourselves, it will change without 'our' attempt to change it." An honest and complete recognition of your type mechanism alone will set the release in motion — not least because you will soon become aware of the price that you pay due to your type and which superfluous and ineffectual habits it's responsible for. In this chapter, I present a step-by-step explanation of a method you can use to take you further along the path of personal development steps while at the same time letting go of your type.

Moving from Type Mechanisms to Growth Mechanisms

The type mechanism is like a bundle of elements that fit together: The elements don't just cling to each other — they also reinforce each other. But you can use the same elements to set a release process in motion. The following sections show you how this works.

Using the type mechanism as a tool for development

Just like what you do in order to untangle a ball of yarn, the trick is to find the end piece so that you can start the detangling process. When you find the starting point, you can then transform the type mechanism into a growth mechanism, turning your type into a helper and good friend. The ingredients that are used in addition to the type mechanism are the defense mechanism and type reactivity. I describe the defense mechanism in Part 2 of this book and present reactivity here.

Reactivity

You have a type, but you are not your type. Even when you have a type, it doesn't express itself throughout the entire day. You spend most of the day in a normal and relaxed state. You have no problems with yourself and, hopefully, none with your surroundings. Your internal observer and your type are both asleep.

They're fast asleep — until your type is suddenly roused. Something happens that jolts your type out of its sleep, puts it into a state of alarm, and forces it to react. Something triggers your type — a button is pushed or an alarm bell rings that moves your type into action. Then the autopilot starts up and you start to show all your automatic behaviors — your typical way of handling things. You become tense or stressed, and at that moment you can't do anything other than what you have always done in such situations. Maybe you want to do something else, but at this moment you don't know how, and you don't have the freedom to do it differently. This is what we call the *reactivity* of the type. When the type becomes reactive, it assumes control over you and the situation. These uncontrolled, type-specific reactions are what cause conflicts, personal problems, and suffering. Something happens in your surroundings that throws you off balance and you can't react any differently. This is reactivity.

What throws someone off balance and makes them become reactive is ultimately type-specific — and the reactivity is expressed in an equally type-specific way. Recognizing this type-specificity is one of the most important areas of self-observation and self-management. Here are a few examples:

>> Type 5 individuals are thrown off balance by others who ask a lot of quite personal questions about private matters (about feelings, for example), by people claiming their time and energy, by undesirable intrusions, by confrontations that bring with them strong emotional reactions, by a lack of personal time to recuperate, and by pushy people.

>> Type 6 individuals are thrown off balance by a lack of transparency, by the feeling that not everything is being expressed or that information is being held back, by political games and an abuse of power, by a lack of loyalty, and by situations where people are stuck in an underdog role and can easily be abused.

>> Type 2 individuals are thrown off balance by (close) people who reject their help, by situations where their help apparently isn't noticed or appreciated, by people who don't respond to their "niceness" and aren't nice in return, and when it's "payday" and the other person doesn't pay back.

Given this type-specificity, how people express their reactivity depends on the situation and the people involved in it. In general, people express their reactivity differently at the workplace than at home, for example. This is also the reason for people often reporting that they are very different at home than they are at work.

As a rule of thumb, it can be said that people in reactivity show more type-specific behavior, especially the negative side of their type. Then the underlying passion often appears most noticeably. Just think about the resentment of a Type 1, the pride of a Type 2, the fear and mistrust of a Type 6, and so on. In the example of how a Type 2 becomes reactive, the pride that emerges when help is rejected appears in the form of wounded pride. Type 2 individuals always report how much other people have disappointed them.

Seeing how you become reactive

To keep training your internal observer and your skill of self-observation, it's a good idea to reconsider a few questions:

>> In your interactions with people, can you think of things that affect you like the proverbial red rag to a bull? Which "wrong" buttons can others push inside you? What triggers you, and what makes you reactive?

>> Can you describe what happens inside you when that occurs?

>> Can you describe how your reactivity is displayed?

Finding your way back

You now have all the pieces in place for an effective growth mechanism:

>> **By handing yourself over to fixations, passions, reactivities, and defense mechanisms, you limit yourself.** Observe how you constrain yourself and engage in a dialogue with yourself to cast doubt on how you're currently reacting. Look at not only what you gain from your type but also what it costs you.

>> **Plan your path forward:** Which development step do you think should be next? What do you want to let go of first? (Always take things one step at a time.)

For each type, I briefly explain how you can find your way back — the way to let go of your type mechanism. You'll notice that a lot of the information may seem obvious, but what I suggest goes completely against the nature of the people who have that type. This information refers to the innermost core of someone's being. The first step consists of accepting the challenge and gradually considering the steps necessary for the type and then experimenting with them in your life and your relationships.

Letting go of fixations and consciously steering your attention

> *Well-being is good luck, or good character.*
> *(But what are you doing here, Perceptions? Get back to*
> *where you came from, and good riddance. I don't need you.*
> *Yes, I know, it was only force of habit that brought you. No,*
> *I'm not angry with you. Just go away.)*
>
> *Marcus Aurelius (121–180 AD), from Meditations, Book VII*

To let go of a **Type 1** mechanism, keep these tips in mind:

>> Realize that your attention is directed toward something that is wrong and therefore needs to be improved.

>> Realize that this is your version of right and wrong.

>> Practice seeing and acknowledging that there's more than one correct method to fix what must be improved.

>> Let go of your mental fixation. Tell yourself, for example: "It's good the way it is." Watch how high other people set the bar, and then set your own to 70 percent of what you normally use as a benchmark. Then pay attention to what actually goes wrong and, particularly, to the reactions of other people.

>> Practice seeing and accepting imperfections in yourself and others.

>> Avoid the urge to prevent criticism or feedback. Practice allowing them now and then. Is it really so bad when other people tell you that they think it could be done differently or better?

>> Ask yourself how much the opinion of other people matters. Let it come — you can handle it!

>> Notice how much time, effort, and energy you save if you set the bar to 70 percent. You can use this leftover energy for leisure activities.

>> Become aware of the internal tension that arises from suppressed anger.

>> Ask yourself what this anger is trying to tell you.

>> Establish contact with your suppressed instincts and impulses, and learn to listen to them.

>> As an exercise, become like a child and follow your impulses.

To let go of a **Type 2** mechanism, do this:

>> Realize that you're directing your attention to the needs of others.

>> Realize that you're doing this to satisfy your own needs and that this is quite a convoluted path to real satisfaction.

>> Imagine that you know what your desires and needs are just as well as you know this about other people. Realize that you're suppressing your own needs and your own will.

>> Take some time to be alone, to ask yourself what your deepest needs really are. Practice telling others what you want, or also ask them for what you need.

>> Picture yourself asking another person for something.

>> Recognize the nice feeling, the pride in yourself, when you know best what someone else needs.

>> Recognize how much time and energy you spend responding to everyone else's needs — and it doesn't even give you the benefits that are motivating you.

>> Acknowledge that a real relationship isn't a one-way street and that you're standing in your own way by only giving and not receiving.

>> Imagine that others might also enjoy giving you something.

>> Imagine that you're standing in your own way because you don't recognize and acknowledge this fact.

>> Complete the task of learning to appreciate yourself, independently of what you might mean to others.

>> Free yourself from your dependency on others and from having to be nice for other people. You'll soon notice that others appreciate you for the person you are, not just because of what you're doing for them.

>> Become like a child again — give and receive freely.

To let go of a **Type 3** mechanism, the following ideas can help:

>> Ask yourself whether you're directing your attention toward a successful image and toward opportunities to score points.

>> Ask yourself whether you're doing this to be noticed and loved, although it isn't really about you, but rather about your achievements.

>> Imagine yourself letting go of this need for achievement — and what you would then experience.

>> Imagine that the people you love will still love you even if you fail.

>> Ask yourself what is important in your life: successful projects or being with your loved ones.

>> Your task consists of slowing down while coming in closer contact with yourself and your feelings.

>> Brake, brake, brake.

>> Practice saying no to a project that offers tempting opportunities to score points.

>> Recognize that you have a tendency to mislead others so that you appear to be in a better position than you are.

>> Ask yourself when was the last time you honestly told someone that you're not doing so well right now.

>> Imagine that you were to free yourself from this habit of hiding your unhappiness, showing yourself as you are even if you're not doing that well.

>> Acknowledge how much you're concerned with painting a positive picture of yourself, your life, your family, and other aspects.

>> Pay attention to your physical sensations (especially tiredness) and learn to listen to them.

>> Take some time to sit still and explore the world of your feelings and what they tell you about yourself.

>> Notice that others think you're nice, even if (or especially when) you're not regaling them with a story of your success.

>> Become like a child again so you can receive appreciation and love as the person who you are.

To let go of a **Type 4** mechanism, keep these points in mind:

>> Realize that this is your version of reality and that others see it differently.

>> Practice seeing yourself and appreciating what you see, and having a positive outlook and presentation.

>> Recognize in yourself the ever-present underlying desire for fulfillment and for achieving an ideal.

>> See in yourself any tendency to expand your emotions, and develop your head center to balance it out.

>> When you see that you're expanding your emotions, practice letting go of this habit, and try shrinking your emotions instead.

>> Acknowledge that you often compare yourself with others, with how things used to be, and with how the place where you are right now compares with other, more beautiful places.

>> Direct your attention to what is present in the here and now. Use your head center.

>> Recognize how, systematically, you are constantly dissatisfied and talk only about your problems.

>> Practice talking to people even when there are no problems that need to be discussed; talk about positive topics; express yourself positively.

>> Recognize in yourself a tendency to keep a distance from others — perhaps because you fear rejection.

>> Practice becoming more stable in your emotions and bonding with others (your loved ones).

>> Correct yourself when you notice that you're distancing yourself from something or someone, and make a point of maintaining the connection in those cases.

>> Realize that you tend to feel inferior or superior to others.

>> Learn to recognize that all people, including you, are equal, even with all their weaknesses.

>> Ask yourself what your jealousy is trying to tell you.

>> Become like a child again and feel fulfilled and connected.

To let go of a **Type 5** mechanism, try the following tips:

>> See that you're directing your attention to what others expect from you and what they might want from you.

>> Realize that this is *your* view of reality and that other people may not want anything from you.

>> Realize that people who want something from you will ask you for it and that you can always say no.

>> Watch what happens when you practice approaching people instead of retreating.

>> Practice feeling where your boundaries are and communicating this info directly.

>> Realize how you isolate yourself from your feelings, from others, and from space and time.

>> Your task is not to isolate yourself but rather to make connections.

>> Recognize how you keep other people and situations in control, by being frugal with information, for example, and by keeping people and situations separate.

>> Imagine letting go of this habit; experiment with it! See that it doesn't cost you any energy; instead, when you let go of control, it ends up freeing you, and your energy won't run out.

>> Allow yourself to experience your emotions and sensations. Don't be afraid of them — they're just as fascinating as your thoughts.

>> Experiment with communicating information about yourself and from within you.

>> Avoid coming up with reasons to avoid such communications. Your development depends on it.

>> Ask yourself what your reticence is trying to tell you.

>> Become like a child again; find your spontaneity and just act (without thinking first).

To let go of a **Type 6** mechanism, follow these suggestions:

>> Recognize that you're directing your attention to what can go wrong, where danger is lurking, what generates distrust, and so on. Come to terms with the fact that this is *your* version of reality and that you aren't perceiving an important part of objective reality.

>> Become aware of your worries, (self-)doubts, and desire for security.

>> Practice directing your attention elsewhere — by thinking that things can also go well, for example.

>> Learn to see and accept that a certain level of insecurity is part of life.

>> Get into the habit of making reality checks and asking yourself which fears might have a realistic foundation.

>> Let go of your mental fixations by saying, "I trust that it will go well."

>> Learn to notice and let go of your projections, also by means of reality checks: Ask the other person what's really going on.

>> Establish contact with your suppressed instincts and impulses, and learn to listen to them.

>> Become like a child again: Have confidence and courage.

To let go of a **Type 7** mechanism, try the following tips:

>> Realize that your attention is directed toward possibilities because they are unlimited, fascinating entities.

>> Become aware of the fact that your fast-paced mind never stands still and is continually jumping from one topic to the next.

>> The development path for someone with Type 7 is concentration, concentration, concentration.

>> Practice moderating yourself and telling yourself to stop — not only when it comes to doing things but also when thinking and speaking.

>> Practice noticing when you no longer listen to other people and interrupt them. Hold back.

>> Determine when you're looking for positive opportunities to avoid fear (of deprivation).

>> Practice working on only one task at a time and finishing tasks before starting something new.

>> Realize that you're self-serving; develop an eye for the feelings and concerns of other people.

>> Practice spending time with others — potentially listening to their pain and negativity without explaining it away.

>> Learn to see joy and suffering as two equivalent sides of life, and accept this fact.

>> Notice when you start to rationalize and pay attention to what you're fleeing from.

>> Become aware of your insatiability in all respects, including in your enthusiasm; restrain and moderate yourself.

>> Become like a child again, and experience joy and sadness when these emotions happen; all sadness will pass again.

To let go of a **Type 8** mechanism, the following tips should help:

>> Realize that you're directing your attention to being strong and invulnerable.

>> Understand that this is just *your* version of reality and truth.

>> Learn to recognize when you see only your own truth; learn to open up to the truth of other people.

>> Pay attention to when you act impulsively, and learn to suppress impulses that are pushing you to act immediately. Think first, act later.

>> Perceive your effect on others; practice giving others room, including in conversations.

>> Learn to recognize how and what you deny — your weaknesses and needs but also other people's interests and ideas.

>> Recognize your tendency to fight all the time, to measure your strength, even if you make this combat appear elegant and playful.

>> Let go of your mental fixation by telling yourself, "The other person isn't my enemy."

>> Practice seeing and accepting that the other person isn't looking to fight with you and doesn't want to hurt you.

>> Don't try to hide your vulnerability in your fortress any longer. Just continue to open the gate. When your loved ones see your genuine, innocent, and vulnerable self, they will also treat you more gently.

>> Recognize and experience the true power of your vulnerability; it doesn't need your protection.

>> Become like a child again, in all openness, innocence, and vulnerability.

To let go of a **Type 9** mechanism, keep the following points in mind:

>> Realize that you're directing your attention toward submitting to others and avoiding even the slightest disruption.

>> Become aware of how much you let yourself become distracted, letting your attention remain vague and your energy trickle away in trivialities.

>> In the presence of others, practice staying in touch with yourself, your priorities, and your ideas. Notice when you're occupied by unimportant matters and what you should focus your attention on instead.

>> Learn to direct your energy and concentration toward your limits, to what you want, to what's truly good for you, and to whichever action is the right one.

>> Realize how you make yourself invisible and try to deflect any attention coming from other people.

>> Learn to see your anger as a sign that you don't feel as if you're being seen, heard, or taken seriously.

>> Let go of your mental fixation; say to yourself, "I'm important, too," for example.

>> Ask yourself what your inactivity is trying to tell you.

>> Your task is to become more alert; recognize when and how you anaesthetize yourself.

>> Remember to think of yourself, yourself, yourself.

>> Recognize that it isn't really so bad if you make a few small waves by stating your opinion. Experiment with making your opinions known; watch how people react. Maybe they'll suddenly notice you, after all.

>> Become like a child again and play. Every individual counts.

Chapter **17**

The Spiritual Enneagram

There is a road, steep and thorny, beset with perils of every kind,

but yet a road, and it leads to the very heart of the Universe:

I can tell you how to find those who will show you the secret gateway that opens inward only,

and closes fast behind the neophyte for evermore.

There is no danger that dauntless courage cannot conquer;

there is no trial that spotless purity cannot pass through;

there is no difficulty that strong intellect cannot surmount.

For those who win onwards there is a reward past all telling — the power to bless and save humanity;

for those who fail, there are other lives in which success may come.
— H. P. BLAVATSKY, COLLECTED WRITINGS, *VOL. XIII*

This poetic summary states that anyone can take a path of development, one that requires thinking skills, courage, and assertiveness. But you don't have to take this path alone; you will meet others on this journey whose support you will need along the way — but also others who need your assistance. (And that last line quietly indicates that you can go back and try it again if you don't succeed in this life.)

Seeking Your Higher Self

In Parts 1 and 2 of this book, I present the Enneagram as represented by its type mechanisms, along with the Lower Self — the type itself, also known as the *ego*. In spiritual work as well as in the Enneagram, your Higher Self plays a significant role. (For more on this aspect as well as its connection to the various levels of consciousness, see Chapter 14.)

The goal of working on personal development is to shift control so that the lower levels of consciousness are directed by the higher ones. You can see this as striving toward mind over body, but the Enneagram goes even further because, with it, you can distinguish between various levels of consciousness — your head center knows a lower level and a higher level, for example. The goal of your development consists of getting the lower mental center (filled with fixations based on wrong assumptions) under the direction of the higher mental center (the higher-minded ideas).

This bringing of the lower center under the direction of the higher center is called *second-level* learning. Your internal observer assumes control of the Lower Self, thus making it possible for the Higher Self to appear and take control. The lower emotional center (passions, vices) is directed by the higher emotional center (the higher, or sacred, virtues). In a seminar, my colleague Hannah Nathans drew the diagram shown in Figure 17-1 on a flipchart to illustrate this process.

In this diagram, the development on a psychological, or type, level — first-level learning, in other words — is shown as developing in breadth. It's still describing action at the type level, but it offers an expansion based on compensating skills and an increase in the set of behaviors. In Figure 17-1, it appears as a horizontal ellipsis.

This chapter is about the spiritual Enneagram and the development of higher levels of consciousness. In Figure 17-1, this development on the second and third learning levels is depicted as a vertical ellipsis. The first step consists of developing the internal observer. You can do this yourself and turn this into practice. The next step leads to the Higher Self, or the transpersonal level. You can prepare for this, but ultimately, it's about reaching an inner receptive state.

Full transformation, the third learning level, means that the Lower Self isn't being controlled by the higher levels, but has been transformed into the Higher Self. Then the Lower Self has dissipated, so to speak. This extraordinary state is what people refer to as *enlightenment.* People are released from their lower selves and no longer have any difficulties with fixations and passions.

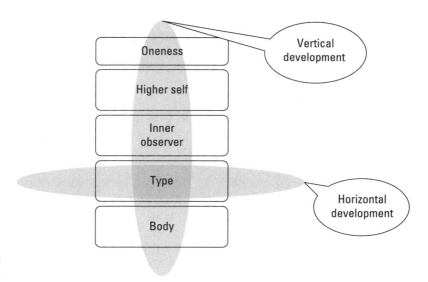

Oneness

Higher self

Inner observer

Type

Body

Vertical development

Horizontal development

FIGURE 17-1:
Your Higher Self.

Acting on your own or being receptive to what comes from without

Part of the path to development consists of recognizing the various states inside you via self-observation and reflection, and to differentiate between them. When do you act and react as directed by your Lower Self, and when are you doing so at the direction of your internal observer or by way of your Higher Self? The state of the internal observer can be trained. When you spend time with this training, it becomes relatively easy for you to enter this state of consciousness.

The fourth century monk Evagrius describes this as the first step of the path, the one where you train your inner observer, as the *praktike*. You can do this too. But you can't take the next section of the path, the *gnostike*, on your own. It's a receptive state of being, something you receive. When you're in the state of the Lower Self, the type blocks the way and you can't — and won't — receive anything. Despite all that, you can still do something — namely, arrange your internal state so that it is receptive to what may come — making receiving possible, in other words. Imagine a field you're preparing for planting in order to improve the conditions for a bountiful harvest. There's no guarantee that a bountiful harvest will come — you "receive" it. But if the field isn't well-prepared, you already know that a bountiful harvest is unlikely.

What's so great about receiving when I can take what I want?

When most people think about an inner state, in which they have to wait for something they can receive, their Enneagram type immediately starts protesting: "What, wait? What is this thing? Is it worth it? Will I actually get it? Isn't it something for special people? I don't need to wait — I can make sure I get what I want myself."

REMEMBER

You're living an illusion if you think that your Enneagram type can ensure that you will get whatever you want. What do most people want? Many people would say happiness, love, acknowledgment, recognition, and being heard and being truly free — and their types do indeed go to great lengths to achieve this in ingenious ways. These are important benefits, which is why all types try in their own way to gain as much control over them as possible. But how well will your type succeed in procuring what it wants? Are you in fact happy? Do you feel acknowledged, appreciated, loved? How free are you in your natural inclinations? Your type has its strengths, but how much freedom to choose do you have in your day-to-day actions?

In reality, your type doesn't really care about your happiness. Its function consists of making it easier for you to survive in this world, not in making you happy. With all kinds of worries and tensions, your type actually blocks the path to your happiness. The Desert Fathers of the early Christian Church already discovered this. The answer to the questions "What stands between me and God? What stands between me and my true self, my nature? What stands between me and others?" is "I, myself. My type stands in the way."

Looking reality in the face

Those things you don't receive because you're standing in your own way are your true self, your God. How can you receive when you're filled up by yourself? When I'm full to the brim of myself — my thoughts, my feelings, and my sensations — I have no room to receive anything. That which you aren't receiving through the filter of your type is an unimpeded view of full reality. With my type, I have a one-ninth view of reality. When I continue to develop, I expand my viewing angle, but I won't reach 360 degrees.

REMEMBER

Your type is your blindness. To what degree does this bother you? It bothers you in your relationships, for example. Maybe you aren't able to recognize the other person's good intention because you tend to judge on the basis of your type. Having a direct experience means encountering reality the way it truly is without the interference of projection, identification, suppression, denial, or other defense mechanisms. Direct perceptions can also be a spiritual experience — direct in the sense that nothing stands between you, your true self, and your experience.

Being receptive

The preparation phase for directly facing reality consists of emptying yourself, emptying the type in yourself. When you're empty, you can receive; you can open up to receive something higher. This higher thing can be God but also the experience of nonduality, of being itself, or the wisdom and love of the higher virtues. It doesn't mean that you will get these higher things instantly. They're still gifts. You can see the state of receptivity as a positive counterpart to the reactivity.

When you're reactive, you have to react; when you're receptive, you can receive freely. Training your receptivity also helps you stay grounded and present, in balance. Receptivity also helps you to accept the feedback, criticism, anger, and other issues that normally throw your type off balance.

Many roads lead to Rome

When it comes to your development, many different paths also lead to the same spiritual goal. In (Christian) spiritual traditions, two main paths are referred to as the *via positiva* and the *via negativa*. From the names *positiva* and *negativa*, you might infer that one is better than the other, but this definitely isn't the case. Both are valuable and can be entered separately or complement each other. They aren't modern inventions — the monk Evagrius Ponticus (345–399 AD) already wrote about this topic.

In Christian mysticism, the *via negativa* is best illustrated by the writings of the 16th century Spanish friar and mystic Saint John of the Cross, especially in his poem *The Dark Night of the Soul,* whereas the *via positiva* is championed in the writings of Saint Teresa of Avila, who was Saint John of the Cross's contemporary. Claudio Naranjo, a cofounder of the Enneagram, wrote about the *via negativa* in his 1971 study *On the Psychology of Meditation.* Together, the *via positiva* and the *via negativa* form what Naranjo calls (borrowing from Saint Thomas Aquinas) the *via eminentiae* or the *via creativa*. Different traditions explain the terms *via positiva* and *via negativa* in various ways and also sometimes use other names to refer to the same things. The next few sections spell out one approach for defining these terms.

Traveling the via negativa

The *via negativa* is the starting point when it comes to the Enneagram practice and is what occupies you most: emptying yourself of the type mechanism — letting go of the ego. The highest level of letting go consists of the ego transforming itself and dissolving.

It's not about fighting the ego. On the contrary, by directing your attention and energy to what you want to fight, you give the ego energy and it will grow.

The goal is to empty yourself by embracing your ego and considering it honestly; as a result, when it's released, it moves into the background. In brief, you attempt this process of emptying by learning self-observation, by seeing what your attention automatically focuses on, and which underlying driving forces and passions define you — and then letting go of it all. This also happens when you train your attention and focus it on something other than the goal that your type is fixated on. You notice when your type turns on the autopilot, when you're fixated, and this enables you to let go. Your fixation dissolves, along with your passion. In *The Dark Night of the Soul*, Saint John of the Cross describes the painful experience of feeling God's absence during his imprisonment (the emptiness), which then led to the mystical experience of being united with God.

THE VIA NEGATIVA AS A PATH WITH THE ENNEAGRAM

In Chapter 6, I talk about the four categories of the head center (remembering, thinking, planning, imagining) and how, depending on the type, the content of these categories differs. The *via negativa* leads to an emptying of the categories. As a Type 1 person, for example, I can make myself unhappy by staying stuck in my resentment about someone or something and try to imagine why something isn't working. But I have a choice and can also train myself to let go of it. This path leads to freedom because ridding myself of this feeling of resentment means it can no longer make me unhappy. Then the unwanted fixation is designated according to its category — a memory or a thought or mere imagination.

By realizing that what bothers me is only a thought, a memory, or just my imagination, I can let it go. Let go of the thought. Let go of the memories — they keep a grip on you and make you unhappy. You tend to leave the control to your type and your ego and adhere to your fixations. Letting go of fixations seems like a loss, as if you were giving up or losing something. And you resist this abandoning of your fixations, even if these fixations cause you to suffer. So the path of the *via negativa* consists of working yourself through your ego pattern, not running away from it, not trying to make it seem better than it is, and not fighting it — but rather going through it. Emptying yourself with the Enneagram leads to the following realizations:

>> I am not my body.

>> I am not my emotions.

>> I am not my thoughts.

PRACTICE SLOWLY AT FIRST

Your type mechanisms work so quickly that it's often difficult to intervene in time. The first step to comprehending your type mechanism consciously is to figure out how to slow it down. Something that moves more slowly is easier to catch. When your "machine" is slowed down, this creates space in which you can observe yourself at that moment and prevent an automatic reaction. You can practice slowing down your type mechanism through meditation, attention training, and breathing techniques. Focusing on my breath is a helpful method for me. When I notice that my type switches to autopilot, I try to turn my attention back to my breathing, because breathing is empty in the sense that it has no content or judgment. Practicing the *via negativa* through breathing is called Vipassana in Buddhism and is now also known as mindfulness or stress-reduction therapy. All these are examples of the *via negativa* — all different names, but at bottom the same principle.

FORMS AND EXAMPLES OF THE VIA NEGATIVA

In his *Original Blessing: A Primer in Creation Spirituality*, Matthew Fox describes some forms of the *via negativa*. He also touches on the example of emptying: You just let images, thoughts, and memories pass — emptying yourself and the categories in your head — and allowing for silence. In the Old Testament, the prophet Elijah didn't find God in an earthquake, nor in a fire or storm, but rather in silence. Fox also describes the *via negativa* as being emptied and as something that happens to you — when you meet and accept pain, for example, not fighting it but relaxing into it so that it slowly fades away. When you accept something as what it is, it becomes bearable over time — the pain dissipates.

One form of the *via negativa* in the Christian spiritual tradition is the lesson of sin and salvation. The word *sin* has a different, deeper meaning in the spiritual sense than in daily use. Sins can be the refusal to let go, for example; the refusal to admit that receptivity is necessary in life; clinging to the ego, control, will, and projection; not letting others be who they are; and not wanting to see the good intentions of others. Salvation isn't a liberation from pain in the sense that you no longer have to feel it, but rather a salvation through the pain, in that life is lived fully and thus experienced in its full depth. Sadness and pain bring you to the here and now.

Via positiva

A simple description of the *via positiva* would characterize it as developing toward the positive by imagining the positive. In this respect, neurolinguistic programming (NLP), a popular approach to communication, personal development, and psychotherapy created by Richard Bandler and John Grinder, matches the *via positiva* method— one succinctly summarized by Rob Schneider in the film *The*

Waterboy with the phrase "You can do it!" One well-known form of trying to achieve something through visualization is an affirmation. My affirmation at the start of the path was, "Is it not good enough the way it is?"

REMEMBER

To be clear, this particular phrasing violates the rules for a good affirmation. The word *not* shouldn't appear here. But this affirmation still worked well enough for me, even in its flawed form. Usually I could answer this question by saying, "Yes, it's good enough." Then I could restrain myself; I no longer had to keep improving and perfecting myself and could keep my energy within myself. I stopped myself from losing myself in the object of the improvement. Today, I tell myself, "It's good enough as it is." This is based on an inner conviction that I wasn't able to feel back when I formulated the first affirmation. This work proceeds in small steps.

You apply the same principle in a guided meditation — in visualizations or in meditation techniques where you focus, for example. The basic principle behind the *via positiva* is this: You can let go of something or empty yourself of something only if it's replaced by something else. An exercise in psychotherapy based on this principle consists of recognizing unhelpful thoughts and learning to replace them with helpful thoughts.

FORMS AND EXAMPLES OF THE VIA POSITIVA

Recognizing a god and believing in him is already a form of the *via positiva* in itself. The recognition that there's something greater than oneself awakens the positive within you so that you can recognize the higher aspect. To commit to a higher goal — to another person, the community, or the country, for example — is also a form of the *via positiva*. Another one is attributing positive characteristics to God: He is good, wise, merciful, gracious, loving, and so on. Principles based on the statements "And God saw everything that he had made, and, behold, it was very good" or "God is in all things, and all things are in God," and that the divine spark resides within you, that the power of love is overwhelming, that the soul is pure, and that life is there for celebrating are also examples of imagining something higher — something positive that has favorable effects on your life.

In the aforementioned *Original Blessing: A Primer in Creation Spirituality*, Matthew Fox presents examples of the *via positiva:* the path of affirmation, gratitude, being conscious and not numb, salvation and healing power, and experiencing the beauty and profundity of creation.

THE VIA NEGATIVA AS A PATH WITHIN THE ENNEAGRAM

The focus of Enneagram practice is on the *via negativa*, on becoming empty and letting go of your type. Your type can comfortably move into the background because you are conscious of the internal observer and are letting it move to the forefront. When you have this emptiness and receptivity, you can direct your attention to whatever you want. It might be a positive affirmation, a positive thought, or something else that you want to visualize and achieve as a goal. With the Enneagram, you also use this space to invite the higher virtues inside you. When the passions or vices of your type move into the background, it creates space for virtues that were also originally active in you when you were a child.

Of Higher Virtues and Ideas

The higher virtues and ideas are a state that you receive. You can't create them on your own from within — you receive them. In this state, your perception isn't colored by your views, fears, projections, or prisms of your type. Your internal awareness isn't blocked. What you're doing goes through you but doesn't set your ego in motion. The higher virtues and ideas have nothing to do with the future and past — they only exist in the here and now.

Moving from vice to virtue: A gift

Transferring control of the lower emotional center to the higher emotional center means changing a vice into a virtue. The authority of the church whose teachings were conveyed as dogmas can make this sentence sound self-righteous: Virtues must be imposed as compulsions. A virtuous life becomes mandatory and may even be further sanctioned by fear when there are threats of hell and damnation.

The virtues that I'm talking about here are more like a gift — not something that has to be, but rather something that you sometimes get as a gift. (See Figure 17-2.) It's also not something that you imitate to maintain appearances, but rather is something that you are — on the level of the true self. The wisdom of the Enneagram shows that what brings you suffering and anger in your life is created from your vices or passions. It's your pride, your deception, your immoderation, and your resentment, for example, that cause you suffering. Your vices are what create internal imbalance. When you let go of these vices (via negativa), you can invite the higher virtues instead (via positiva). Then you get to a place within yourself that is free of suffering.

Mary (Type 1) can let go of her resentment toward others in certain situations, in the process becoming a more cheerful person. That's because resentment in no way makes her happy — it's negativity that Mary is stuck in. The emptiness after the resentment, which disappears in the background along with her type, is already a pleasant state in itself. The absence of obsessive thinking and compulsive acting brings a great deal of inner calm, yet inner calm isn't yet serenity, the higher virtue that a Type 1 person can achieve. Experiencing serenity means having a deep feeling that things are good as they are now; that things will be different again tomorrow and that will be equally good; you experience the unmistakable fact that everything in nature is in motion and that everything is good. The impulses, needs, and wishes that live within you stand revealed as part of your nature, and you see that it's good as well, and that you can act accordingly while everything is in flux. Serenity is more than a sense of calm — it's a deep experience of the fact that everything is good, in a pure, light, and quiet manner.

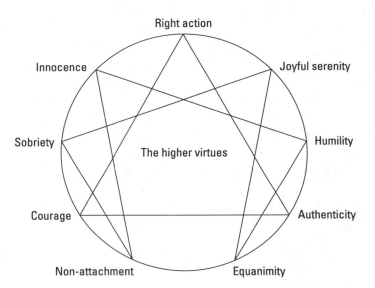

FIGURE 17-2:
The higher virtues
in graphical form.

When **Roy (Type 2)** gets his true self to control his reactivity — his pride — he can experience the higher virtue of humility within himself. Of course, humility doesn't sound like much of a virtue in our Western society. In the present day, it's not at the top of most people's lists of desirable characteristics. But the spiritual meaning of the term — the idea that humility stands for "knowing your true value" — is actually quite nice. It's not about humility in your day-to-day language, which is roughly synonymous with "making yourself small, or obeying." It's about knowing your true worth, feeling no more but also no less valuable than you really are. Experiencing how valuable you are in a qualitative sense is also part of this. The Type 2 person who knows and experiences their true value deep inside no longer has to get it confirmed by others. Their self-worth doesn't depend on the possibility of giving something to other people. Then Roy can give and receive freely and without expectations — to the degree that is actually necessary and as Roy himself wants. Humility is a deep internal experience and acceptance that he also has needs and that this correlates with the laws of nature. Fulfilling these needs in roundabout ways is no longer necessary because he can fulfill them himself. He no longer depends on others to feel good; he no longer needs to strive for a sense of value by making himself indispensable.

Tina (Type 3) can perceive her deception and let it go. This is an important step in her development into being more free as a human being. When her true self takes control of her particular reactivity — deception — she can experience the higher virtue of truthfulness and sincerity within herself. This frees her from constantly having to maintain her image, her masks, and her success stories in the changing roles that Tina assumes. No longer having to do this compulsively seems like a liberation. As soon as the energy is no longer lost through the deception, Tina can come to rest. As a gift, she receives the higher virtue of truthfulness: She experiences who she really is deep inside, that her best self is her true self, that she no longer needs any masks, and that she is loved as the person she is.

Tim (Type 4) can let go of his envy, in the process becoming a more cheerful person. His constant comparisons of himself with others and his feelings of envy don't make him happy. Tim is stuck in this negativity. The emptiness that arises when envy retreats into the background with the type is pleasant. The absence of ups and downs and his abandonment of the hunt for what others have so that the ever-present sense of desire can be satisfied creates inner peace. This isn't equanimity yet, the higher virtue that Type 4 can achieve. At the level of the Higher Self, equanimity for Tim means experiencing that he is fulfilled, whole, and complete deep inside, here and now. He can then look upon what others have and what he lacks without distress, seeing that any gap or emptiness inside him can be filled by himself and that nothing important is in fact missing.

When **Alice (Type 5)** can get her true self to take control of her reactivity — greed — she can experience the higher virtue of non-attachment within herself. Her restraint fails to make her happy and gives her the feeling that she has to isolate herself from others, from life, from her own feelings. To no longer need this is freedom and a source of enrichment in her life — an enrichment because she can be in connection with herself, with others, and with life. As a gift of the higher virtue of non-attachment, Alice experiences deep inside that she doesn't have to hoard her life energy and knowledge and that she experiences her feelings and her life energy precisely when she connects with others and with life. She realizes that this doesn't make her "empty" but rather, on the contrary, fulfilled and enlivened.

Ian (Type 6) can let go of his fear, becoming a free person. The emptiness that arises within him when the fear retreats into the background with the type is a pleasant experience. To no longer have to be compulsively vigilant, no longer turning negative ideas into disaster scenarios, and no longer keeping one foot on the brake creates space to go through life without biases. The gift of the higher virtue of Type 6, courage, is something quite different. At the level of the higher self, courage for Ian means experiencing deep inside that he is safe and secure, here and now. It's that he doesn't have to be vigilant, that there is enough courage inside him to go his way without biases, that he can cope with whatever happens to him on the way, and that his body can also act without thinking.

Louise (Type 7) has her insatiability under control and thus experiences herself as a freer person. At first glance, the insatiability seems quite funny, but it wastes a lot of energy. Until now, it ensured that Louise was dominated by her type, that her mind was constantly active, and that her exhaustion kept increasing. The emptiness after letting go of the insatiability is a freedom and enrichment of her life. As a gift of the higher virtue of sobriety, Louise experiences deep inside that she no longer needs or wants everything. There is space to focus on the here and now. Sobriety and setting limits are now accompanied by calmness and profundity, which enable her to appreciate the full spectrum of life deep within her.

When **Stan (Type 8)** gets his true self to control his lust, he can experience the higher virtue of innocence within himself. At the level of the Higher Self, innocence for Stan is the deep internal experience, here and now, that he can let life happen without biases, without needing to keep anything in control or to protect anything — the innocence that he lost at some point as a child. He also learns that he can remain vulnerable without sensing the danger that others are out to get him. Deep inside, he knows he's fine and no longer needs his fortress.

Margaret (Type 9) has let her true self take control of her inertia and is open to receiving the higher virtue of right action. The mental inertia that kept her from standing up for what would be important for her has not made her happy. As a gift of the higher virtue of right action, Margaret gains a deep inner sense of what she wants and what is good for her and her situation. The right action isn't something that she does but is something that flows through her by itself. She sets something in motion and the right action emerges as if on its own. Deep inside, Margaret experiences the energy to do what is good for her and her development, and she does it without worries, without hesitation, without detours.

The higher mental center

At the level of the higher mental center, the higher or sacred ideas can be found as counterparts to the fixations. Oscar Ichazo calls the higher ideas in his system the psychocatalysts because he believes that higher ideas accelerate the transformational process just like catalysts do in chemistry. Naranjo defines the higher ideas as nine aspects that have the power to correct individual fixations as well as implicit cognitive errors. Each of the higher ideas describes an aspect of the direct, objective perception of reality as it is — objective in the sense that no subjective distortion or type-specific veil influences this perception. The reality experienced from the Higher Self is the spiritual reality of nonduality. The higher ideas are the gifts of nonduality, the gifts of being.

The higher ideas of the individual types

The following sections contain descriptions of the higher ideas of the individual types. I've taken these from a number of different sources, including A.H. Almaas' *Facets of Unity: The Enneagram of Holy Ideas*, Sandra Maitri's book *The Spiritual Dimension of the Enneagram: Nine Faces of the Soul*, and my training with Helen Palmer as well as from my colleague Hannah Nathans. I supplemented them slightly and rephrased them to make them easier to understand.

Type 1: Higher perfection

At the level of the Higher Self, deep within, persons with Type 1 experience that what they are at this moment is real and that this is good and perfect. This perception isn't distorted by a judgment. They experience things in this moment just as they are. Higher perfection is the deep inner experience of what is referred to in Zen Buddhism as *kono-mama*, the "being as it is." It means accepting reality as it is, deep inside, and seeing and experiencing perfection in it. One recognizes and accepts the fundamental nature in everything, each person, and yourself; it's good as is. Every manifestation in the universe is an expression of the fundamental nature of things and the experience that this fundamental nature is good.

REMEMBER

It's difficult to process this idea when one considers all the suffering that exists in the world. Humans can somewhat accept suffering as a result of illness and catastrophes, however terrible they might be, because they consider it part of nature. The most difficult part to understand is the suffering that people do to each other, to animals, and to nature. This suffering caused by people is created by the alienation of humans from their inner being, by their acting on the level of their type. Even if it's hard to accept, it's often the case that it's precisely the experience of suffering that makes people want to follow the path of development toward goodness, peace, and wholeness. Nothing good comes from evil.

Type 2: Greater freedom and higher will

At the level of the Higher Self, deep within, a Type 2 person feels that their needs are being adequately met. The deep realization that they are, through their true selves, able to be alone, to care for themselves and to receive, is a higher freedom — the realization that the universe satisfies real needs and requirements. It doesn't take more or less than is actually necessary. The higher will is the realization that the meaning of everything happening in your life lies in experiencing it and participating in it. The higher will is the awareness that reality is happening just as planned. The easiest way to deal with it is to go with the flow. Surrendering yourself to the higher will is freedom.

SACRED IDEAS

In the spiritual reality of a God or Oneness, there exists sacred perfection, sacred will and freedom, sacred hope, sacred primordial nature, sacred omniscience, sacred power, sacred faith and trust, sacred work, sacred truth, and the highest of all: sacred love. I usually write *higher* instead of *sacred*, but here I thought the word was fitting. The sidebar figure shows this in graphical form.

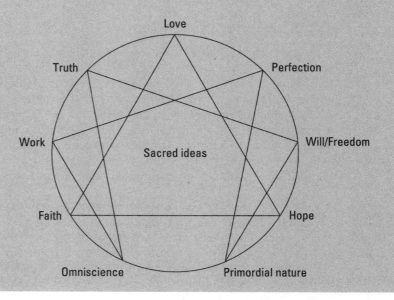

Type 3: Greater hope or higher law

At the level of the Higher Self, deep within, a Type 3 person can relax in the knowledge that their life is proceeding according to universal rules. You get what you need without having to set the universe in motion. The universe moves on its own. Then a Type 3 individual can allow real feelings to arise, because they no longer stand in the way of their own goals. The body expresses what is true. Hope isn't the prospect of things getting better — greater hope means experiencing that it's already in order. Higher hope is the realization that you can't and don't have to organize it yourself, that this order is being created according to the higher laws of the universe, just as planned, and that God acts for you and can do it better than you can. You don't have to do everything yourself.

With this realization at the level of the Higher Self, you can surrender to the flow of life and of being. The realization of the existence of this higher law is the realization that the universe, the world, and life are always in motion, never at rest, that you are part of this motion and you flow with it.

Type 4: A more profound connection to primordial nature

At the level of the Higher Self, deep within, a Type 4 person experiences a connection with the true self, with the primordial source, with all things, with unity. Everything comes from the same source and returns to it. It's the objective experience that the true self, your nature, has always been there and that you have never been separate from it — although you experience this differently if your consciousness is active at the level of your type.

A more profound primordial nature refers to the deep inner experience that this primordial state exists in everyone and is the home of the soul. It's the realization that the connection exists even when you don't feel it and the experience that all people share this connectedness with each other at the original source. Here every person is connected to the others and to the greater whole. A more profound primordial nature means the experience that you arose from being and consist of being.

Type 5: Greater omniscience

At the level of the Higher Self, deep within, a Type 5 person experiences that they are an inseparable part of the rest of reality. You experience that the whole consists of its parts and that everything is connected — the realization of oneness. You experience yourself as an inseparable part of this whole. Higher omniscience is the recognition that knowledge is present and available in this connectedness — the perfect insight. It's the complete understanding of your nature and the knowledge of who you are. It's omniscience about yourself and your life, nature, and nonduality — the realization of yourself as an expression of the greater whole.

Type 6: Higher power, higher faith, and higher trust

At the level of the Higher Self, deep within, a Type 6 person experiences a higher power that exists within them. They discover a foundation of strength and steadfastness inside themselves. On this basis, deep within, Type 6 individuals experience confidence and faith in themselves, in others, in the world, and the universe. They feel supported and carried. This trust isn't based on hope but rather on the experience of having solid ground beneath them. Nothing can destroy the essential safety that you experience deep inside yourself. That is the higher power, the higher trust. The higher faith transforms your consciousness. It's not a mental concept but rather a reality based on experience. Deep inside, you recognize your inner being, its existence, its presence. It's the recognition of the origin of everything that exists, the divine spark within you, of your true nature, of God. You recognize exactly what suits your spiritual insight and language.

Type 7: Higher work

At the level of the Higher Self, a Type 7 person experiences that higher work is the attainment of the true self today, in the here and now. In this state, Type 7 individuals accept all of life, with its joy and sadness, fun and pain, possibilities and limitations. They experience concentration, work, and purposeful activity without being distracted by new plans. Their work is internal work in the present. Their lives are a sequence of moments in the present of which they are aware. Focused on continuity in the present, they experience the unfolding of their souls. This process is inseparably connected with the unfolding of their whole being, of life, of reality. Self-realization is part of the realization that takes place in everything and at every moment. It's part of the natural development of being, and it functions through devotion. This is the higher work.

Type 8: Higher truth

At the level of the Higher Self, deep within, a Type 8 person experiences the truth that everyone shares with each other instead of possessing just their own, personal truths — truths that are tied to their own interests. The higher idea of truth is the experience that the cosmos forms an indivisible unity. It's the actual experience rather than a denial of how things belong together, how everything and everyone is connected.

The higher truth lies in the direct experience of your own being as the true self, in the realization that there's more than just what is material or physically perceptible. You experience the essential truth as objective and unchangeable, not dependent on a situation or opinion but as something valid equally for everyone. In a Type 8 person, the higher truth dissolves the source of the struggle through the realization that the other person's truth is part of the perfect truth. This is true, and the other is true as well.

Type 9: Higher love

At the level of the Higher Self, a Type 9 person experiences themselves as a completely accepted part of the universe. There is love. The perception of reality without the filter of the Type 9 ego shows that love exists by nature and that nature is lovable, that love enchants you. People recognize that the pleasures in life and the joy of living are an expression of love. You don't have to make an effort to receive this love; it's simply there, and you only need to accept it. People love themselves and others, and they have a sense of self-worth. They experience the love that exists and has always existed. People are active without making an effort. The activity happens through Type 9, and nothing that must be done according to the universal will is left undone. Action is an expression of universal love. Reality is an expression of love.

5

The Roots of the Enneagram

Chapter **18**

The Origin and Development of the Enneagram

The exact origin of the Enneagram — who came up with it and when — is unknown, partly because *the* Enneagram doesn't exist: The Enneagram has evolved from different sources and developed in different ways. In this chapter, I look at the more recent sources of the western Enneagram.

Believing That Older Is Better

For one reason or another, people like to believe that insights are better the older they are — maybe because people generally attribute more wisdom to their ancestors than they do to themselves. But people had the same problem even at the beginning of our era.

The Persian prophet Zoroaster, or Zarathustra, is said to have lived 5,000 years before the Trojan War began. He is assumed to be the author of the *Chaldean Oracles*, which provided important inspiration to philosophers and spiritual seekers of the time. Another scripture that is said to be ancient is the *Corpus Hermeticum*, which originated in Egypt. It became a kind of Bible to those seeking to immerse themselves in the spiritual tradition. Just like the *Chaldean Oracles*, the *Corpus Hermeticum* originated around the beginning of our calendar. Apparently, people attribute more authority to a scripture when it's old. This is also evident in the Enneagram: It's true that some people tend to elevate it into a millennia-old wisdom. But the fact that the scriptures aren't as old as people often claim doesn't make their content less interesting or valuable.

YOU OFTEN FIND THE SAME THING UNDER THE SAME ROCK

I considered the subject of cultural anthropology an important part of my education, partly because it taught me a few valuable ways of looking and thinking. An important research method in this area is (participatory) observation, which includes critically interpreting your own observations. This is how you learn — or at least try to learn — to distinguish sense from nonsense and illusion from reality. When studying cultures, for example, you can observe how practices are transferred from one culture to another; interpretive carriers such as language, symbols, and myths are part of the research.

Precisely because no clear origin of the Enneagram and its symbol is known, many (including me) have started the fascinating process of searching for traces in our human history. Who learned what from whom? A lot of knowledge is shared this way, but not everything. Sometimes, comparable items are found in different places — often, even at about the same time. Sometimes, people search in the same place and in the same source, so it isn't surprising that some of them find the same things independently of each other. When observing natural phenomena, neither is it surprising that different people considering the same phenomenon perceive the same result. This is true for the natural world around you, the *cosmos* — and when you search and research inside yourself. When two people look under the same rock, they'll probably find the same thing. People are crazy about the old-time wisdom.

There are myths and there are gossips

Since time immemorial, wisdom has been passed down by the telling of myths. That's why myths are often stories containing a moral. Myths fit in well with the figurative way of thinking that still characterizes you as human. You have probably had the experience of seeing a teacher or trainer explain an insight by using a picture. But *myth* also has another, often negative meaning: a story that's considered true only because many people repeat it.

Myths are formed when someone tells something to two others, for example. Those people tell others in turn. We humans tend to believe something if it's said often enough, because that person and this one and that person's brother say so, too. The same is true of things set down in writing. Take the story of creation, for example. I consider it a wonderful mythological story. Other people take it literally because it's in a book that they consider authoritative. That's why these people find confirmation in the fact that hundreds of variants of the same story appear in scriptures in so many places around the world: "If it's in so many books, there must be something to it."

It ain't necessarily so

Why is this insight so important to me for this book? Humans share truths with each other, but they also share falsehoods in the same way. The falsehoods quickly develop a life of their own. That's why you must always critically examine — also internally — what you can and can't accept as the truth. Keep asking yourself questions. If someone in the Enneagram world announces that a certain Mr. Gurdjieff brought the Enneagram to the West, dare to ask whether that was really the case — because it's also claimed that a certain Mr. Ichazo must have gotten it from Gurdjieff. Then there's this question: "Oh, really — is that true?"

Maybe you think, "Is it so important who passed what to whom or who came up with what? The Enneagram works for me, and that's all that matters." That is also a truth. This perspective applies to me as well, and I continued my search more as a hobby anthropologist. From others, I know that many people consider origin stories to be important. That's why a book offering an introduction to the world of the Enneagram must also mention this story.

The First Versions of the Enneagram Symbol

The oldest writings I can find that contain symbols similar to the Enneagram are by Ramon Llull, a Catalan Christian mystic (1235–1316). He drew various circles in which he tried to capture certain kinds of knowledge: from the order of the cosmos and from consciousness to a circle containing the various virtues and vices. He felt that this was the best way to summarize knowledge from all areas of science, including theology. Llull based this belief on the notion that a limited number of basic, undeniable truths exist in all fields of knowledge and that you can understand everything about these fields of knowledge by studying combinations of these elemental truths. In his *Ars Generalis Ultima (The Great Art)*, the first figure of his teaching depicts these elemental truths arranged around a circle divided into nine sections, with an alphabet of nine letters. (See Figure 18-1).

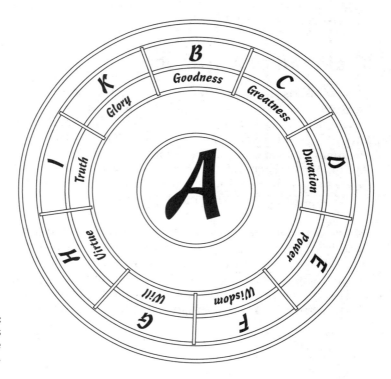

FIGURE 18-1:
Ramon Llull's circle of nine elemental truths.

Figure 18-2 shows Lull's second elemental figure: three closed triangles drawn inside the circle. Now, Llull's circle is starting to look much more like the Enneagram of today. In Llull's time, Christians, Jews, and Muslims lived together in

Spain, sharing knowledge and influencing each other. It therefore isn't unreasonable to assume that Llull was inspired by the figurative art of the Muslims as well as by Jewish theories of numbers and letters, which attributed special properties to these signs. This is still evident in the Jewish mysticism of the Kabbalah. (For more on the Kabbalah, see the "Oscar Ichazo" section, later in this chapter.)

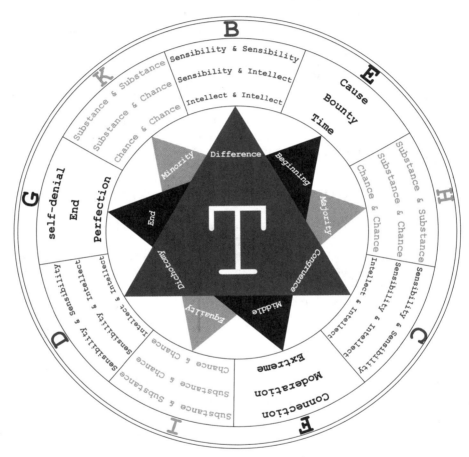

FIGURE 18-2: Coming closer to the present-day Enneagram.

The man who knew everything

The Enneagram symbol appeared in Western writings for the second time in 1655, in the work of Athanasius Kircher (1602–1680), a Jesuit priest. In the 17th century, he was called the "man who knows everything." Considered one of the most influential universal scholars of his time, Kircher studied Hebrew, philosophy, and theology and then became a professor of ethics and algebra at the University of Würzburg, where he also taught Hebrew, Aramaic, and much more.

Kircher was a follower of *syncretism*, a doctrine that aimed to unite different beliefs and religions. He also worked on reconstructing the universal language that he believed came before the linguistic confusion that followed the destruction of the Tower of Babylon. Thinking that he would find the key to it in Egyptian hieroglyphics, he carried out in-depth research on Egyptian antiquity.

Similar to Ramon Llull, Kircher believed that the foundations of all knowledge could be summarized by a small number of logical symbols, which was the topic of his book *Ars Magna Sciendi (The Great Art of Knowledge)*, the first book on symbolic logic. (With the coming of the 20th century, the philosophy of language and the field of computer science developed from Kircher's work done many years earlier.) Kircher also drew an Enneagram in which not only the sides of the triangle 3-6-9 were closed, as in Llull's, but also those between the corners 2-8-5 and 1-4-7. He called it an Enneagon. (In view of his broad interests and extensive research, he was likely familiar with the work of Ramon Llull, but I personally cannot attest to it.)

Pioneers of the Enneagram in the West

The Russian-Armenian mystic and philosopher G.I. Gurdjieff has been credited with bringing the Enneagram symbol (back) to the West, but I would argue that he in fact wasn't the first, and he wasn't the only one — he simply had more of an impact. Similar to Ramon Llull and Athanasius Kircher, Gurdjieff didn't attribute to it the same meaning of the personality theory that's in use today. However, people still use the version of the symbol introduced by Gurdjieff, in which only the triangle 3-6-9 is closed and there's no connecting line between points 2-5 and 4-7. Through the work of Gurdjieff — and maybe even more so through the book by his student P.D. Ouspensky, *In Search of the Miraculous: Fragments of an Unknown Teaching* — the Enneagram became known to a wider audience.

Georges Ivanovitch Gurdjieff

It's known that Georges Ivanovitch Gurdjieff (1877–1949) was born in Alexandropol in Russian Transcaucasia, a region near the Iranian border, in what is today the city of Gyumri in Armenia. Gurdjieff already proved to be a seeker of truth at a young age, striving for perfect awareness and self-realization in his life. His search took him on a journey that lasted about 20 years and included travels in the Middle East, Africa, and, above all, Central Asia. Around 1914, he began to share the results of his search with his students in Moscow. (This book contains many of his lessons.)

Searching for the origin of Gurdjieff's teaching and the Enneagram, many people have retraced his paths, which lead through the different forms of yoga practiced by Hindus on to Buddhism, Eastern Christianity, Sufism, Kabbalistic mysticism,

Judaism, Zoroastrianism, and the ancient Egyptian religions all the way back to a mysterious, unknown primal source. In exploring all these spiritual traditions, you encounter elements that Gurdjieff has incorporated into his teaching.

Those with a knowledge of yoga will recognize that the greatest similarities to the Enneagram can be found in the Eightfold Path tradition of raja yoga. (Raja yoga is also called *royal* yoga.) It's the path of *karma* yoga (the union with God through physical work and dedication to others), *bhakti* yoga (union with God through piety), and *jnana* yoga (union with God through wisdom, mental activity, and discernment).

In the past, it was said that disciples followed the path of karma yoga in their first life, bhakti yoga in the following life, and jnana yoga in their third life. Later, thanks to the evolution of human consciousness, the practice of raja yoga made it possible to follow all three paths in just one life. This can be compared to what is described as Gurdjieff's Fourth Way in other chapters of this book: the teaching to develop all three centers — head, heart, and gut — simultaneously and in a balanced way.

WHAT WAS THAT ABOUT SECRET BROTHERHOODS?

It's often reported that Gurdjieff learned about the Enneagram from a secret Sufi brotherhood, the Sarmoung, in a monastery hidden away in northern Afghanistan. A certain Desmond Martin also described a visit to this brotherhood in 1965. I wasn't able to pin down how much of this is true — all I'll say is that it's been verified that the name of the brotherhood means "the bees" in Persian and its motto is "Work yields a sweet essence." Martin describes seeing the Enneagram symbol depicted on a wall, that the Sarmoung call it "No-Koonja" or the nine-pointed Naqsh (which means *seal* or *imprint*), and that this symbol means "Reach for the innermost secret of humanity."

The nine-pointed Naqsh lives on today in the name of the Naqshbandi, a prominent Sufi order. Although I don't consider the poetic, pictorial language of the Quran easy to understand, you can read in plain English on the order's website at https://naqshbandi.org that it was visited first by Gurdjieff and then by his student John G. Bennett. In his *Principles of Reality*, Bennett describes the Enneagram as the secret of the spider web, a reference to the spider web in front of Mohammed's cave, where the cave is a symbol for the presence of God. In the 36th chapter of the Quran (the Surah Ya Sin, also known as the heart of the Quran), the ninth verse mentions the barriers confronting humans — which the Naqshbandi masters, seeing the significance of this warning coming in the ninth verse, interpret as nine spiked points of the heart keeping people at bay. When you search for reality, you encounter these barriers, which you can't see through. It's also said that the reality of these nine spiked points of the heart falls under the authority (or knowledge) of the nine great Naqshbandi masters.

The website of the Naqshbandi order also states that the order shared much of its knowledge with Gurdjieff — but not everything, because the time had not yet come. According to the Naqshbandi brothers, Gurdjieff swore to them that he would keep this knowledge secret, as he himself always insisted. Gurdjieff later met sheikhs from this order in Damascus and Turkey.

GURDJIEFF'S TEACHINGS

Although Gurdjieff claimed that you understand something only if you can incorporate it into the Enneagram, he didn't incorporate a personality theory there. He didn't teach his students anything about personality structures. Gurdjieff was known to believe that people weren't ready yet. This isn't surprising, considering the spirit of that time.

Around the time in which Gurdjieff broke through the buffers and defense mechanisms of his students, Freud was formulating his own theory of defense mechanisms. Freud started his work with psychoanalysis, in which patients for the first time were included as part of their own healing process and asked and encouraged to practice self-observation and self-reflection. It was fitting for that period that Gurdjieff didn't involve his students in his own learning process, but instead instructed them as a master.

REMEMBER

As interest in the Enneagram grew, so did interest in the work of Gurdjieff. Many things that are considered parts of his teachings are excerpts from the works of Pythagoras (astronomy, music, number theory, and more), Plato, and other philosophers. This isn't surprising because Gurdjieff never made a secret of the fact that he had traveled far to gather his wisdom. The value of his work probably lies in the fact that he didn't just bring wisdom from the East to the West; he also brought ancient wisdom to the West of the 20th century — wisdom that was brought back to life and, thanks to his efforts, was allowed to reach many people who would never have known about it otherwise.

As for Gurdjieff's teachings proper, he argued that the Enneagram represents two universal laws: *The law of three* refers to the three forces (active, reactive, neutral); *the law of seven* describes how all processes and transformations follow natural laws.

Gurdjieff assumed that humans think linearly, according to cause and effect. Because people live in a three-dimensional world, they can't precisely observe and see through the processes of the world with linear perception and thinking. Only when people incorporate the processes in the Enneagram is it possible for them to see through and understand these processes. John G. Bennett describes the law of three and the law of seven as three sources and six steps. The Enneagram as a process model helps you understand processes and also recognize when and where processes stagnate. According to Gurdjieff, people understand the Enneagram only after they can imagine it in motion. It describes dynamics within you and in the outside world.

Here's a summary of a few important aspects of Gurdjieff's teaching that relate to the inner work with the Enneagram:

>> Humans are automatons; they act mechanically and as though they were asleep.

>> Humans can't remember because they act on the basis of their ego rather than on the basis of their true selves.

>> Deception is humans' greatest sin; people can't and don't want to see themselves as they really are. As a result, people can't develop their full potential.

>> All people have a dark spot in their character, which causes them unnecessary suffering. Their false personality hinders them in their lives.

>> The harmonious development of humans is tied to the fulfillment of natural laws.

>> True thinking and knowledge take place in the heart.

>> There can be no development without internal struggle (internal jihad).

>> Gurdjieff's goal was to break through the buffers (defense mechanisms) of all people because these buffers conceal their negative character traits from them.

>> Inner work requires you to follow the traditional path under the guidance of a teacher, in a group.

>> Inner work means real work; good intentions won't get you anywhere; it requires effort, investment, dedication, and discipline.

>> The Enneagram is a mirror image — an *archetype* — of the cosmos that is always in motion.

>> Humans are part of this cosmos.

>> The Enneagram is an intelligent summary for spiritual teaching.

>> The Enneagram offers a path to transformation and enlightenment.

Oscar Ichazo

The fourth place where the Enneagram appears in the West is in the work of the Bolivian native Oscar Ichazo (1931 to the present day). In his teachings, he works with various geometric figures or seals from the school of Pythagoras, such as the pentagon, hexagon, heptagon, enneagon, and dodecagon. In the 1960s, he developed the idea and practice of integrating personality structures in the Enneagram and using them for self-observation, self-reflection, and spiritual development.

Based on what my research is telling me today, Ichazo could rightly be called the father of the Enneagram in the form and with the theory as it is known and used today. The elements he used weren't new, but the combination in which he placed them was, as were his placement of the passions, fixations, holy virtues, and ideas. His teaching goes far beyond the Enneagram, which is why I can't go into detail with regard to that work in this book. As far as the Enneagram is concerned, among other things, he accommodated the nine divine qualities in the Enneagram, just as he had encountered them in Neoplatonism, the Kabbalah, and Christian mysticism. He contributed to the theory of the wings and the ideas behind the stress and comfort points of each type. (Incidentally, he used the term *Enneagon*, just like Kircher did. For more on the wings theory and stress and comfort points, see Chapter 14.)

Ichazo also has an extraordinary life story. At a young age, he was fascinated by the medicine men of the Bolivian Indios and their use of the hallucinogenic Anahuac. He learned from them, became acquainted with their drugs, and had his own series of special out-of-body experiences. At the age of 19, he met an older man and went to Buenos Aires with him. A group of mystics met regularly there; Ichazo served them coffee and learned from them. These mystics were representatives of very different traditions — from Zen Buddhism, Sufism, and theosophy to the Kabbalah and numerous forms of yoga. There he also acquainted himself with P.D. Ouspensky's *In Search of the Miraculous: Fragments of an Unknown Teaching*.

Ichazo founded study groups in Santiago and traveled to the Middle and Far East each year. He studied in the north of Kashmir and in the south of Iran. He studied Sufism in a school of the Suhrawardiyya order in Kandahar, and then studied with the Bektashi order, the Naqshbandi, and the followers of the renowned Sufi Jamal ad-Din al-Afghani in Kabul. He also traveled to Asia and learned about the Chinese classics in Hong Kong. In 1969, Ichazo taught at the Institute of Applied Psychology in Santiago, Chile. In 1970, he founded study groups in the city of Arica, in the northernmost corner of Chile; a group of Americans from the USA participated in a ten-month training course with him. One of the course participants was the Chilean psychiatrist Claudio Naranjo. In 1971, Ichazo went to New York and founded the Arica Institute, where he taught until 1981. Today he lives in Hawaii with his wife and dedicates himself mainly to writing.

According to Ichazo, people don't direct their thinking if their consciousness isn't clearly developed. As long as their consciousness hasn't been freed, people will continue to suffer. The spiritual path is that path where you live a normal, everyday life and a spiritual life at the same time. It's therefore comparable to raja yoga or Gurdjieff's Fourth Way. On this path, you're aware of yourself at every moment. You're also aware that you don't do your deeds for yourself but that your actions are in the service of a higher goal that goes beyond you. Only then does what you do and how you do it have real value.

Ichazo was never a teacher of the Enneagram; the Enneagram was part of his teaching, which he calls protoanalysis. The goal of *protoanalysis* is to reach the state of enlightenment and union with the divine. Ichazo adopted many methods from the spiritual traditions in which he was trained. From Sufism, for example, he uses the Nine Kinds of *Dhikr*, a powerful meditation technique in which certain affirmations (such as *La ilaha illallah*) are chanted repeatedly while certain movements are performed. This meditation technique addresses all three centers, leading to a silent state of being. This state of inner stillness creates an inward calm.

Claudio Naranjo

Claudio Naranjo (1932 to the present day) was born in Chile, studied medicine there, and later became a psychiatrist. He has also practiced all kinds of professions: He worked as a professor and was trained as a Gestalt therapist and worked as such. Today he lives and works in the USA, where he also publishes his works.

Naranjo learned about the personality Enneagram in 1969, when Ichazo gave his lectures at the Institute of Applied Psychology in Santiago. Naranjo worked at the Esalen Institute in California, which had become the center of the human potential movement (HPM). Over 20,000 people came to attend seminars there each year. In 1970, Naranjo took 50 Americans to Arica to attend a course with Ichazo there. In 1971, he founded his own study group in Berkeley, California. This made Berkeley the cradle of the modern Enneagram movement. Many important Enneagram authors and teachers still live there today. The program pursued by Naranjo's group developed an increasingly detailed profile and was given a name: Seekers after Truth, or SAT. *SAT* means "truth" in Sanskrit.

Naranjo integrated the personality Enneagrams he learned from Ichazo into character descriptions. Naranjo also incorporated into the Enneagram the knowledge he brought with him from his broad training as a psychiatrist and Gestalt therapist. From this he developed a systematic psychology of Enneagram types, creating a holistic reproduction of the personality traits, motives, cognitive styles, and existential dimensions of each Enneagram type. Thanks to his background as a psychiatrist, he recognized and described the neuroses of the individual types and also saw similarities with the personality disorders listed in the *Diagnostic and Statistical Manual of Mental Disorders,* or *DSM.*

Naranjo realized that some of Freud's defense mechanisms were related to certain types of the Enneagram. Naranjo formulated a theory about the disintegration of consciousness and the healing and transformation process. He worked with meditation, music, and other therapeutic techniques and was the first to conduct panel interviews with representatives of the individual types to demonstrate their characteristics and the validity of the theory.

Chapter **19**

Current Enneagram Schools and Movements

O ne goal of this *For Dummies* book is to present a guide to the world of the Enneagram to people who are exploring it for the first time. The kinds of questions often posed by participants in my introductory Enneagram workshops indicate that there's a need for such a guide: "There are so many authors. How are they different? Which one should I read? One person says this, another says that — who's right?" The various approaches have many similarities, but they definitely have differences as well. They all add something new, develop their own stories and approaches, and specialize in certain parts of the Enneagram that appeal to them and that they have discovered to be meaningful to them.

Seeing That the Readers Are the Winners

A preliminary note: It wasn't easy for me to write this chapter, simply because I didn't read every book by all the authors I mention and I most assuredly didn't take a course with every single one of them. It was inevitable that I would perform an injustice to the authors and trainers. My goal, however, is to give you, to the best of my abilities, an overview of Enneagram work that is as broad as possible.

To fill in the gaps of my own knowledge, I asked the following authors and teachers — big names in the world of the Enneagram — to contribute some writing that is based on a few of my questions. I was also able to ask students of most of the movements to report about their experiences. I'm touched by the cooperation and the enthusiastic support I received from so many. The readers are the winners because, this way, I gained further inspiring information.

Sorry, completeness is not an option

The study of the Enneagram has grown so large that many trainers are engaged with it all over the world. This chapter isn't intended to be a business directory of all Enneagram authors — instead, in this chapter I introduce you to the most important movements and their most famous representatives. When the movements are introduced, I also explain those new aspects of the Enneagram associated with each movement. This gives you an overview of what is out there and indicates which direction might suit you.

The Sufi Enneagram: Laleh Bakhtiar

Since the Sufi Enneagram is so often mentioned as the source of the Western Enneagram, this book is not complete without telling you something about it. Even if this assumption about how the Enneagram has been passed down to others isn't shared by everyone, the Sufi Enneagram can't be omitted.

Laleh Bakhtiar wrote three books about the Enneagram and offers lectures and seminars all over the world. The title of her trilogy is *God's Will Be Done*. This approach to the Enneagram is quite different from the one we know, because it isn't based on the traditional line of the teachers Ichazo and Naranjo. This is why I like to refer to Bakhtiar's work, because she displays a version of the Enneagram without Western influence. I find it fascinating and valuable to learn about the Islamic perspective in her work. Although our models use different approaches, I find more common aspects than separating elements regarding the spiritual path in her books.

Laleh Bakhtiar wrote the following letter to me:

> When the Enneagram flourished in the 1990s, many books spoke of the "Sufi connection." Enneagram teachers gradually distanced themselves from this view and integrated their own definitions and methods into their teaching. All these methods are far removed from the original Sufi concepts. The Sufis also integrated the Enneagram into their teaching, so it isn't quite correct to say that the Enneagram is originally from Sufism. It originates with Plato, St. Thomas Aquinas, Moses Maimonides, Abu Hamid al-Ghazzali, and many others.

Until the 13th century, there was no nine-pointed Enneagram, because practical philosophy spoke of only six points. The discussion among philosophers referred to the three virtues of Plato (courage, wisdom, and temperance) and whether there was too much or too little of these virtues. The person who was centered in virtue was considered an honest and righteous person (the fourth virtue, according to Plato), but only if someone else confirmed it. In the 13th century, Nasir al-Din Tusi realized that a discussion of too much or too little virtue concerns only the quantity. He introduced the possibility that virtue can also be lacking in quality, meaning that it can't be a question of only whether a virtue was developed too strongly or weakly — it can also be developed incorrectly. This added three vices, and the result was nine. The center of the Enneagram, the zero point, stands for the person without an ego, whose honesty and integrity are thus confirmed.

Subsequently, several Sufi orders started to use this psychological method to determine where someone new should start on their spiritual path. In this Enneagram, the head center is at the top, the heart center on the right side, and the gut center is on the left. The head center then contains three points relating to wisdom, of which there is too much or too little or which is incorrectly developed.

It works the same way for the other two centers. Sufis can accurately determine a student's state and thus begin the practical application of the Enneagram. A person can display the points one to nine at any time, but it isn't the case that this person is then that number or type, as is wrongly taught today. What is specific to the Sufi Enneagram is that one person can manifest all nine numbers at different times. The goal is to reach the center 0 and be as egoless, honorable, and honest as possible — a person who can see reality just as it is.

According to Laleh, and also confirmed by her students, one strength of this model is that it helps you see where you stand at any time and see what you have to work on. In her opinion, when types are assessed according to the Western method, there is a danger that someone will increasingly identify with their type and continue to find confirmation of themselves in the type's negative aspects. As a result, someone can increasingly live out the stereotypical image of the type. Laleh may be right with this concern; my colleagues and I do see this increasingly in practice. However, we expressly teach it differently.

Here's a sample of Bakhtiar's writing:

The process of the great struggle means relating oneself in a balanced and honest way to reality, to truth, to the Supreme Being, to God, and to nature in all its forms created by God. The learning process starts with learning who we are, gaining knowledge about ourselves, and then becoming conscious of our place in the universe. Starting with ourselves, we learn how important it is to use our reasoning to control our desires and needs. We then learn to apply balanced reason in our relationships with others and in our relationship with reality. The goal is to be centered and able to control our passions by using balanced reason. Like spiritual warriors, we will treat others honestly and honorably and put others and their needs above ours.

Kabbalah and the Enneagram: Howard A. Addison and Hannah Nathans

It's not surprising that there are striking similarities between the Enneagram and Kabbalah, because the people who invented the Enneagram were inspired by the teachings of Kabbalah, among other contributors. I can hardly imagine what the Enneagram can additionally offer to people who are following the mystical path of Kabbalah. I asked Rabbi Howard Avruhm Addison and the rabbi-in-training Hannah Nathans of the Dorshe Neshamah Institute their views on the subject. Addison has written two books about the Enneagram and Kabbalah. They teach this subject together in America.

Hannah Nathan and Howard Addison wrote the following letter to me:

> There is a striking similarity between the Enneagram types and the manifestations of the divine in the Kabbalistic tree of life (Etz Chaim). We explore the Enneagram through the lens of the Jewish mystical tradition. By creating a synthesis of the wisdom of the Enneagram and the insights and spiritual exercises of Kabbalah, we hope to reach a deeper understanding of reality and the paths toward personal transformation. We help students to become aware of how each soul is rooted in both the radiant and the shadow side of the divine and which unique developmental tasks *(tikkunim)* each soul is meant to fulfill.
>
> In accordance with the Kabbalistic belief that we exist simultaneously in four worlds, or four layers of reality *(arba'ah olamot),* we help students to recognize the existence of several levels of consciousness. We invite them to expand their connection to the higher levels of awareness by means of contemplation exercises and studies so that they become able to consciously move from one level to another and manifest their true self more fully in professional and personal relationships.
>
> Although we are primarily trained as rabbis and Jewish pastors, our interreligious experience and studies of wisdom traditions from around the world have taught us that there is a common contemplative core that transcends the divisions between the spiritual systems. We emphasize the universal wisdom of the Enneagram and Kabbalah and invite students to recognize their own identity in relation to what they understand to be sacred. We consider the psychological insights of the Enneagram and Kabbalah to be extremely important and also value what they teach us about the higher qualities. Why? Because every student can strive to become a worthy embodiment of the higher states of consciousness by gaining awareness and self-knowledge and by practicing receptivity.

Rabbi Goldie Milgram says the following about Rabbi Addison and Hannah Nathans:

> Rabbi Avruhm Addison and Hannah Nathans helpfully and spiritually incorporate the Enneagram into the field of Jewish psychology. Surprising and effective correlations between the Enneagram and the very longstanding Jewish approaches to human development lead to a positive and useful integration.
>
> In 1812, Menachem Mendel from the Jewish settlement Sataniv (at the time, part of Poland and now part of Ukraine) published *Cheshbon ha-Nefesh (Moral Accounting)*, a model for individual ethical development (called *musar* in Judaism). In their classes, Addison and Nathans introduced the Enneagram and taught the correlations of the Enneagram with strategies for mapping the mind from the texts and methods of the original Kabbalists, especially the tree of life model. This way, they enabled us to study Hasidic teachings about the *midot* — those qualities that we want to purify or appreciate more. By observing panels where individual fellow students talked about their place in the Enneagram and by watching a series of videos, we were better able to assess the function of the Enneagram and connect it to the thorough teachings of the Jewish tradition. Above all, the course offered an important and refreshing initiative within the cognitive-behavioral approaches of psychology as found in Judaism. This is wonderful, because spiritual growth is only possible after thorough individual purification, so that the mind is not misperceived and misapplied.

Rabbi Goldie Milgram is the author of *Reclaiming Judaism as a Spiritual Practice: Holy Days and Shabbat* and the publisher of *Seeking and Soaring: Jewish Approaches to Spiritual Direction*.

The Enneagram: A Christian Perspective, Richard Rohr

The Enneagram was quickly adopted by many people within the Christian tradition. Richard Rohr, one of the better-known authors and teachers from the Catholic side, is a Franciscan friar who wrote a bestseller about the Enneagram. According to Rohr, each Enneagram type is characterized by a fundamental sin that causes a separation from God. The false self of the human must die so that God's love can flow freely again. The Enneagram shows people the way toward a conversion, according to Rohr.

Richard Rohr wrote the following letter to me:

> The authority you attribute to me arose from the fact that I was probably one of the first to publish a book on the Enneagram (together with Andreas Ebert), and due to the integration of the wisdom of the Enneagram with the Judeo-Christian concept of spiritual transformation.

The Enneagram describes perceptible manifestations of the strengths and weaknesses of each type. I hope that I may accompany people on their way to a wonderful self-awareness that makes them kneel before the grace, devotion, and healing they receive. I hope that our books help people laugh at every automatism that tries to dominate them and laugh at themselves as well. We give examples, the actual experiences of people, Bible texts, and other narratives that illustrate both the positive and the negative sides of each type. This way, we also try to contribute to the necessary relativization and exposure of our human ego in today's highly egocentric Western culture.

Our approach aims to expose and dissect our illusions and thus create a desire for transformation. In general, my seminars focus more on the wings than on the arrows of the stress and comfort points. I also get greater support from the wings in my work.

As a Christian, I strive to connect the Enneagram with the eternal tradition that we once called the purifying path, especially with the teachings of Evagrius and my Franciscan brother Ramon Llull. When used wisely, the Enneagram is an ideal tool to lead us to the enlightened path (to the path of grace, not as the final goal) and awaken the need inside us to find a connecting or unifying path (our need for a higher power, for grace and God).

Here's what some students have said about Father Rohr:

I was very touched not only that Rohr is returning to universal Christianity but also by the way he is doing so. The inward path is important, not the path to the church. In itself, the path inward is a natural step in the Christian tradition. I see Rohr more as a spiritual master and priest and less as a teacher. He teaches much more comprehensively than just about the Enneagram. His language from the Christian tradition appeals to me, as do Rohr's words about the fundamental sin and the invitation of the spirit.

He speaks the same way about the nine faces of Jesus and (like Bennett) places the Lord's Prayer on the Enneagram. He integrates psychology and religion. He questions many things, for example, and makes a distinction as to whether a monk retreats because of his spirituality to lead an ascetic life or whether it's a monk with Type 5 who simply lives by his type.

We also participated in workshops from other Enneagram teachers and with Rohr. We think it is advantageous that he pays so much attention to the three centers. He doesn't just give information about the centers but also emphasizes how important it is to strive for more balance between the centers and how that can be done. When you read his books, he already assumes that you know the Christian terminology, since he doesn't explain it. I think the best thing about Rohr is that you feel his (Franciscan) spiritual foundation so strongly — his real life energy.

The oral tradition: Helen Palmer and David Daniels

The Enneagram had its breakthrough to the general public thanks to instructors who had learned about the Enneagram in Berkeley in the 1970s. One of the early and better-known authors is the psychologist Helen Palmer. Her first book about the Enneagram appeared in 1988. She taught psychology at Berkeley University and also offered meditation exercises for the students. During her own psychology studies, she had already started her meditation training, her self-exploration, and her spiritual journey with her Buddhist teacher.

Palmer came in contact with the Enneagram in the 1970s and read the book *Transpersonal Psychologies* (edited by Charles T. Tart), where John Lilly presented a brief overview of Ichazo's typology. Palmer began exploring the Enneagram with her students on this basis. She worked with the panel method, in which she interviewed several students who recognized each other in the same type. One subject of the study was the obstacles the students encountered during their meditation exercises. Palmer discovered only much later that Evagrius Ponticus had already studied this topic, about 1600 years earlier.

The oral tradition can't be mentioned without also naming someone who accompanied Helen Palmer in her initial steps. In 1988, Helen Palmer and the psychiatrist David Daniels established a training program for Enneagram teachers: the Enneagram Professional Training Program (EPTP). At the time, Daniels was still a professor of psychiatry at Stanford Medical School and had long had his own practice as a psychiatrist. EPTP training is now organized by way of Enneagram Worldwide, where David Daniels still plays a leading role. Daniels played a key role in the development of the training program.

The Helen Palmer and David Daniels approach

The main characteristic of the work of Helen Palmer and David Daniels is what they call the *narrative* tradition. Among other qualities, this one includes self-exploration and knowledge transfer through the type assessment interview and the panel interview. The method taught at their school, Enneagram Worldwide, is also called the *psychospiritual integration* method, which is the method you read about in this book. Palmer integrates into the method the knowledge and experience from her job as a psychologist and her broad spiritual training. The sources of her knowledge and inspiration are quite different: the Vedas, Jung, Sufism, Gurdjieff, Christian mysticism, as well as Kabbalah. Palmer has a scientific orientation and is still studying, writing, researching, and publishing whatever is related to the Enneagram and inner work. She is familiar with a wide range of meditation formats and breathing techniques and explains exactly what the various forms have to offer and how their effects are different, and also which forms work well for which person and which do not.

Palmer tries to introduce people to what she calls direct experience and show them how to get there. The only thing that stands between humans and a direct spiritual experience is their type. Palmer doesn't just lecture — she lets people experience the various states of consciousness in her seminars. She brings people into contact with their inner knowledge and helps them to train their intuition and receptivity to enable direct experiences. In her seminars, Palmer almost exclusively teaches beyond the type.

Here's what some students have said about Helen Palmer:

> As soon as Helen starts to speak at a seminar or a reading, I feel that she is in a class of her own. I have heard a lot of people talk about the Enneagram, but no one brings nearly as much depth, precision, integrity, education, and, most important, spirituality to it as she does. I always had problems with meditation, but a meditation led by Helen transports not just me but the entire room into a deep state of being. Thanks to Helen, I learned how exciting my inner being is and how wonderful it is to spend time there during meditation. I meditate, thanks to Helen.

Here's what some students have said about David Daniels:

> A seminar with David Daniels was my first contact with the Enneagram. It made a strong impression on me, and as a result I took part in the EPTP training two months later. David doesn't just talk about compassion and goodness — he embodies them. He has clinical and therapeutic experience in guiding people; he not only offers a lot of knowledge and vivid stories and anecdotes but also has a sense of humor. When he interviews a panel, there is always room for tears and laughter. At one panel, I received a great gift from David: He taught me compassion for myself — not a mental concept of compassion, but rather the deep, inner experience of it.

The diamond approach: Hamid Ali and Sandra Maitri

Sandra Maitri and Hamid Ali were members of Naranjo's group Seekers After Truth (SAT) in Berkeley in 1971. For four years, Naranjo taught the group about Theravada and Tibetan Buddhism, Hinduism, Sufism, Confucianism, and the Fourth Way — with a focus on using the Enneagram as a tool. The group was strongly oriented toward Gurdjieff. The focus was on "overcoming the personality, the conditioned feeling of an independent self that consists of mental constructs from the past in order to connect with spiritual depth" (taken from Maitri's *The Spiritual Dimension of the Enneagram: Nine Faces of the Soul*).

Hamid Ali, born in Kuwait, came to the United States at age 18 and studied at Berkeley University. He received a bachelor's degree in algebra and, later, a master's degree in the natural sciences. He completed his doctorate in psychology with a focus on Reichian therapy. Ali develops an approach to inner work that he calls the diamond approach to inner realization. This doesn't explicitly teach about the Enneagram, but students who know the Enneagram can see how it is implicitly used for self-exploration. I consider his book *Facets of Unity: The Enneagram of Holy Ideas* (published under his pen name, A.H. Almaas) to be one of the best books about the Higher Self in the Enneagram. Ali teaches the diamond approach at the Ridhwan School, an institution he founded in 1976, principally based in Berkley, California, and Boulder, Colorado. Maitri, in addition to giving readings and lessons on the Enneagram all over the world, is connected to the Ridhwan School as a lecturer.

Here's what some students have said about Sandra Maitri:

> It inspires me that Sandra touches a deeper spiritual layer through her nature. It's hard to describe, but it's evident that she has lived through the Enneagram. Her lectures aren't cerebral. They touch you on a different level — they speak to your heart. She tends to activate the unconscious, in the area of my subject, and makes the state of being beyond this tangible — what is possible for me in terms of growth. She uses the Enneagram as a compass, to let us use self-exploration to experience how the different Enneagram aspects work within us, with the aim of letting go of the ego more and more. In working with Maitri, a student senses the emphasis on the spiritual path, letting go of the ego, and working at the level of the heart center.

The levels of development: Don Richard Riso and Russ Hudson

The second well-known Catholic Enneagram author is the former Jesuit Don Richard Riso. He works with Russ Hudson at the Enneagram Institute in New York. Riso studied the Enneagram with Bob Ochs (a student of Naranjo) at the Jesuit Seminary in Toronto in 1973. At the time, material on the Enneagram was still quite limited, and just like others, Riso began to research, develop, and elaborate it further. He discovered that certain parts of the psychological description of the types were missing — a description of how the types act at a healthy, developed level, for example. As a nonpsychologist, he was inspired by Freud, Jung, Karen Horney, Erich Fromm, and other psychologists.

One of the contributions by Riso and Hudson to the development of the Enneagram consists of the nine levels of development they prepared in detail for each of the nine types. The levels are divided into three healthy, three average, and three unhealthy ways of acting on a psychological level. The authors see this not just as an indispensable contribution to the Enneagram but also to personality research in general. They named every type on each development level — 81, in total. Starting out from the familiar approach in psychology that every person knows of a basic fear and a basic desire, Riso and Hudson worked out the motivational basis for each of these 81 types. As a result, they added many elements to the original work of Ichazo and Naranjo and worked out detailed type descriptions. They also developed the Riso–Hudson Enneagram Type Indicator (RHETI) and other personality tests (QUEST–TAS).

Here's what some students have said about Riso and Hudson:

Don and Russ immediately made a lasting impression on me when I met them for the first time: warm, compassionate, and inspiring. I appreciate their openness and commitment, combined with their inner peace, which is immediately noticeable during a seminar. Everything indicates that they have reached the healthier levels of development. They motivate and challenge you to remember how you really are. They make it clear that we aren't our egos, that we are much more, and with their engaging sense of humor they make this very acceptable.

Don and Russ clearly show respect for the nine types. They never typecast anyone or say that someone has assessed themselves incorrectly. They leave you time and space to discover your own type. This creates a sense of safety. Their approach is intellectual, theoretical. and thorough. Everything starts with a clear introduction of the types, which also becomes profound: The exercises usually consist of monologues and repetition questions. There is also a short panel now and then to demonstrate certain concepts.

I think that the phase the model is in and the recognition it has received in broad psychological circles would not have come about if Don and Russ hadn't done so much groundbreaking work. The development levels in particular explain the differences within the types and clarify the dynamics of a type. In individual coaching, the development levels are an indispensable tool for me. As soon as the levels enable people to realize which negative spiral they're in and where this will take them, many consciously decide not to further follow the chosen path. It's often a dramatic turning point. The process of becoming aware now happens more quickly than before.

Chapter **20**

The Inner Work Tradition

I n this chapter, I tell you about my personal search for the origins of the inner work at the core of the Enneagram as well as what this search has yielded in the form of concrete knowledge and insights. The inner work that is once again gaining in popularity is rooted in centuries-old traditions. I talk about Evagrius Ponticus and Plato in several places in this book, but in this chapter, I take a closer look at the ideas of the era in which they lived and about their possible sources of inspiration.

REMEMBER

To get to know yourself, do everything you can to discover your own roots, especially your cultural and spiritual roots. On the other hand, it isn't necessary to know all that prehistory in order to work with the Enneagram. This information is for you whether you're an enthusiast or you're just interested in the origin and background of the Enneagram. Think of this chapter as a source of inspiration (the dessert!) or as a way to deepen your understanding.

Assessing the Truth and Value of Ancient Texts

Every letter, symbol, ritual, or book was once thought of or written by a human being, even texts that many people consider sacred, such as the Tanakh, the Bible, the Quran, the Vedas. I always keep this in mind when I search for the truth. The fact that something has been repeated by many people over a long period doesn't make it any truer for me. What makes something true for me is a confirmation via my own inner experience, among other things. By perceiving within myself how my fixations and passions reinforce each other, for example, I was able to integrate that fact into my understanding of the Enneagram. In any case, it was a clue that made me want to take a closer look at the Enneagram, simply because if the Enneagram were right about this aspect, then maybe it was right about other aspects as well.

When I read books about ancient scriptures or ancient spiritual traditions, I recognize many things that I've learned on my journey of discovery with the Enneagram as well as insights I've gained along the way. With my background in social and cultural sciences, it's not surprising that something like this fascinates me, but there's even more. During my studies, I found insights that complemented what was written in modern books and helped me on the path of my personal development.

I learned from Pythagoras, from Evagrius Ponticus, from Plato, from Plotinus, and from many others. Even though these insights aren't part of the Enneagram practice, they're important enough for me to mention in relevant places in this book. I consider this to be valuable knowledge from individuals who have contributed to all the earlier development. There are also descriptions of insights and experiences that I can't accept as true simply because they don't speak to my personal experience. Maybe they'll speak to me at some later date, or maybe they've already spoken to you. I don't consider these things impossible, and I find them interesting enough to take a closer look, because they were written by people who also described experiences that I have already encountered.

On the trail of the Egyptians

Not so long ago, I thought of Egypt in terms of pyramids, pharaohs, hieroglyphs, and sphinxes. I had no idea about the religion of ancient Egypt. While searching for the roots of the Enneagram, I discovered how much the ancient Egyptian religion, the Judeo-Christian tradition, Islam, and modern spirituality have in common.

In the next few sections, you can find a small selection from the many, many aspects, comparable insights, and characteristics my encounter with the ancient Egyptian religion has yielded. I now feel a connection to the people who were already busy with their inner work 4,000 years ago in ways comparable to what is happening today. I also realize that people are probably rediscovering things now that were already known then — that they're remembering them again, in other words. Maybe you can learn even more from them in this area.

Tangible and intangible, visible and invisible worlds

Many ancient peoples had a well-defined philosophy of nature: It was assumed that imperceptible forces were at work behind all perceptible events. This isn't an absurd consideration, because even though you can perceive the effect of gravity, for example, the force itself that triggers it isn't perceptible.

Because it was possible to recognize the effects of causes that couldn't be seen, it was also assumed that there lay an immaterial, nonmaterial, and invisible world — the world of the spirit. — next to the material and visible world. If something couldn't be explained by what you saw, you attributed it to higher forces and powers. These were called gods, or God in monotheistic traditions. For the Egyptians, it was self-evident that everything that could be perceived by the senses was an expression of the immaterial world, that the immaterial world expresses itself as a form in the material world. The ancient Egyptians therefore thought that humans also carried all the elements of the material and immaterial world within themselves. This is not wrong, either: Humans are structured by the forces and properties of nature and the cosmos. Conversely, everything that is in humans and can be perceived in humans can also be found in nature and in the cosmos. This is the basis of the view that human beings, as microcosms, are copies of the macrocosm.

The divine system of Heliopolis

Several divine systems existed in ancient Egypt; the most widespread one — and the one that proved to be quite significant in its time — was the system represented by Heliopolis. In this system, the gods represent the structure of the world of the spirit.

The spiritual world was divided into three levels, and the same three principles always worked together on each level. These three principles were presented to the people as a triad of gods. The first and highest level was that of the cosmic spirit: the creative primordial law that underlies everything that exists. The first god in this system was Re, or Atun, the sun god. He awakened new life in the second god, Nut, the primeval ocean, which resulted in the birth of the third god, Geb, the original form of the earth.

These three principles of the triad of gods match the universal law of threes (with its three forces) that is at the heart of the Enneagram. (For more on that topic, see — naturally — Chapter 3.) Re or Atun is the symbol of the fertilizing, providing, active, male principle. The symbol of Nut is the principle that is present in everything and that manifests itself as the receptive, passive, feminine. The collaboration between the two creates a new form in which primeval will and primordial law are revealed: Geb. The third principle is a neutral principle in that it lets the active and the passive work together — the two can become aware of themselves precisely because they take shape in this form.

Students of the ancient spiritual traditions noticed that these three primal principles — creative information, realizing energy, and the expression of both of these principles when they become the new form — were active everywhere and in everything (including themselves).

The third level: The human mind

By engaging with the human mind, you're making the leap down from the first level to the third level of the system of gods at Heliopolis. At this level, the creative principle was named Osiris. Here, Osiris stands for the true self of humanity — a true self that you can recognize from the Enneagram. Acting as the creative principle on the spiritual level, Osiris urges people to become conscious and be active. Osiris is a symbol for the law or destiny of humanity, for the latent core of the true self, for the destiny of humans to become aware of themselves. This is why Osiris is never depicted in animal form, but rather always as a human being.

The second, receptive principle at this level is called Isis. It stands for the soul of humankind. Combining the first and second principle — the receiving soul accepting the spirit striving for consciousness — leads to insight and self-knowledge in the form of the consciously realized true self: Horus, the falcon god, child to Isis and Osiris. A parallel to the Enneagram can be seen here as well, when someone speaks of the Higher Self, in which higher thinking (Osiris) and the energy of the higher virtue (Isis) come together.

Seth and Nephthys, Egyptian symbols for fixation and passion

Interestingly, two other symbols are known in the system of gods at the third level: Seth as the half-brother of Osiris and Nephthys as the half-sister of Isis. As is often the fate of half-brothers and -sisters, they take a lower position. They also represent the active and the receiving principle but on a sensual level, in the sensual world, which — in contrast to the nonmaterial, spiritual world — is subject to transience and passes through cycles of development bound to time (birth and death, spring and winter, and so on). In the ancient Egyptian religion, the suffering of Isis (the human soul) was caused by Seth's active intervention in the sensual world. This can be explained as humanity's inclination toward evil — the inclination to align oneself not with the spirit but with matter, with all the consequences that this has.

In the Egyptian religion, Seth and Nephthys stand for what is called the *Lower Self* in the Enneagram. Seth represents the thinking of the head center (the fixations), and Nephthys the feeling of the heart center (the passions). In the Enneagram, you see Seth's intervention in the sensual world as the suffering caused by the fixations that drive humans to act and that block the way toward (receptive) being.

The Sphinx holds up a mirror to humans

Blessed is the lion that is eaten by a human,

thus the lion becomes human.

But wretched is the human who is devoured by the lion,

thus the human becomes a lion.

—Saying from the Gospel of Thomas in the Nag Hammadi scriptures

The approach used by the ancient spiritual traditions is that humans are dual beings. On one hand, humans are animals with animal characteristics and primary reactions, filled with passions, desires, and the tendency to assert themselves, to distinguish themselves, to mark their territories, to rule, and to possess (their reptilian brain). On the other hand, humans are beings of a higher order, with the capacity to become conscious and reflect, to contemplate their thoughts, feelings, and actions, and to perceive (the neocortex).

The Sphinx reflects these two aspects of a human and does so in the correct, desired relationship. The majestic face of the Sphinx reflects this latter, higher aspect in the nature of a human: the head and the knowledge of the spiritual order are the leaders. From there, the lion's forces are directed and used. If it's the other way around, if the animal leads inside the human, this has serious consequences: The spiritual being isn't used, the primary reaction and functioning in the material world are all that remains, and all you're left with is suffering.

EXAMPLE

Humans still carry the lion inside them. Let's look again at Stan (Type 8) and Margaret (Type 9). As children, they dealt with their insecurities in their own way. Margaret finds it hard to assert herself; she has trouble accessing the energy of anger that gives people assertiveness. Stan, on the other hand, often shows the anger with which he asserts himself quite clearly in order to protect himself and to hide his vulnerable inner self and his fears. Stan's parents taught him that he is carrying a lion inside who takes good care of him, sometimes too well; sometimes, the lion also needs a break and needs to sleep for a while. But Stan can awaken it whenever he needs it. These same parents taught Margaret that she also carries a lion inside herself, just like her brother Stan. This particular lion is a bit of a slacker, however; he should help Margaret more often. All she really has to do is consciously call on this lion within her whenever she needs its help.

About the mystery schools

The mystery schools of the ancient world are probably comparable to what are called spiritual schools today — training institutes for development and awareness. Every era and every place has its own language. The Greek Plutarch (first century AD) was a priest of the Mystery Temple of Delphi and wrote about the myth of Isis and Osiris as well as the evolutionary path of humans. In his opinion, the goal of the mystery schools was to recognize "the primary ruling entity — the one being that can only be perceived through the spirit."

Mystery schools were institutions where — in the language of the Heliopolis system of gods — the consciousness of Osiris could unfold. The mystery schools aimed to restore the balance in the world that was disturbed by Seth — a disturbance that led individuals to direct their thoughts, feelings, and interests exclusively toward the exterior world rather than toward their interior selves.

People are familiar with this lack of balance because they see it acted out in Enneagram seminars, where the whole point is to learn how not to be so easily knocked off balance by the outside world. In seminars, you learn how to restore your inner balance and to focus your attention more on yourself instead of on the outside world. This is also based on a higher goal: the idea that you contribute to a better, restored world by restoring your inner balance.

REMEMBER

The Egyptians believed that the world was out of balance. People were too focused on the world of the senses and on material goods, which are at the root of all evil. When you look at the consequences of your actions as they have played out in the present state of the world — in the environment, for example — the Egyptians might not have been all that wrong 5,000 years ago. As long as humans permit their governments to be guided only by economic goals and developments, Seth will continue to rule.

The myth of Isis and Osiris

The myth of Isis and Osiris is the story of the development path on the third level, that of the spirit of humanity. This story is found in the Pyramid Texts, the oldest of the ancient Egyptian funerary texts, dating from the period of the Old Kingdom (2650–2150 BC). The development path is illustrated in symbolic language and seems to be comparable to what is still practiced today.

The path of development was once called the path of mysteries, which can be divided into different phases. It starts by reestablishing the desire for the lost unity with the spirit. Even the earthly aspects of the soul (Nephthys) will then play a part because they feel that even in the sensual world, fulfillment can be experienced only when it's aligned with the spiritual order.

Based on this renewed desire, the student of the mystery school prepares for the second phase — the one that will awaken Osiris so that the student's true self can be realized. In a sense, the students detach themselves from the many parts of the sensual world and the shadow world during the third phase and receive impulses from the spiritual world on their own.

When Horus defeats Seth, this means that the students overcome their inner tendencies that bind them to the sensual world and lead them toward evil. Then the students reach the stage of freedom; they're no longer bound to the material world. They live in the world but are no longer of it. In the fourth phase, a harmonious relationship is established between the material and the spiritual worlds; the students are at the service of their true selves and function as an expression of the spiritual world. The eye of Horus that was stolen by Seth, that thing which enables the discernment of the true self, is recovered and given to the true self, Osiris.

REMEMBER

This ancient wisdom has thus not lost any of its timeliness. You can also find these aspects of development in this book expressed in the language of the Enneagram — just think of the different levels of consciousness and the need to train one's self-observation, reflection, and discernment.

The wisdom of the Greek philosophers

At first glance, moving from the wisdom of the ancient Egyptian religions or mystery schools to the Greek philosophers seems like quite a leap. When you look at how knowledge was actually transferred through the ages, however, it looks more likely. When you know that story, it becomes even more clear why you can recognize so much of the ancient wisdom in the Enneagram practice today. In earlier chapters, I describe only a few short examples, but of course there is much more. This chapter makes up for the brevity of earlier discussions.

The Greek philosophers contemplated questions that you would now consider part of the theological domain. In ancient Greece, no distinction was made between philosophy, psychology, and theology. The spiritual well-being of human beings was — as you might say today — considered holistically. *Philosopher* literally means "lover of wisdom" — all wisdom, not just one corner of it.

For Plato, philosophers were people who were filled with the love of wisdom, a kind of wisdom that gives immortality to those who fall under its spell. In the upcoming sections, you'll find out more about the inspiration Plato found in Pythagoras. But first, continue reading about the places where wisdom was sought and found. For that, you need to return to Egypt.

The cradle of wisdom

Humans know from numerous sages, philosophers, and mystics of the ancient world that many studied in Alexandria (Egypt) and Babylon for many years. A few centuries before the birth of Christ, Alexandria was a cosmopolitan city — a bustling economic and spiritual center of the Eastern Mediterranean. The best scholars from all over the world — logicians, astronomers, healers, and philosophers — were meeting there. The city's library was so substantial that it was only surpassed in the number of volumes it contained late in the 19th century.

Alexandria was also a melting pot in terms of religion; the old Egyptian religion was interwoven with Greek and Eastern teachings. (Trade with India was flourishing at the time.) Allegedly, a Buddhist mission was already under way in 250 BC and the Buddha is mentioned. Alexandria can be considered the origin of movements such as Gnosticism (more on this later in this chapter) and neoplatonism.

Pythagoras, Euclid, Archimedes, Plotinus, Clemens (founder of scientific Christian theology), Origen, and Valentinus taught in Alexandria over many centuries. The Desert Fathers, who were the first Christian monks who retreated to hermitages for study and prayer (including Evagrius Ponticus), also lived in the desert south of Alexandria.

ORIGIN OF THE THERAPISTS

From a text by Philo of Alexandria (a Jewish religious scholar), it's known that an Egyptian-Jewish group called Therapeutae settled at Lake Mariout near Alexandria. They were regarded as the forerunners of the later (Christian) monastic communities.

Philo writes that their name meant "healing," among other things, and that they practiced a healing method superior to that of the city. Though only the body was healed in the city, the Therapeutae also healed the soul, which is subject to severe suffering and almost incurable diseases, including being plagued by lust, desire, fear, greed, injustice, and immoderation.

In a region where, and at a time when, one imagined gods to be real or believed, it's remarkable that Philo sees the healing power of the Therapeutae as the result of their own efforts — the way of life they chose and the spiritual exercises they practiced. Because of their ascetic life, by the way, some folks have hypothesized that the Therapeutae were influenced by the Buddhist mission. The ascetic way of life that is characteristic of Buddhists wasn't previously known in the Jewish tradition. The linguist Zacharias Thundy therefore speculates that the name Therapeutae is a Hellenistic malapropism of the Indian word for traditional Buddhists: Theravada.

When you're looking for the origin of words and names, you can also consider whether the current (psycho-)therapists owe their name to the Greek word for "healing" or to these ascetically living healers of the soul. Just like these soul healers, modern psychotherapists are focused on a person's inner self. It's equally striking that the ailments of the soul as distinguished by ancient therapists like Philo of Alexandria correspond to the passions or vices that form the basis of each type in the Enneagram. By this I don't mean to imply that the Enneagram might have had its origin there — there's no evidence of that — but the correspondences are striking. It's more logical, however, to assume that in a comparable exploration of the inner being — through self-observation and meditation, for example — the same causes of human suffering can be found.

Pythagoras — God seeker and spiritual guide

What was so exciting about Pythagoras? He founded a mystery school from which his teachings found their way into many other mystery schools — and inspired movements that still exist today. His exploration of the cosmos and numbers was part of his search for God. He was convinced that God is expressed in everything in creation, and he hoped to come closer to unraveling the mystery of God by exploring the secrets of creation. The theory of numbers thus originated in a spiritual search.

Now, Pythagoras's view that the spiritual world is expressed by the sensual and material world is no coincidence. In Alexandria, Pythagoras studied everything that was sacred to the Egyptians: astronomy, geometry, number theory, and music as well as all divine mysteries. Among other things, the merit of Pythagoras lay in that he passed on to the West what he learned in Egypt.

PYTHAGORAS — MORE THAN JUST A THEOREM

Pythagoras is mainly known as a mathematician, but he was much more than that. He was born on Samos, a Greek island in the eastern Aegean Sea, and lived from about 582 to 507 BC. Like many geniuses, he has been credited with both great wisdom and madness. No writings from his hand have been preserved, so what is known comes from oral tradition and from what others — Herodotus, Plato, and Aristotle, for example — have written about him. Two biographies were written about Pythagoras (by Iamblichus and Porphyry of Tyre) only in the third century AD. It says a lot that even after seven centuries, Pythagoras was still so well-known and considered to be so important that people wanted to record his life. Plato was credited with having said, "There are men and gods and beings like Pythagoras."

Number theory as the consequence of a spiritual search

Following in the footsteps of the Egyptians, Pythagoras believed that the world of the senses reflects the world of the mind — but also that the world of the mind consists of harmony and numbers and that the world of the senses is also determined by numbers. He strove for harmony and the purity of the soul, which he thought could be supported through the knowledge of numerical ratios, among other things. His teachings therefore focused on numbers. This is difficult for people to imagine today because numbers are used exclusively to express quantities.

At that time — and even more so for the Pythagoreans — numbers also had a qualitative meaning because they were considered an expression of the spiritual world. You can still find this today, for example, in the Jewish alphabet: Each letter has a number and a corresponding symbolic meaning. For example, 18 stands for *life*. Numbers don't just have a quantitative and functional value but also a qualitative, symbolic one. From that perspective, the number represents a state rather than a quantity. In Pythagorean number theory, the numbers had the following meanings:

>> **1** stood for the highest thing imaginable, the invisible spirit, the unity from which everything has been and still is created, the point from which all expansion unfolds, the point at which all characteristics are laid out as in a seed; in the tradition of the Egyptians, it also stands for creative thinking.

>> **2** results from the division of 1. In a quantitative approach, 2 is seen as the sum of two 1s; in the qualitative approach, 1 breaks into two poles when it's divided: an active and a passive one, a fertilizing and a receiving one. In this respect, 2 is the state of polarity. It also stands for the beginning: Where the division begins, time also begins. In the Egyptian tradition, it stands for consciousness.

>> **3** is the third principle, the form, which emerges as a result of this creation and of the possibility of joining an active, fertilizing force and a passive, receiving force. In the sensual world, the form is the child in which father and mother take shape together. In the spiritual world, these are Re, Nut, and Geb. In the tradition of the Egyptians, 3 also stands for insight.

Every number thus has a qualitative meaning. The perfect number of the Pythagoreans was 10, resulting from 1 + 2 + 3 + 4, the tetractys. It was considered the expression of the highest perfection and holiness, and the Pythagoreans saw it as a perfect description of the structure of reality. It was the symbol of the constantly repeating and continuing creation, which projected itself onto a lower level at every repetition. This makes sense when you look at nature: In each unit, you always find smaller units at a lower level. The Milky Way contains solar systems as smaller units, and the laws of the higher unit apply in the same way here as well.

Pythagoras also imagined the numbers as forms, for example, as triangular or square numbers. Square numbers, for example, are

1	4	9	16
x	xx	xxx	xxxx
	xx	xxx	xxxx
		xxx	xxxx
			xxxx

Triangular numbers are

3	6	10
x	x	x
xx	xx	xx
	xxx	xxx
		xxxx

Mathematical harmony in music and scale

According to Pythagoras, numerical relationships dominate the universe, but their laws are also expressed in other ways in music, for example. When you pluck a string and then the halved string, you hear two tones that sound good — harmonious — together. The harmonious note known as E is produced by dividing the length of the A string into 2:3 (fifths); the D, by dividing the string length into 3:4 (fourths); and so on. Pythagoras defined the musical scale that is still known and used today.

But for Pythagoras the most important aspect of musical tones was the spiritual one. Because humans experience a pure tone as harmonious, his fundamental belief was that humans seem to react to the oscillations of the tones. It was and still is thought that the soul of a human can also be healthy or sick and is thus in a state of harmony or disharmony.

Precisely because humans react to the oscillations of tones, it was assumed that harmonious tones or music could help pacify a soul in disharmony and bring it into balance. According to his students, Pythagoras was a master who could strengthen wounded souls through music. A modern example of this principle is a singing bowl massage. I don't know much about its effect, but I have heard that people experience healing from this and find inner peace.

Of acousticians and mathematicians

Two aspects played a role in the way Pythagoreans approached the sciences: their relationship to the world of the mind and their expression in the sensual world. This is an example of duality: the distinction between two worlds.

In contrast to the modern view of scientific research, Pythagoras considered thinking to be an expression of the spiritual and thus superior to sensual perception. He thought that pure knowledge was directed toward the immaterial, toward a higher order than the material. The earthly is only a (lower) imitation of the spiritual.

Mathematicians today don't really understand this perspective and share it even less. By the way, they also owe their job title to Pythagoras. The *mathemata* were truths that could be seen, so they were derived from what could be perceived with the senses. Pythagoras saw them as one side of a coin. The other side consisted of the so-called *acousmata* — traditional sayings or formulas that referred to important rules of life and were related to the spiritual world.

After the death of Pythagoras, acousticians and mathematicians began to dispute. The latter felt superior to the acousticians and looked down on them because, they argued, the acousticians simply believed what they heard, not what they themselves perceived or recognized. But the mathematicians had only understood part of Pythagoras's teachings — it had escaped them that a good student of the mystery school had to know and apply both aspects of Pythagoras's teachings, not just the part that appealed to them personally. The dispute alone was completely contrary to the teachings of Pythagoras: By looking only at the visible world, you inevitably became the plaything of human passions and contentiousness. And that is precisely what happened.

Other examples from Pythagoras's teachings

According to Pythagoras, the disharmony that humans experienced was caused by the fact that the worlds of the spiritual and the sensual were off balance. This in turn was caused by the fact that people focused primarily or even exclusively on the sensual world. Because they could no longer experience spiritual unity, humans directed themselves toward the strangest things in the material world. For Pythagoras, the soul's attachment to the sensual world was precisely what explained the existence of reincarnation. Pythagoras proclaimed that everything that is created is reborn. According to him, nothing is completely new, and everything that is born alive is therefore related to each other. Pythagoreans therefore didn't eat animal products. It is said that Pythagoras also preached to the animals, as St. Francis of Assisi did later. That might be why he was accused of madness. Given the connectedness between everything and everyone, men and women were considered and treated equally and they held community property. These aspects also reappear in later mystery schools. At least at first glance, the rules of the Pythagorean order were rather strange. Here are a few items from the long list:

>> Don't eat beans.

>> Don't pick up anything that has fallen.

>> Don't step over crossbars.

>> Don't start a fire with iron.

>> Don't walk on main roads.

It's easy to smirk at these regulations and see them as primitive taboos. I'm fascinated by the profundity of the remaining regulations; I want to know what's behind them. Knowing that the language of the time was rich in images and symbols, you might ask what was meant here. For example, the rule of not starting a fire with iron can be interpreted to mean that the anger of another person shouldn't be stirred up with sharp words. Given that interpretation, this would be an example of a rule for a life without strife and in harmony. Imagine how different the world might look today if everyone made an effort not to let other people's anger flare up.

No friendship comes close to the Pythagorean one

Another wonderful example of what the school of Pythagoras stood for is a community rule related to friendship. The unbreakable bonds of friendship among the community members didn't just come about on the basis that they considered each other nice. It affected all members of the community, for these two reasons:

>> **They all had the same goal.** They wanted the goal of unity and connectedness with the world of the spirit.

>> **They recognized the divine possibilities of each person.** The friendship among Pythagoreans has assumed mythical and proverbial forms.

The path of development in the Pythagorean school

For the Pythagoreans, it was particularly important to break the earthly ties that bound them to disputes, disharmony, and desire. When Pythagoreans felt anger rising inside, their goal was to command themselves to stop. They would make an effort to let go and relax in order to regain their composure.

After inner reflection, if the Pythagoreans came to the conclusions that the cause lay with the other person, they could explain the situation to the other and rebuke them, if needed. The Pythagoreans called this a *reorganization*. This was the nice way in which conflicts were handled, not through reactions that led to an escalation of the dispute, but rather by changing the conflict situation with the help of insight, patience, and mindfulness. Nowadays, this approach is used professionally by mediators.

The mystery path of Pythagoras was conveyed in his holy speech, which was at least partially recorded in *The Golden Verses*, a collection of Pythagorean sayings compiled by one of his disciples in the first century AD. Although this work contains some wonderful sections, it would be too much to include the entire text in this book. Here are just two excerpts:

> *Of the others, you make a friend of the one who is the most excellent. Let yourself be converted to leniency through gentle words and useful deeds. Don't get into a fight with your friend over a minor incident as long as you can, because ability lives close to necessity.*

> *Don't flaunt appearances at the wrong time, like someone who doesn't know what is appropriate. But also don't be petty: Moderation is the best in everything. Do what will not harm you, and think before you do it. Don't let sleep drop upon your tender eyes until you have considered each of your works of this day three times: "Where did I fail? What have I done? What have I left behind?"*

About exoterics and esoterics

It wasn't easy to be a student of Pythagoras. Before Pythagoras accepted a student, he first checked how this person talked about his parents and peers and then observed his behavior and what made him happy or sad.

If the student was accepted, he was tested during the first three years. He received all kinds of tasks. Above all, however, Pythagoras apparently took every opportunity to show his contempt for the student. This was how he tested stamina and zeal. Only after this trial phase was finished were you considered a true student of the mysteries. In the following five years, the student was only allowed to learn and listen in silence, because the most difficult form of self-discipline is to keep the tongue in check. During this time, the students followed Pythagoras's lectures behind a curtain; they were exoterics, from the Greek word *eksôterikós*, or "outside the circle." After these five years, they were allowed to continue their journey behind the curtain in direct contact with Pythagoras. Now they were esoterics (from *esôterikós*" — belonging to an inner circle") for the rest of their lives.

Plato

Plato (428–347 BC) was destined for a political career, but he switched to philosophy after meeting Socrates. He became convinced that humanity must develop wisdom, justice, and moderation in order to survive. With the current economic and environmental crises caused by greed, this assumption still seems relevant.

Plato taught that people must first identify what they're oriented toward before they can develop the qualities they need. So they first need to know what these qualities are: justice, courage, temperance, and wisdom. In his striving to recognize the essence of things, Plato developed what is today known as his theory of ideas. (In Chapter 19, I talk about how these four virtues are central to the Sufi Enneagram. Greek philosophy, gnosticism, and neoplatonism had a great influence on various movements in Islam — hence the similarities in thought.)

According to Plato, true philosophers are those who detach themselves from the ephemeral and material world and strive for perpetual wisdom out of love — thus following the mystery path that Pythagoras already taught in his strictly ascetic school. It's well-known that Plato was greatly inspired by Pythagoras. In Plato's time, this also involved the step from teaching behind the closed doors of the mystery schools to taking the mystery path in plain sight and for sharing with others. (This is comparable to G.I. Gurdjieff's Fourth Way, which I discuss in Chapter 18.)

As a successor to Pythagoras, Plato believed that the entire material cosmos was permeated by mathematical relationships that led to perfect order and harmony. This resulted in the belief that although the superficial everyday world was chaotic, it was based on a perfect, mathematical world that could not be perceived by the senses.

The allegory of the cave

Plato's allegory of the cave, in which he depicts the teachings of all the mystery schools, has become famous. Plato uses this metaphor to describe two worlds: the world of light and knowledge and the world of darkness and projections.

Imagine a cave that's connected to the outside world by a passageway, but where no daylight enters. People are trapped in the cave; they sit with their backs to the entrance and can see only the rear wall of the cave. That's all they have ever seen in their lives. Because they're tied up, neither can they see each other or themselves. Behind them is a wall, and behind the wall is a fire. People are moving between the wall and the fire. The fire causes the shadows of the moving people to be projected onto the cave's rear wall, where the prisoners can see them. The sounds of the movements are also reflected by the rear wall.

Plato claims that the chained people only perceive shadows and echoes and accept these as reality because that's all they know and see. Assume that one prisoner gains the necessary willpower to free himself and turn around. Then he would still be so tensed up, and it would be so painful and blinding for him to look into the fire, so confusing to see the moving people, that he would quickly want to turn back around to the reality that he understands. It takes time to be able to stay in the world of freedom and light, to get used to it and come to terms with living there.

Plato also used this as a warning to the mystery schools: The people who have experienced the world of light and talk about it are considered insane by the people who live in the "reality" of the sensual world. The other prisoners can't even imagine what that one person has seen, simply because they themselves have never experienced anything like it. It goes beyond what they can comprehend. Plato knew two examples of how his predecessors had fared in such cases: Pythagoras was exiled when his teachings from the mystery school reached the outside world; Socrates was actually murdered because his perceptions and teachings were incompatible with the insights and rules of the sensual world.

About gnosis

In the period after the Romans destroyed Jerusalem (70 AD), the gospels of the New Testament were written down. This was also when the dogmas and the teaching authority of the Roman Catholic Church first took hold. But there's another movement as well: Gnosticism is also a philosophy that has its roots in the first century after Christ.

In the book *The Hermetic Gnosis Through the Centuries,* the editor, Gilles Quispel, mentions that, in addition to the Judeo-Christian tradition and Greek philosophy, a third tradition had an influence on cultural heritage: the gnostic tradition. Quispel writes that "Gnostic Manichaeism has existed for over a thousand years and had millions of followers. It wasn't just limited to one people but spread among different peoples from the Atlantic to the Pacific Ocean. It was rightly called a world religion." It was an extremely peace-loving movement, and significant scriptures about it are still found to this day, such as the Nag Hammadi scriptures, a collection of early Christian and gnostic texts discovered near the Upper Egyptian town of Nag Hammadi in 1945.

Why this is relevant for getting to know the Enneagram's version of inner work becomes clear when you consider what is meant by *gnosis*. The Greek word *gnosis* means knowledge or insight. A student of the early gnostic theologian Valentinus (AD 100—c. 160) put it this way:

> *Gnosis is*
>
> *the knowledge of who we were*
>
> *and what we have become,*
>
> *where we were*
>
> *and what we were thrown into,*
>
> *where we are rushing*
>
> *and what we are redeemed from,*
>
> *what birth is*
>
> *and what rebirth is.*

In this context, the word *gnosis* stands for inner knowledge and one's conscience. The belief of the gnostics isn't one in the sense of a particular church or religious movement. They place their inner knowledge and experience above any external authority. The inner authority arises from their knowledge. It isn't rational knowledge but rather the inner experience of human beings — an inner knowledge.

Gnosticism became an umbrella term for various mystical-religious movements — the hermetic gnosticism (Egypt), for example, but also the gnosticism of early Christianity. They share the recognition of an inner authority — an inner knowledge that is greater than any external authority. Early Christianity and the Apostolic Age were also oriented toward the gnostic. Only later did the Roman Catholic Church reject this doctrine as heresy. Nevertheless, several important figures of the Early Church, such as the great church father St. Augustine, were followers of gnostic movements for some time.

The discovery of the spirit within oneself is the path of *gnosis.* To this end, humans must overcome the material and the psychological within themselves. In this regard, the Enneagram shows similarities with the gnostic tradition — the focus, for example, on the way inward and the recognition of a higher entity as the inner authority. It also shares the gnostic tradition's emphasis on the uniqueness of the personal path each individual follows in their (spiritual) development and growth. In this respect, the Enneagram can be considered a modern version of gnosticism.

Plotinus and the Enneads

The Hellenistic philosopher Plotinus (204–270 AD) lived during the period when gnosticism flourished. He was considered one of the most important representatives (or even a founder) of neoplatonism. It's evident that Plato had a strong influence on him, among other sources. As a successor to Plato, Plotinus also believed in a dualistic reality — the existence of a spiritual world that is essentially different from the perceptible, sensual world.

However, Plotinus put more emphasis on a supreme, totally transcendent "One," containing no division, multiplicity, or distinction and beyond all categories of being and nonbeing. He placed all knowledge in the service of getting closer to the One. This is again comparable to Pythagoras. There's no explanation of what emerges from the One, but it's illustrated in many ways: as a never-ending source from which all kinds of rivers spring, as a tree that sends life from its roots into the branches and leaves without itself changing, or as the sun that always shines without losing its strength and brightness.

The fact that his student, Porphyry of Tyre, recorded the life and teachings of Plotinus and titled the book *The Enneads* in itself has nothing to do with the Enneagram. At that time, numbers were also considered significant in terms of quality and content. The number nine was considered sacred and so was the Ennead, a nine-pointed star, an ancient sacred symbol. That is probably why Porphyry and the unknown founders of the Enneagram chose this sign.

Plotinus was one of the first to connect the experience of happiness *(eudaimonia)* to human consciousness. This was another reason for his great influence on Western civilization, where the happiness and well-being of the individual is fundamental.

According to Plotinus, it's possible to experience real, true happiness by identifying with what is best in the universe. Happiness isn't dependent on physical things. On the contrary. Plotinus describes in *The Enneads* a different way to happiness and fulfillment — or to God, as Plotinus sees it. Recognizing the virtues and seeing that human suffering is caused by the vices has an effect on a deep (and difficult to understand) level. The transformation of vices into virtues is considered to be the way to happiness and to God. This is how human beings develop wisdom, moderation, courage, and righteousness. It can be compared to what is still practiced today in the method of psychospiritual integration with the Enneagram and what I describe in this *For Dummies* book.

THE HOLY NUMBER 9 AND THE STAR WITH NINE RAYS

Why was the number 9 considered holy? I think that someone could write an exciting book with all the explanations that are available. Here's just a summary:

- The number 9 is the highest of the single-digit numbers.

- It therefore symbolizes completeness and perfection.

- It's considered to be the number of transition and conversion.

- It's the last working period before the end, after which a new period or series or cycle starts again. (This is probably why the 9 was once placed at the top of the Enneagram symbol.)

- When you calculate the checksum of the numbers divisible by 9, the result is again 9 (2 x 9 = 18 and 1 + 8 = 9; 35 x 9 = 315 and 3 + 1 + 5 = 9). In Hebrew, the number 9 stands for the unchanging or universal truth; 9 is the result of 3 x 3, and even the 3 is a significant number.

Many spiritual or mystical traditions — Egyptian, Celtic, Greek, and Christian — include an Ennead of nine gods or goddesses or angelic choirs that represent an archetypal set of principles. The nine Egyptian gods were also called Enneads because it was said that they revealed the nine faces of God. (You might have met some of them earlier in this chapter.) The kabbalistic tree of life also has nine mystical levels. The Sufis call their 9-ray star No-Koonja or the Naqsh (seal).

REMEMBER

The philosophy of Plotinus still yields a powerful influence. His thoughts as passed down by his student Porphyry in *The Enneads* make for inspiring reading today. In the books and ideas of Ken Wilber (see Chapter 22) you can find great similarities and a strong influence of Plotinus' *The Enneads*.

The Desert Fathers

In the fourth and fifth centuries AD, monks moved into the desert in places such as Egypt. There, they dedicated their lives to prayer and to their striving to come closer to God. They worked hard to fight their inner vices and to assimilate the virtues. Their efforts still make them an important source of inspiration, especially for Christians who practice the Enneagram or write about it. The monk Evagrius Ponticus wrote a lot about his disciples, monasticism, and the inner path.

Evagrius Ponticus

Evagrius Ponticus (345–399) is considered a gifted monk and an outstanding philosopher. His thinking was strongly influenced by the early Christian theologian Origen of Alexandria (c. 184–c. 253). Evagrius explored a way of uniting with God and developed his teaching on this subject. To this end, he analyzed the disturbances that occur within humans. His experience as a frequently consulted spiritual guide gave him many psychological insights.

Evagrius considers the four main virtues to be these: mindfulness, righteousness, strength/power/courage/will, and moderation. He distinguishes between primary vices and simple vices that are derived from the former. He divides the primary vices in ascending order from substance to spirit: gluttony, lust, greed, sadness, anger, sluggishness, vanity, and pride. Evagrius believes that asceticism is the way to fight movement (through vices) and reach inner silence, or dispassion (*apatheia*). This belongs to the highest of all virtues: love. In their classification by Evagrius, the vices became known as the Christian mortal sins, or root sins. His vices and their transformation into virtues are also central to the Enneagram.

Although Evagrius lived in the desert as a hermit, he proved to be a true gnostic in his teaching. For him, the way to reach God was the way within. When the so-called fathers of the Catholic Church consolidated their dogmas and their authority, one result was that the teachings and writings of Evagrius were still banned 250 years after his death. Many of his works were preserved because they appeared under other names. His teachings were consistently studied and appreciated, especially in non-Catholic Christian circles, such as the Byzantine and Syrian churches. Today, about 1600 years after his death, Evagrius and his work are gaining interest again and are becoming better known. His reputation is being rehabilitated and, following in-depth research, his works are appearing under his name again.

Finding scriptures believed to have been lost

Many ancient writings have been rediscovered in the 20th century, some of them at Qumran, an archeological site on the West Bank on the edge of the Dead Sea. (Their hiding place gave the writings the name the Dead Sea Scrolls.) In 1945, another trove was discovered near the small village of Nag Hammadi in Upper Egypt and became known by the name of this location. A German translation with commentary was published by Hans-Martin Schenke and the Working Group for Coptic Gnostic Scriptures in 1960. It's possible that Athanasius, the archbishop of Alexandria, was involved in the disappearance of these works. Around 367 AD he wrote an Easter letter in which he listed which texts belong to the canon. This list corresponds exactly to what is known today as the New Testament. In this letter, he also warned against heretical writings. Anything considered gnostic — texts that talk of finding a path toward God with no interference from the church — were quickly labeled heretical. It's likely that monks hid writings that weren't on the approved list. It's possible, for example, that the scrolls of Nag Hammadi were hidden by monks from the nearby St. Pachomius Monastery. Christian and non-Christian, gnostic and non-gnostic scriptures were found at Nag Hammadi. The Christian texts contain revelations that were considered secret teachings and were intended only for initiates.

These early Christian writings are valuable because, thanks to them, you're introduced to a powerful spiritual tradition from the first century of the era. You can rediscover the roots of the Western culture that were branded as heretical by the dominant church institutions and thus extinguished. One of these texts is *The Secret Book of James*, supposedly written by the purported brother of Jesus. In this book, Jesus doesn't spare his disciples; instead, he confronts them with their mistakes. This scripture teaches that humans are the ones who actually hurt and persecute themselves. When you cleanse your energy — your force field, as it were — you can radiate purity.

My sense is that *The Secret Book of James* is profoundly relevant and inspiring for the Enneagram practice. For me, it was a joyful recognition. My search didn't lead me to the discovery of a centuries-old Enneagram symbol, but it made me feel at one with the people who worked on their inner beings over the centuries. On truly intriguing quote from this ancient scripture reads as follows:

> . . . I myself have not yet fully understood the book, which is also revealed to you and yours. Therefore, make an effort to understand it and search for its meaning. Then you will achieve salvation and reveal it to others in turn.

This shows how important it is to deal with the material found in these writings, and it describes the inner search for meaning for the purpose of further development. It's not much different from Enneagram practice — including the appeal to individuals that they pass it on to others after experiencing its benefits. Here's another quote:

> The savior answered and said: "Thus I said to you, be fulfilled so you may have no deficiencies. For those who have deficiencies cannot be redeemed. Because it is good to be fulfilled and bad to have deficiencies. Just as, conversely, it is also good to acknowledge your own deficiency and bad to nonetheless feel fulfilled. Because if the fulfilment does not increase and the deficiency does not decrease, the deficiency will be filled but the fulfilment will not lead to perfection. That is why you will have deficiencies as long as it is possible to fill yourselves and fulfill yourselves, as long as it is possible to have deficiencies in order to ultimately benefit in the end. So let the spirit fill you, but give way to rational argument. Because the argument is the soul, it is psychic.

This is a call to confront one's own deficiencies and change something about them. Enneagram practice also teaches that nature won't stand still. You can choose from only two movements: development and growth or death. The choice is just as limited for your inner path: further development or disintegration.

But there's also a great danger in thinking that you're already fully developed. In inner work, this seems to be a phase or an experience that everyone encounters. They have taken so many steps forward, and the great pain they suffered because of their personality structure seems to have vanished. When you sense this, it does truly feel like a salvation. I'm speaking of personal experience: This is quickly followed by your falling asleep again. Because I truly (temporarily) experienced no suffering, my practice of self-observation slowed down and the deficiencies reappeared — at first slowly and hardly noticeable, but soon faster and more visibly again. This was a good wake-up call to get back into practice.

The gospel of truth and C.G. Jung

It's assumed that the Gospel of Truth was written by Valentinus around the year 145 AD. After its discovery at Nag Hammadi, the text was passed around many times and then was purchased by the C.G. Jung Institute in Zürich, Switzerland, and made inaccessible to scientists until 1956. Strictly speaking, this isn't a gospel but rather a meditation that revolves around a central theme. It wants to teach you the truth about your true nature — who you really are and what you have forgotten:

> We, the people from the middle, are the people of choice; we can choose between the spiritual world and the material world. Liberation lies in the spirit, and captivity lies in the material. The salvation lies in the psychic experience of finding ourselves, our inner peace.

C.G. Jung was quite interested in gnosticism and saw many connections with his archetypal psychology. The central theme of *gnosis* — self-knowledge — aligns with what Jung calls the *individuation* process — the healing process of the soul. For Jung, salvation arises from a person's subconscious through their confrontation with their shadow and its integration into their true self. Suppressing the shadow only makes it stronger while the inner gap between shadow and self grows wider and wider.

Back to the Future

The phrase "As above, so below," attributed to the (mythical?) sage Hermes Trismegistus, sums up the fact that what you know here on Earth can also be attributed to what is above you. In line with this idea, your abilities to think, experience, desire, and be conscious must also be present in nature and in the cosmos. What exists in the cosmos can be expressed in an organism only after a suitable organ has developed for it — the brains of humans with their neocortices, for example, which distinguish them from animals. You see the internal observer as an inner sense organ, which in the Enneagram practice is trained specifically for further development.

Plato assumed that it's necessary to create justice, courage, moderation, and wisdom in humans in order to develop. Jung believed that the necessary step toward a harmonious development of humanity is the development and opening of the heart center. Gurdjieff also taught that true transformation knows only one path — namely, through the heart or heart center. It's the path of love, wisdom, and justice but also of courage and moderation.

From the human perspective, evolution seems to be proceeding exceedingly slowly. Yet when you consider that the big bang probably took place 6 billion years ago, that the Earth was created 4 billion years ago, that the first hominid appeared 4.4 million years ago, and that the spiritual wisdom of the West was first put into words and pictures in the Old Kingdom of the Egyptians around 2650 BC, then the evolution of the (spiritual) human, and especially of the part of the human brain where consciousness develops, has been fairly rapid in the past 4,000 to 5,000 years. This certainly arouses curiosity about how human consciousness might develop in another thousand years. Will humanity use its chances and opportunities to transform into a loving and righteous people?

Participate in this process. Listen to Plato, Evagrius, Jung, and Gurdjieff — go to work and do your part.

The Part of Tens

IN THIS CHAPTER

» **Personal growth**

» **Change management**

» **Developing lasting relationships**

» **Tips for managers and teachers**

» **Recruitment and personnel selection**

» **Education and parenthood**

Chapter **21**

Ten Ways to Apply the Enneagram in Daily Life

T he Enneagram can be used in many different ways. Because it deals with your actions as a human being, the Enneagram can be applied in every area of your life — from the personal sphere to the work sphere and everywhere in between. There's one thing you most likely deal with every day: your relationships with one or more people. Every time I'm requested to do professional work with the Enneagram, such as for a (management) team, I notice that, after an hour, the conversations revolve around the home and family of origin (my-mother-this, my-father-that, my brother, my sister, and so on).

The following sections describe ten major issues. I could write a separate book about each of these topics and their connections to the Enneagram (and some of these books already exist). You can find a brief depiction of each topic here to show the benefits of applying the Enneagram in this area. I hope that, with a little imagination, you'll be able to expand the examples to areas or topics that are of particular interest to you.

Starting with the Personal

The Enneagram starts with the idea of self-management as the basis for becoming more effective in all possible areas. You can create room for more personal effectiveness when you become self-aware and discover that it's your type that's controlling you, rather than you yourself.

You learn to recognize how selective your perception is through the prism of your type. With that realization, you can also see how much your choices to act are being limited by your automatic reactions and patterns. People who learn to see these limitations can gain effectiveness just by learning to perceive holistically and without judgment. They see the full 360 degrees, not just one-ninth of the panorama, which leaves room for a much broader range of possible actions — room to coordinate with another person rather than fall back on one's circumscribed set of actions based on one's own implicit principles. The Enneagram offers this widened perspective as a benefit when it comes to personal effectiveness.

Dealing with Change

When people feel insecure, they're actually more likely to show their type-specific behavior. And what makes people more insecure than experiencing all kinds of changes at their company? This isn't surprising: When you work full-time, you spend most of your time at the workplace each week and gain in return your livelihood, your income, and your sense of security.

Some of the types virtually blossom during a restructuring process. They like changes or short-term projects. For those who manage change processes at an organization, it can be useful to know the employees' type-specific behavior. In change processes, overcoming resistance and managing personnel requires a great deal of attention during the change, which means a lot of time and energy can be saved in this area. The change process also runs more smoothly, and the employees are able to follow the process more easily.

Putting Relationships On a Solid Foundation

When it comes to maintaining lasting relationships, the Enneagram is extremely useful and valuable. Learning to recognize, acknowledge, and appreciate the differences between people may be the greatest benefit of the Enneagram.

In seminars, people are often suddenly touched by the fact that they now truly recognize and understand important people in their lives. They suddenly understand why their mother does what she does, why some things are happening with a partner, why it's so difficult to communicate with a brother, why it's sometimes exhausting to talk to a colleague — in short, what is going on in the other person. Understanding how things are different in other people automatically leads to more patience and compassion — a greater understanding, in other words.

The Enneagram offers the possibility of building bridges between people. With that in place, you can then cross the bridge to the other person. People often tell me that they had a completely different, wonderful conversation with their partner at home in the evening after an Enneagram seminar. If your type doesn't get in your way, you can apparently understand each other reasonably well and be truly connected.

Achieving More Success in Mediation

There's a good reason that this *For Dummies* book includes an entire chapter about the value of the Enneagram when it comes to mediating during conflict situations. (See Chapter 12.) The Enneagram was already discovered by coaches and therapists some time ago. The value of the Enneagram for their work is obvious. For me, one of the most valuable and effective applications involves mediation and other situations where conflicts have to be resolved.

The causes of conflicts and the difficulties in resolving them are often related to clashing personalities, a lack of understanding for each other, or emotions working below the surface. The Enneagram offers a shortcut to sound knowledge of human nature and empathy to mediators who haven't studied psychology.

The more mediators can get a handle on the human and emotional side of a conflict, the more often they can achieve a satisfactory outcome. In divorce cases in particular, this can help with processing the pain and finding meaning, which in turn can help both former partners stay on good terms with each other after the divorce. This is extremely important, especially if children are involved.

Gaining Effectiveness as a Manager

The Enneagram offers a shortcut to sound knowledge of human nature and empathy not just to mediators but also to managers. Managers also tend to lead others on the basis of their own implicit principles, meaning they pull the strings and push the buttons that work for themselves, just as they themselves want to be managed. This probably works more or less for many of the employees on the team — but maybe not.

Sooner or later, all managers encounter employees on their teams whom they can't relate to well or whom they can't understand. They can't find the buttons that they need to push. Then the Enneagram acts like a kind of manual on how to deal with other types of people. In essence, it's a manual for situational management that helps to let go of one's own implicit principles and convictions and thereby gain new options for action.

Learning Organizations, Successful Project Management, Winning Teams

Peter Senge, in his 1990 study *The Fifth Discipline: The Art and Practice of the Learning Organization*, defined the learning ability of an organization — the ability of managers to mobilize learning within the organization, in other words — as a decisive factor for successful organizations of the future. Other authors stress the need for a process-oriented approach, such as the organizing of feedback processes, self-organization processes, and interaction processes — working with people, in other words. Knowledge of human nature helps with these tasks.

The Enneagram offers sound knowledge of human nature and a vehicle for reflection. It supports managers in designing a learning organization, in successful project management, and in creating winning teams. Management guides often describe what managers should do. The question of how they should do it remains open. How can they overcome their own limitations in order to do what's necessary and what they might not be inclined to do by nature?

Instruction

Through their profession, teachers are involved in the education of children. After the parents, they often play the largest and most intensive role in the daily life of children and adolescents between the ages of 5 and 18. Accompanying adolescents in this crucial stage of their lives cannot be done carefully enough.

During the social-emotional development in particular, the children need someone (a professional) who supports them. If these professionals know the Enneagram types, they're better able to understand the difficulties they have with some of the children. A class of 25 to 30 pupils always has children with whom the teacher can naturally work more easily than with others. Those who are honest with themselves (and the child) may be able to notice that they find it difficult to work with a certain type of child. The Enneagram helps with learning to perceive what's happening and — even better — in which direction the solution can be found (including with the teachers themselves).

Staff Recruitment

Is the Enneagram a practical tool for recruitment? Yes and no. We know that it's being used for this purpose. Some personnel offices even advertise it. I think that it's not a good idea to use the Enneagram for stereotyping — if creative qualities are desired for a certain job profile, for example, in no way should you limit your pool to just Type 4 people. Not every Type 4 person is creative, and other types can also be creative in their way. I don't consider this approach to be advisable — on the contrary, I would avoid it.

In staff recruitment, the level of personal and professional development and the ability to learn are particularly important. The Enneagram can help to determine this in candidates. Working with the Enneagram is also useful when two suitable candidates have been selected and the goal is to determine which of the two is better suited for the future boss and the rest of the team in their personality structure.

Education

For me, one of the greatest applications of the Enneagram is in the education of children, where it opens up great opportunities. The social-emotional development during adolescence has a particularly strong influence on your later behavior as an adult — whether you're able to build and maintain lasting relationships and how you act in society, for example. In the education area, the Enneagram offers the chance to better adapt to the individual child. The child's personality structure is still developing, but even at a young age it's apparent how the temperaments differ. Knowing that the Enneagram helps to empathize with what is going on in the child allows for more targeted guidance. Attentive educators who can truly see and hear the children can usually do this without the Enneagram, but the Enneagram makes it easier to see one thing or another more quickly and clearly.

Parenthood

Education and parenthood seem to be the same topics at first glance, but there's a difference: *Education* is what you do with, and offer to, the children in your life. You educate and teach the child. Developing yourself in your parenthood is different. This is about your own development as an educator and as a human being; you might say that it's about how you educate yourself and what you teach yourself.

Your development as a parent enables you to learn about yourself in this role, along with your strengths and weaknesses as an educator. When it comes to a set of parents, the Enneagram is a good vehicle and tool to consciously grow into parenthood and education together. This means that rather than solve problems that get in your way on a day-to-day basis, you jointly make a conscious plan of which strengths you have together as parents, how you complement each other, what your weaknesses are, and — above all — what you both as parents want to give your children for later. Put another way, it's all about how you as parents can complement, support, and appreciate each other in this wonderful and difficult task.

Chapter **22**

Ten Books for Your Enneagram Library

With so many Enneagram books out there worth recommending, I find it difficult to limit myself to just ten, but that's the task I've set for myself. In this chapter, you can find recommendations for books about the Enneagram as well as recommendations for related books and authors. These books complement this *For Dummies* title and dig deeper into the subject.

The Enneagram

By Helen Palmer

In this handbook, which was my introduction to the Enneagram, the depth and accuracy of the type descriptions came about as the result of what people themselves said in the author's panels. When you read your own type description, you'll ask yourself how it's possible that the author knows all this about you. I have heard this reaction many times by now. *The Enneagram* is not so much a book that you read from cover to cover as it is a reference book. The most popular part of the book that makes it unique to this day is the relationship guide: It shows the relationships between all possible combinations of Enneagram types in terms of their most important mechanisms and issues — for not only romantic relationships but also those in the work environment.

The Enneagram: Nine Faces of the Soul

By Richard Rohr and Andreas Ebert

The Enneagram: Nine Faces of the Soul emphasizes the spiritual side of the Enneagram. The authors clearly integrate their Christian background into their discussion. Practical applications of the Enneagram are described mainly in the context of personal relationships and not as much for the workplace, unless you work in the ecclesiastic sector. Retreats, discussion groups, and community work each receive their own chapter.

The Spiritual Dimension of the Enneagram: Nine Faces of the Soul

By Sandra Maitri

Sandra Maitri is a student of Hameed Ali (A.H. Almaas), who in turn studied with Claudio Naranjo. Some colleagues find the books by Almaas easier to understand, but Maitri's books are also enjoyable. Even though the content overlaps with Helen Palmer's *The Enneagram*, it's still pleasant to read about how she describes the spiritual side of the types and their formation as well as the way back to a connection with the Higher Self. This fits seamlessly into the views of the mystery schools that I present in Part 5 of this book. Furthermore, what Maitri writes about the child's soul is beautiful and enlightening.

The Enneagram Field Guide: Notes on Using the Enneagram in Counseling, Therapy, and Personal Growth

By Carolyn Bartlett

The Enneagram Field Guide is probably the most practical and readable book available about using the Enneagram in psychotherapy. What's interesting and new about it is that Bartlett interviewed numerous people who knew their Enneagram type. She asked what works for them in therapy and what doesn't, which provides invaluable information to therapists in particular, enabling them to align their therapy even more precisely with what helps other individuals.

Character and Neurosis: An Integrative View

By Claudio Naranjo

Claudio Naranjo has published many books, including *On the Psychology of Meditation* (with Robert Ornstein), which has been an important source of inspiration for many people and is helpful in better understanding certain aspects of meditation. His better-known work, however, is *Character and Neurosis: An Integrative View*, because it appeals to a larger target group — precisely because here he provides insight into using the Enneagram in therapy from his perspective as a psychiatrist and Gestalt therapist.

Essential Enneagram: The Definitive Personality Test and Self-Discovery Guide

By David Daniels and Virginia Price

This short and easily comprehensible book focuses on the Stanford Enneagram Discovery Inventory and Guide (SEDIG). It offers a pleasant, quick start along with a clear path to further development and tips for every type. For each combination of types, it also describes how the two can be similar and how they ultimately differ. This helps many people in assessing their own types when they're still wavering between two possible choices. It's also quite helpful for consultants who want to assess their clients' types.

Wie Anders Ist der Andere?

By Wilfried Reifrath

Available only in German, this book focuses less on the exploration and further development of one's own inner life and more on the complications that can arise in the relationships between the types, their causes, and possible solutions. He focuses especially on applying the Enneagram in professional work with others, whether as a consultant, an educator, or a manager.

The Meditation Handbook

By Dr. David Fontana

The title says it all. *The Meditation Handbook* is an enlightening book that is engaging for several reasons, even if there's more to learn and discover about meditation. It's not just a handbook — it also presents different meditation methods and their effects in a clear and concise way. It discusses which methods you find and in which form and under which names in all spiritual traditions. I highly recommend it if you're interested in the topic.

In Search of the Miraculous

By Peter D. Ouspensky

People who feel inspired to practice and explore the Enneagram often also become interested in getting to know the work of G.I. Gurdjieff, not because Gurdjieff would have taught the Enneagram — it didn't exist in its present form at that time — but to better understand the background of the concepts. *In Search of the Miraculous* was written by a disciple of Gurdjieff's — his righthand man, in fact — about his life and teachings. It's not easy reading, but it's still an inspiring book and one that you can keep perusing over time.

No Boundary: Eastern and Western Approaches to Spiritual Growth; The Spectrum of Consciousness

By Ken Wilber

I can highly recommend these two books by Ken Wilber, first and foremost because they make the philosophy of Plotinus once more accessible. Moreover, Ken Wilber presents detailed and in-depth explanations for each of the various spiritual principles he covers in these books. You'll learn more about duality and nonduality, being, the now, oneness, and the path to growth. You can also read about your persona and your shadow. Wilber explains difficult concepts such as the transcendent self in terms a layperson can understand. You'll also find many exercises and tips in his books.

Ich Bin Anders — Du Auch?

By Pamela Michaelis and Ingrid Meyer-Klemm

Available only in German, *Ich Bin Anders — Du Such?* is written in the spirit of the oral tradition. Through childhood stories, it presents nine different Enneagram styles and gives a precise and differentiating description of how you experience them in the world, often with a liberal smattering of quotes. In addition, through the authors' profound knowledge about the Enneagram, you'll receive practical guidance to support your personal growth and to accompany that of others.

Das Enneagramm: Neun Weisen, die Welt zu Sehen, Neun Typen der Persönlichkeit

By Jürgen Gündel

Available only in German, *Das Enneagramm* is another example of a book written in the oral tradition. Nine people were interviewed.

Chapter **23**

Ten Further Enneagram Resources

The Enneagram is a worldwide phenomenon. Here's a taste of workshops, seminars, and training courses on the Enneagram that are out there.

Enneagram Holland

Jeanette van Stijn

Benoordenhoutseweg 23, 2596 BA Den Haag, Netherlands,

office@enneagram–nederland.nl

www.enneagram–nederland.nl

You can book lectures and Enneagram activities at your company with the author of *Enneagram For Dummies* at:

Reflexxi | Jeanette van Stijn, Benoordenhoutseweg 23, 2596 BA Den Haag, Netherlands

Enneagram USA

Enneagram Studies in the Narrative Tradition

Helen Palmer, David Daniels, Peter O'Hanrahan, Terry Saracino,

PO Box 18701, Fairfield,

OH 45018, USA,

www.enneagramworldwide.com

Enneagram Germany

Pamela Michaelis, Isestrasse 55, 20149 Hamburg,

pamela @ enneagramgermany.de

www.enneagramgermany.de

Enneagramm@work (Germany)

Jürgen Gündel und Partner, S6,25, 68161 Mannheim,

juergen.guendel@enneagramm-at-work.de

www.enneagramm-at-work.de

The Enneagram at Work (USA)

Peter O'Hanrahan

enneagramatwork@gmail.com

https://theenneagramatwork.com/

Typology

A podcast with Ian Morgan Cron

www.typologypodcast.com/home

The Enneagram Journey

Another podcast, this time hosted by Susan Stabile

www.theenneagramjourney.org/podcast

The Enneagram Institute

Created in 1997 by the late Don Richard Riso and by Russ Hudson

www.enneagraminstitute.com/

The Diamond Approach

Sandra Maitri and A. Hameed Ali,

www.diamondapproach.org/users/2286

The Naranjo Institute

Dr Claudio Naranjo (1932-2019)

www.naranjoinstitute.org.uk/

Appendix

Summary of the Enneagram Types

I designed this book so that you can learn, step by step, something about the individual types as I address each specific topic in this book. The idea is to give you a picture of the Enneagram as a model for its nine personality structures and as a roadmap for your own, personal development. Still, I thought it would be helpful for you to have a place where you can briefly look up information about a particular type. This appendix is that place — it's an overview of the individual types that lists their most important aspects.

Type 1

Names

Perfectionist, reformer, moralist, teacher, social justice warrior

Pays attention to

Right and wrong; what can be improved; what kind of order must exist; clear, careful and responsible action; asking "What do I do, or what does someone else do, correctly or incorrectly?"

Energy flows into

Improvements; doing things right and thus avoiding reproach and criticism; acting responsibly and independently; acting only when success is ensured; paying attention to internal criticism and avoiding external criticism; swallowing anger that can be directed (in an uncontrolled way) against others; suppressing personal impulses, needs, and small pleasures

Conviction

Many things must be improved in the world; people aren't appreciated as they are.

Lower Self		Higher Self
Fixation Resentment	< = mental = >	Higher idea Perfection
Passion Anger	< = emotional = >	Higher virtue Cheerful serenity

FIGURE A-1:
The Higher Self/
Lower Self of
Type 1.

Resentment as an emotionally charged thought

A Type 1 individual believes that they have to be perfect and flawless in order to be seen, appreciated, and loved. That's why it is horrifying for them to make a mistake. They often remember how nice it was as a child to receive confirmation for perfect behavior or a perfect performance. Their own spontaneous impulses become secondary to their striving for perfection. The mental fixation of resentment arises when — despite their best efforts — something doesn't turn out well, gets sabotaged, or isn't seen and appreciated. The person or object sabotaging this objective becomes the target of the resentment. This can be the Type 1 themselves or another person or the situation. In the latter case, the person follows it up with an analysis of who can be blamed for these circumstances.

Anger as a passion

Type 1 individuals are called *perfectionists* because they tend to make a dedicated effort to improve things, make them right, or make them perfect. These often idealistic people want to do something particularly well, especially when it concerns them personally. Becoming angry isn't part of the plan. This is why Type 1 people tend to suppress their own rage. When anger arises, a Type 1 person tends to pass it off as mere annoyance and shows only irritation, if anything. Those around Type 1 can easily sense this resentment or tension. Anger can arise, for example, when others don't act just as responsibly as the Type 1 person.

Strengths

Has integrity; likes to improve; energetic; idealist; independent; eager; quality-conscious; self-control and discipline; high standards; strong sense of responsibility and accountability

Strategies for further personal development

A Type 1 person has to acknowledge that several roads lead to Rome and that the term *different* or *imperfect* doesn't always mean "worse" or "bad." They must also accept imperfection in themselves and in others; be forgiving; give themselves time for relaxation and joy; learn to question their own rigid rules and high standards; recognize feelings of resistance as signals of suppressed desires and needs; and keep in mind that the meaning of life is being human, not being perfect.

Serenity as a higher virtue

When a Type 1 person can let go of resentment toward others in certain situations, they become a more cheerful person. Resentment won't make you happy. Type 1 individuals are stuck in this negativity. Letting go of obsessive thinking and compulsive behavior provides true inner peace. It isn't serenity yet, the higher virtue that Type 1 people can achieve. Experiencing *serenity* means sensing deep inside that everything is good as it is right now, and that it will be different tomorrow and also good. Serenity is more than calmness; it's a deep experience that things are good, in a pure, light, quiet manner.

Perfection as a higher idea

Reality is in the here and now. Things are already perfect as they are. This perception is no longer distorted by a judgment. People experience things in this moment, just as they are. Sacred perfection is the deep inner experience of what is called *Kono-mama* in Zen Buddhism: "It is what it is." Deep inside, reality is accepted as it is, and perfection is recognized and experienced in it. The fundamental nature in everything and everyone, including oneself, is recognized and acknowledged. Every manifestation in the universe is an expression of the fundamental nature of things and an acknowledgement that it is good.

Type 2

Names

Provider, helper, seducer, caregiver, manipulator

Pays attention to

The needs of others; being attentive and available; reciprocating; investing a lot in a relationship; being friendly, kind, and helpful; receiving appreciation and confirmation; saying "It's my turn."

Energy flows into

Giving; helping; sensing the feelings and needs of others; being needed; earning the acceptance and appreciation of other people seen as important; feeling important in relationships by meeting the needs of others (pride); adapting to meet those needs; creating positive feelings; saying no and avoiding conflict

Conviction

The world is full of people who need me; you have to understand others, be nice, and offer something in order to receive something in return.

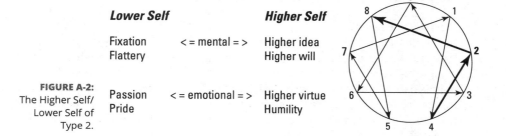

Lower Self		*Higher Self*
Fixation	< = mental = >	Higher idea
Flattery		Higher will
Passion	< = emotional = >	Higher virtue
Pride		Humility

FIGURE A-2: The Higher Self/ Lower Self of Type 2.

Flattery as an emotionally charged thought

Type 2 individuals believe that they have to earn being seen, appreciated, and loved and that they must first help others or compliment others before they themselves have a right to the same treatment. They often remember how nice it was when they made themselves useful as children and when this was seen and appreciated. Their spontaneous will becomes secondary to serving others. It is terrible for Type 2 people if their help is rejected, because they see this as a personal rejection. The mental fixation of flattery occurs when a Type 2 individual wants to be perceived and esteemed by an important or interesting person.

Pride as a passion

Type 2 individuals are also called *providers* because they are highly oriented toward other people and are available to others — and they sense their needs. When you compliment a Type 2 person, they often think this is only fair. They think in line with an earnings model: They have given something and have thus earned appreciation. At the same time, they aren't attuned to receiving anything, not even compliments. Their mechanism is designed so that it's the Type 2 person who gives. Their pride immediately comes to the surface to ward off compliments: "Oh, doing that wasn't a big deal." But deep inside, they think differently: Type 2 individuals feel a secret, considerable pride in their indispensability and achievements. Their pride stands in the way not only when it comes to receiving compliments but also when others offer help. The earnings model of Type 2 is only about the person giving something; it doesn't include receiving anything without having done something for it. Furthermore, Type 2 is convinced that they know what other people need better than do these other people themselves.

Strengths

Helpful; generous; sensitive to the feelings and needs of others; supportive; appreciative of others; energetic; romantic; exuberant and extroverted; cheerful; enthusiastic

Strategies for further personal development

A Type 2 person has to realize that being loved doesn't depend on their bending over backward for others. They have to keep track of who they really are and become aware of their own goals and needs and figuring out how to fulfill them. They also need to understand that their feelings of anger and disappointment are signals that they're losing sight of their needs. More importantly, a Type 2 person needs to see that they're not indispensable and that this is good. Allowing others to give them something and help them should be seen as perfectly fine. Learning to set limits and say no is also crucial. They also need to train themselves to notice when their helpfulness becomes annoying to others. Type 2 individuals simply need to feel valued as the persons they are, not because of the help they provide.

Humility as a higher virtue

When Type 2 people get their true self to control their reactivity and pride, they can experience the higher virtue of humility within themselves. Of course, *humility* doesn't sound hip in Western society, but its spiritual meaning is "knowing your true value." It's not at all about humility in day-to-day language, which is roughly synonymous with "making yourself small obeying." It's all about experiencing your true value, feeling no more but also no less valuable than you really are. Experiencing how valuable you are in a qualitative sense is also part of this concept.

Type 2 people who know and experience their true value deep inside no longer have to get value or have it confirmed through others. Their self-worth doesn't depend on the possibility of giving something to other people. Then they can give and receive freely, without expectations — giving and receiving to the degree that is actually necessary and how they themselves want to do it, without being dependent on others.

Freedom and will as a higher idea

At the level of the Higher Self, deep within, Type 2 individuals experience that their needs are being adequately met. The deep realization that Type 2 people, through their true selves, are able to be alone, to care for themselves, and to receive, is a higher freedom — the realization that the universe satisfies real needs and requirements. Type 2 doesn't take more or less than is actually necessary. The *higher will* is the realization that the meaning of everything happening in life lies in experiencing and accepting it as it is — it's the awareness that reality is happening according to a higher plan. The easiest way to move in life is to flow with everything that happens. Surrendering yourself to the higher will is freedom.

Type 3

Names

Achiever, performer, initiator, maker

Pays attention to

Drawing applause; collecting points; achieving goals; finding efficient solutions; being the best; being seen; asking "Which performance is required?" and "Who or what demands my commitment?"

Energy flows into

Performing goals or tasks; achievements; being efficient; being active and remaining so; adapting to create the desired image; eliminating obstacles to performance; eliminating negativity and emotions; winning; looking good; earning status, prestige, and power; avoiding failure

Conviction

In this world, the successful people are valued for what they do.

Lower Self   *Higher Self*

Fixation   < = mental = >   Higher idea
Vanity   Hope

Passion   < = emotional = >   Higher virtue
Deception   Authenticity

Vanity as an emotionally charged thought

Type 3 individuals believe that they have to be perfect and flawless in order to be seen, appreciated, and loved, and that they have to achieve success and be the best because only then will they attract attention and applause. They often remember how nice it was to draw applause for an achievement as a child. Contact with themselves and their own feelings and interests are pushed aside now. Instead, Type 3 people look at themselves through the eyes of others and attune themselves to what they must do in the eyes of others to be seen and appreciated. Other people must also make a strenuous effort and dedicate themselves to achieving something, just like the Type 3. They also believe that someone who fails — including Type 3 — doesn't deserve to be seen and loved. This is why failure is horrifying for people who recognize themselves in this type. The mental fixation of vanity occurs so that the person can create a successful image.

Deception as a passion

The deception of Type 3 people is more a kind of self-deception or self-concealment. They are also called *performers* because they like to present a beautiful image of themselves, their relationships, their families, and their work. Type 3 needs to be *seen*. They have developed a strategy for literally making themselves visible in all kinds of ways, being successful, and deserving of applause. Type 3 does this in all areas, at work as well as at home, and plays different roles in the process — perhaps as the ideal in-law, partner, parent, or boss.

A Type 3 individual fears that their true self isn't good enough and therefore prefers to play different successful roles. Type 3 people mislead themselves and others because they hide behind the facade of successful roles. The deception of Type 3 consists of identifying with accomplishments and external aspects to fulfill their image of being successful and to be appreciated.

Strengths

Enterprising; leadership qualities; enthusiastic; encouraging; solution-oriented; practical; intrinsic motivation; well-groomed and professional appearance; self-confident; competent and efficient work methods; motivator.

Strategies for further personal development

A Type 3 person has to slow down and permit their emotions and interests to appear. They need to ask themselves which things really play a role in life. They should practice getting in touch with themselves and their true identity and not let themselves be influenced by what others think and expect of them. Set limits at work. Allow themselves to listen to others. Realize that people like them because of who they are, not because of their work or possessions.

Honesty and sincerity as higher virtues

Recognizing and letting go of their deception is an important step in the development of Type 3 into a freer human. When people with this type get their true self to control their reactivity, they can experience the higher virtue of truthfulness within themselves. This frees them from having to constantly maintain their image, masks, and success stories in all the roles they play. No longer having to do this compulsively seems like a liberation. The enormously high energy expenditure is stopped and Type 3 individuals can finally come to rest. As a gift, they receive the higher virtue of truthfulness: Deep inside, they experience who they really are — that their best self is their true self, that they no longer need masks, and that they're loved for who they are.

Hope as a higher idea

At the level of the Higher Self, deep within, Type 3 individuals can relax in the knowledge that their lives are proceeding according to universal rules. People get what they need without having to set the universe in motion. The universe moves on its own. Then Type 3 individuals can allow real feelings to arise because they no longer stand in the way of their own goals. Hope is not the prospect of things getting better. Greater hope means experiencing that the world is already in order.

Hope is the realization that you can't organize it yourself — that order is being created according to the higher laws of the universe, just as planned. People don't have to do everything themselves. With this realization, on the level of the Higher Self, you can surrender to the flow of life and of being. The realization of the higher law is the realization that the universe, the world, and life are always in motion, never at rest, and that you are part of this motion and you flow with it.

Type 4

Names

Individualist, artist, romantic, idealist

Pays attention to

Longing; relationships; rejection; asking "What is missing here?," "What do I long for, in the future or in the past?," "What am I separated from?," and "What do others have that I don't have, and vice versa?"

Energy flows into

Comparing; increasing feelings, especially sadness; avoiding the ordinary and mundane; striving to exaggerate and dramatize; avoiding mediocrity; serving as a yardstick for the world; searching for what is missing and for originality and authenticity (seduction)

Conviction

In this world, people experience pain because their primal connection has been lost.

Lower Self		Higher Self
Fixation	< = mental = >	Higher idea
Melancholy		The primordial
Passion	< = emotional = >	Higher virtue
Envy		Equanimity

FIGURE A-4: The Higher Self/ Lower Self of Type 4.

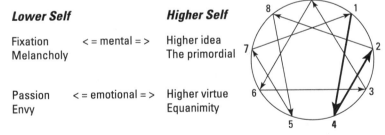

Melancholy as an emotionally charged thought

People with Type 4 want to feel that they are seen and loved. They strive for the ideal of an intense and genuine love, for the unique special love or situation that will fulfill them completely. The habit of continually comparing reality with an idealized image makes Type 4 individuals create their own disappointments. They often remember how painful it was to be different as children, as outsiders. The mental fixation of melancholy occurs when reality (once again) doesn't correspond to the Type 4 person's idealized image, when striving for a deep sense of connection (again) leads nowhere, and when the person feels validated in feeling different, unique, misunderstood, or separate from other people.

Envy as a passion

Type 4 individuals often have a subliminal feeling that there's a lack inside them and in their lives. It makes them feel empty inside. The feeling of absence is accompanied by a deep longing to feel complete and valuable and to drive away the inner emptiness. Through their prism, these individuals see that other people have what they lack. It's the classic case of the grass being greener on the other side of the fence. A Type 4 person doesn't care about superficial things like a stylish car, but rather about the important things in life. A single person with Type 4, for example, can idealize a partnership and be envious of others who live in a so-called ideal relationship. Conversely, a Type 4 person who has a partner might idealize the solitude shown by good friends. These persons don't feel resentful in the sense that they don't want others to have this joy; they just see what others have and also want that for themselves — they want what they imagine as an ideal, but this isn't available or present.

Strengths

Creative; highly sensitive to atmosphere, emotions, and feelings; empathy for suffering; living with depth and passion; romantic idealism; emotional depth; sincere and authentic; analytical and reflective

Strategies for further personal development

A Type 4 person has to learn to focus on what is good and positive rather than on what is missing; to do activities consistently despite their changing, intense feelings; to participate in physical activities and help others so that they become less preoccupied with themselves; to postpone reactions until the strongest emotions have subsided; and to appreciate ordinary, everyday pleasures.

Innocence as a higher virtue

Someone who can let go of their envy literally becomes a happier person. Comparisons with others and feelings of envy don't make Type 4 happy. They are often stuck in this negativity. The emptiness that occurs when envy retreats into the background with the type structure is a pleasant feeling. No longer having emotional ups and downs, chasing after what others have, or the constant longing for this creates inner peace. This isn't equanimity yet, the higher virtue that Type 4 can achieve. At the level of the Higher Self, equanimity for these people means experiencing that they are fulfilled, whole, and complete deep inside, here and now; that they can easily see what others have and don't have to have it; that the emptiness inside can be filled by themselves; and that nothing essential is missing.

The primordial as a higher idea

At the level of the Higher Self, deep within, Type 4 individuals experience a connection with the true self, with the primordial source, with all things, with unity. Everything comes from the same source and returns to it. The objective experience is that the true self, your nature, has always been there and that you have never been separate from it — although you experience this differently if your consciousness is active on a type level.

The sacred primordial is the deep inner experience that the one original source is present in every human being and forms the home of the soul. It is the realization that the connection also exists when you don't feel it, and the experience that all people share this connection with each other at its origin. Here every person is connected to the others and the greater whole. The sacred primordial is the experience that you arose from being.

Type 5

Names

Observer, thinker, researcher, analyst

Pays attention to

Rational solutions; facts to understand; analysis; asking "What do I need to know?," "Who or what is invading my privacy?," "Who demands my time and energy?," "What can I offer or bring to others?," and "What do I *want* to offer and do for others?"

Energy flows into

Observing; retreating to think; maintaining boundaries; keeping a safe distance; controlling time and space (hoarding); minimizing individual needs and desires; keeping strong emotional control (especially fear); protecting myself from emotional expectations and attacks; gaining control and predictability in life; keeping my own energy and using it sparingly; having enough knowledge to explain life

Conviction

More is demanded of people than can be expected in this world; little is given back in return.

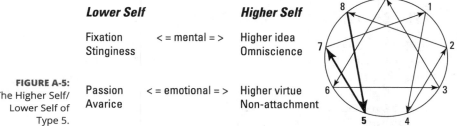

Lower Self		Higher Self	
Fixation	< = mental = >	Higher idea	
Stinginess		Omniscience	
Passion	< = emotional = >	Higher virtue	
Avarice		Non-attachment	

FIGURE A-5: The Higher Self/ Lower Self of Type 5.

Stinginess as an emotionally charged thought

Type 5 individuals believe that people and the world around them expect everything from them and that they can't fulfill this expectation. They have come to the realization that they prefer to be left alone and stay in their private sphere, where they don't have to meet other people's expectations. They often remember how nice it was to be alone as a child, in their own world of thoughts. Isolation from others and their own feelings become more important than any relationship with others. Their principle is "live and let live." This is why people who recognize themselves in this type often see others as overwhelming, pushy, or bossy. The mental fixation of stinginess occurs when they get the sense that people expect something of them.

Greed as a passion

Type 5 individuals often show in panels that they place great value on the precise use of language. Instead of greed, they prefer to talk about restraint. Because the passions are about the kinds of energy related to the types, I agree with the opinion of Type 5 that restraint describes their energy better. They don't necessarily restrain their money, but rather their own person.

Type 5 people perceive what happens around them from a restrained — safe — position. They have a subliminal feeling of absence; they believe they aren't good enough and don't have enough to offer. This is exactly why Type 5 people are concerned with other people's expectations. They worry that they can't offer what is expected of them, that people always demand more when you meet their expectations. These individuals are afraid that it will never end, and thus they act frugally with themselves, their time, their energy, and their knowledge. The object of the greed of Type 5 depends on what is important to that person. Some are quite generous with money but reserved when it comes to information about themselves, their work, or their interests.

Strengths

Eager to learn; true expert; knows many facts and details; calm in crisis situations; thoughtful; perceptive; respectful of others, also in the sense of "live and let live"; keeps other people's secrets and confidentiality; reliable; appreciates simple things

Strategies for further personal development

A Type 5 person needs to allow feelings to emerge rather than retreat with their thoughts. They need to realize that their reticence only makes others feel more prone to intrude. They should try more activities and realize that they have enough energy and support to do what they want to do; participate in physical activities; and find ways to be more active in conversations, to express themselves, and to talk more about personal matters.

Non-attachment as a higher virtue

When Type 5 individuals get their true self to control their reactivity and greed, they can experience the higher virtue of non-attachment within themselves. Their own restraint doesn't make them happy, and it gives them the compelling need to isolate themselves from others, from life, and from their own feelings. To no longer need this isolation is freedom and an enrichment of life — an enrichment because those with Type 5 can then be connected to themselves, with others, and with life. The gift of the higher virtue of non-attachment enables Type 5 to experience deep inside that there is an abundance of life energy and knowledge and that they can experience this exactly when they connect with others, with life. The fact is, others won't leave them feeling "empty"; it's just the opposite — fulfilled.

Omniscience as a higher idea

Deep inside, at the level of the Higher Self, Type 5 individuals feel that they are an inseparable part of the rest of reality. They experience that the whole consists of its parts and that everything is connected — the realization of oneness. They experience themselves as an inseparable part of this whole.

Higher omniscience is the recognition that knowledge is present and available in this connectedness — the perfect truth. It is the complete understanding of your nature and the knowledge of who you are and omniscience about yourself, your life, nature, and unity — the realization of yourself as an expression of the greater whole.

Type 6

Names

Loyal, skeptical, questioning, devil's advocate

Pays attention to

Threats; risks; dangers; hidden intentions; what can go wrong; asking "Whom and what can I trust?" and "Can I trust myself?"

Energy flows into

Being vigilant; categorizing and avoiding risks; doubting and testing; seeking ambiguous messages; rebelling; testing the goodwill of others; avoiding anger by attuning to others; logically analyzing behavior; being critical and acting as devil's advocate; feeling ambivalent about authority; identifying with the underdog; addressing possible dangers (counterphobic) or avoiding them (phobic) to reduce fears

Conviction

The world is threatening and dangerous; people can't be trusted.

Lower Self		**Higher Self**
Fixation Doubt	< = mental = >	Higher idea Faith/trust
Passion Fear	< = emotional = >	Higher virtue Courage

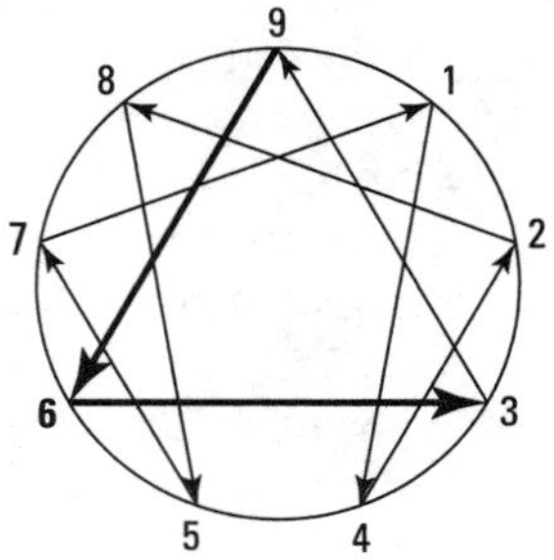

FIGURE A-6: The Higher Self/ Lower Self of Type 6.

Doubt as an emotionally charged thought

Type 6 individuals believe that people and the world around them aren't trustworthy, that dangers, risks and secret intentions are just around the corner. They often remember how unpredictable people's actions can be and how this made them feel insecure and ambushed as a child. Their own spontaneous trust becomes secondary to the alertness that is needed to protect themselves. The person (subconsciously) becomes convinced that a feeling of safety can be achieved by being constantly on guard and scrutinizing everything, by predicting possible negative scenarios and eliminating or actively fighting risks.

The mental fixation of doubt arises as soon as things occur that trigger alarm in Type 6. This can also occur when decisions have to be made. In this head type, the mental fixation is almost consistently active.

Fear as a passion

In contrast to the passions of the types I describe earlier, the fear of Type 6 is the most basic kind of fear: fear of insecurity and of living in a dangerous world. It's the primal fear that causes people to be on guard when it comes to their physical survival. Everyone has this fear, but for Type 6 individuals, it defines life to such a degree that their vigilance never wanes and is focused on all aspects of their lives. This concerns not only situations but also people and relationships. Type 6 people have the habit of always being on guard.

Strengths

Thoughtful; warm; loyal to others; trusting after trust has been developed; intuitive; sensitive; sharply perceptive; honest; humorous; reliable; persevering; responsible; defensive of others; protective

Strategies for further personal development

A Type 6 person has to become their own authority and act accordingly. They need to regain confidence in themselves and others; learn to accept that a certain amount of insecurity is just part of life; check the reality of the fears and doubts they experience through others; recognize that being under pressure is a way of suppressing fears and that fighting is a reaction to fear just as much as fleeing is; continue to take positive action even though they feel danger.

Courage as a higher virtue

When you know your fear, you can let it go and become a freer person. It's pleasant to experience the emptiness that arises in people when their fear retreats into the background along with the type structure. To no longer have to be compulsively vigilant, no longer think in terms of disaster scenarios, and no longer be restrained creates space to go through life with an open mind. The gift of the higher virtue of Type 6, courage, is something very different. For Type 6 individuals, at the level of the Higher Self, courage means experiencing deep within that they are safe and secure, here and now — that they don't have to be vigilant, that there is enough courage inside them to go their way without biases, that they can cope with whatever happens on the way, and that their body can also act without thinking.

Faith and trust as higher ideas

At the level of the Higher Self, deep within, Type 6 individuals experience a higher power that exists within them. They discover a foundation of strength and steadfastness inside themselves. On this basis, deep within, they experience confidence and faith in themselves, in others, in the world, and in the universe. They feel supported and carried. Nothing can destroy the essential safety that they experience deep inside. That is the higher power, the higher trust. The higher faith transforms their consciousness. It's not a mental concept, but rather an experienced presence deep inside where they recognize the existence of their true being.

Type 7

Names

Optimist, epicurean/connoisseur, visionary, generalist, planner

Pays attention to

What restricts them and what is unpleasant; interesting, pleasant, and positive thoughts; new possibilities; projects; fascinating things; new beginnings; freedom and space

Energy flows into

Keeping options open; redefining toward the positive; linking things and information; developing small thoughts into big ones; thinking in pictures; imagining and acting; enjoying life; focusing on positivity; orienting toward pleasant opportunities or extremes; searching for internal control

Conviction

The world is full of opportunities and possibilities; nonetheless, people are constricted and suffer as a result.

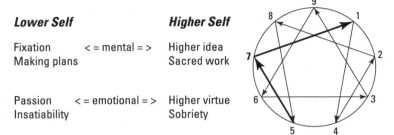

Lower Self		*Higher Self*
Fixation	< = mental = >	Higher idea
Making plans		Sacred work
Passion	< = emotional = >	Higher virtue
Insatiability		Sobriety

FIGURE A-7: The Higher Self/ Lower Self of Type 7.

Making plans as an emotionally charged thought

Type 7 individuals have learned that the world around them is frustrating and restrictive and causes pain. They can escape this by fleeing into the many beautiful possibilities that exist in their minds. There is a mental craving for opportunities, possibilities, and joy, for transforming anything that might become unpleasant into something positive. After all, you can look at anything from two sides, especially with the mental skills that this child has developed. The mental fixation of making plans occurs as soon as something happens that fascinates or inspires Type 7 but also something that might trigger reactions caused by a potential restrictive effect. This immediately creates the need to retreat, even if only mentally.

Insatiability as a passion

In Type 7 individuals, this insatiability relates to life itself. They have the fundamental desire to live and experience life in all its richness. They have developed a craving for opportunities, experiences, and joy. The energy of this insatiability brings a desire for freedom, for being free, which is why Type 7 has an aversion to restrictions. The immoderation of this head type is also a matter of the mind; the potential and joy of planning for pleasant activities can be lived primarily in the mind without anything having to be implemented in reality.

Strengths

Positive; inventive; imaginative; energetic; love of life; recognizes possibilities; playful; cheerful; helpful; inspiring and exhilarating; creative

Strategies for further personal development

A Type 7 person has to always keep in mind that by always searching for pleasant alternatives, they are actually responding to the fear of deprivation, pain, or the desire to shirk responsibilities that might limit their freedom. They need to practice focusing on one task in their work and finishing it before they start something else; to live life more in the here and now and less in the future; to take the feelings and interests of others more seriously and appreciate them; and to realize that it's actually a limitation to seek only the positive and avoid the negative.

Sobriety as a higher virtue

Those who allow their true selves to control their immoderation will experience themselves as freer persons. At first glance, the immoderation seems rather entertaining, but it represents a great loss of energy. It ensures that the persons are under the dominion of their types, that their minds won't rest, and that they feel increasingly exhausted. The emptiness that is felt after letting go of their immoderation is a piece of freedom and an enrichment of life. Through the gift of the higher virtue of sobriety, Type 7 can experience deep inside that they neither need nor want new experiences. It's possible to focus on the here and now and to stick with it. Now sobriety and restriction are accompanied by peace and depth.

Sacred work as a higher idea

At the level of the Higher Self, people with Type 7 experience that sacred work is the attainment of the true self in the here and now. In this state, Type 7 individuals accept all of life, with its joy and sadness, fun and pain, possibilities and limitations. They can concentrate, work, and perform goal-oriented activities without being distracted by fascinating new plans.

Their work is internal work in the present. Their lives are a sequence of moments in the present of which they are aware. Focused on continuity in the present, they experience the unfolding of their souls. These are inseparably connected with the unfolding of all of being, of life, of reality. Self-realization is part of the realization that takes place in everything and at every moment. It's part of the natural course of things and lives in devotion. This is the sacred work.

Type 8

Names

Boss/protector, fighter, leader, challenger

Pays attention to

Who needs protection; who has the power and strength; (in)justice; all or nothing; truth; receiving respect and being able to give it to others

Energy flows into

Being strong, protecting others, fighting; controlling yourself, other things, and the people around you; taking action and taking a stand; choosing all-or-nothing; fighting injustice and falsehoods; earning respect; denying your own weakness

Conviction

The world is unjust; the strong abuse the weak.

Revenge as an emotionally charged thought

Type 8 individuals believe that the world is tough and unfair, a jungle in which you must show your strength, in which you can't be innocent and vulnerable, and that you have to protect yourself. They often recall situations in which they were vulnerable and abused, when they decided that they would never again let anything like that happen. Their own spontaneous impulse to be innocent becomes secondary to the desire for invulnerability, strength, power, and respect.

The mental fixation of revenge sets in as soon as Type 8 feels that something violent is inflicted on the truth or if this type is affected by a (deeply buried) sense of vulnerability or need for fairness. The general response of Type 8 is to fight.

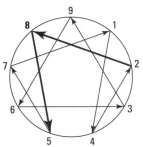

Lower Self		**Higher Self**
Fixation	< = mental = >	Higher idea
Revenge		Truth
Passion	< = emotional = >	Higher virtue
Lust/Excess		Innocence

FIGURE A-8: The Higher Self/ Lower Self of Type 8.

Lust as a passion

What is lust for a Type 8 person? When it comes to the Type 8 personality structure, the passion or energy of lust isn't only sexual. Type 8 individuals have a lust for life, a lust for action. They seem to have an unlimited supply of energy. Because they have so much energy, Type 8 people are often seen to have a strong presence. Other people reckon with them, even when they don't do or say anything. Type 8 individuals have developed a strategy to make themselves big and strong, to belong to the powerful group, the group of people that protects others, not the one needing protection. For this, Type 8 can mobilize a lot of energy from within. The energy of lust is a sensuality affecting all areas of life important to Type 8.

Strengths

Strong; determined; assertive; protective of others; fair; clear; direct; intense; friendly; honest; decisive; fearless; self-confident; able to inspire others.

Strategies for further personal development

A Type 8 person has to become aware of their power and its effect on others. They need to realize that they use their power to hide their vulnerability. They need to learn to allow what looks like weakness and see progress in showing their vulnerability; learn to wait and listen before taking action to dampen their impulsiveness; learn to apply the right amount of power in every situation; learn to allow and welcome an inner sense of peace; learn to look for win-win situations; and learn to compromise.

Innocence as a higher virtue

Those who can get their true self to control the passion of lust can experience the higher virtue of innocence within themselves. At the level of the Higher Self, innocence for Type 8 individuals is that deep internal experience, in the here and now, that they can let life happen without biases, without needing to keep anything under control or to protect anything — the innocence that they lost at some point as a child. They also learn that they can be vulnerable without sensing the danger that others are out to get them. Deep inside, they are fine and no longer need their fortresses.

Truth as a higher idea

At the level of the Higher Self, deep within, Type 8 individuals experience the truth that everyone shares with each other instead of their own, personal truths that are tied to their own interests. The holy idea of truth is the experience that the entire cosmos forms an indivisible unity. Nothing is denied any longer. It's the experience of how things belong together, how everything and everyone is connected. There's more out there than just the material and physically perceptible.

Type 8 people experience the essential truth as objective and unchangeable, not dependent on a situation or an opinion, but rather as something valid equally for everyone. In a Type 8 person, the higher truth dissolves the source of the struggle through the realization that the other person's truth is part of the perfect truth. This is true and the other is true as well.

Type 9

Names

Mediator, connector, peacemaker, negotiator

Pays attention to

Balancing controversial opinions; plans; requests; positions and wishes of others; distraction from their own wishes; maintaining harmony; (not) being seen.

Energy flows into

Going along; merging with others; avoiding and preventing conflicts; being open to others and their interests (and so it's difficult to say no); following structures and routines so that life remains predictable, comfortable, and familiar (harmony); conquering one's own anger; doing less important but reassuring things instead of more important and unsettling ones

Conviction

The world turns people into unimportant beings; it doesn't matter what I mean or what I do.

Lower Self		Higher Self
Fixation	< = mental = >	Higher idea
Forgetting yourself		Love
Passion	< = emotional = >	Higher virtue
Sloth		Right action

Forgetting yourself as an emotionally charged thought

People with Type 9 believe that they have to maintain peace and harmony in order to be seen, appreciated, and loved and that they therefore can't make even tiny waves. They often remember how they already made themselves invisible as a child and were literally overlooked. Their own spontaneous impulse, the wish to be seen and heard, becomes secondary to striving for harmony. Mediators often have problems with people who are loud and distinctive and energetically stand up for themselves. It interferes with their internal serenity, peace, and harmony. This is why Type 9 individuals have a hard time becoming visible, clearly asserting themselves and maybe even becoming angry in the process. The mental fixation of forgetting themselves appears as soon as Type 9 is triggered, which often occurs around others. Type 9 individuals can be completely absorbed by another person, their ideas and desires, and thus forget themselves.

Slothfulness as a passion

Here as well, this is not about the general meaning of the word *slothfulness*. Type 9 individuals are no more and no less work-shy than others. On the contrary, they are often industrious and forget themselves in the process. The slothfulness here is a mental or spiritual energetic state that prevents Type 9 people from doing what would be good for them, from identifying their own needs and wishes. In their striving to maintain harmony, Type 9 has the automatic tendency to merge with others. This is easier and takes less energy than asserting themselves. They can forget themselves when they merge like this. They are generally easily distracted and decide on the more convenient path instead of the one that might be best for them. This is the way in which Type 9 is slothful. Even thinking about what might be good for them takes an effort, which is why they prefer to delay that for a while.

Strengths

Consideration of others; empathetic; great sympathy and adaptability; accepting; supportive; reliable; sensitive; stable; calm; receptive; nonjudgmental; easily accepts circumstances

Strategies for further personal development

A Type 9 person has to learn to pay more attention to their own needs, priorities, and well-being. They have to learn to recognize anger as a signal that they weren't properly considered, and they need to remember that they certainly matter. Type 9 needs to realize that they block or shut out feelings when they let themselves be distracted from their actual priorities by less important things, and they have to learn to accept change and a lack of harmony as parts of life. They have to learn to love themselves as much as they love others.

Right action as a higher virtue

Those who have let their true self take control of their slothfulness can receive the higher virtue of right action within themselves. The mental inertia of not standing up for what is good and important for them doesn't make them happy. As a gift of the higher virtue of right action, they develop a deep inner sense of what they want and what is good for them. The right action isn't something they do, but rather something that flows through them by itself. Deep inside, Type 9 experiences the energy to do what is good for them and their development, and they do it without worries or hesitation, and without a detour.

Love as a higher idea

At the level of the Higher Self, Type 9 individuals experience themselves as a completely accepted part of the universe. There is love. The perception of reality without the filter of the Type 9 prism shows that love exists by nature and that nature is lovable — that love enchants us. A Type 9 person doesn't have to make an effort to receive this love; it's simply there, and they can only accept it. They love themselves and others, and they have a sense of self-worth. They experience the love that exists and has always existed. They are active without making any effort. The activity happens through Type 9; nothing that must be done according to the universal will is left undone.

Index

E

Ebert, Andreas
  The Enneagram: Nine Faces of the Soul, 310
education, Enneagrams and, 307–308
ego, 238
Egyptians
  about, 278, 299
  Heliopolis, 279–280
  human mind, 280
  Isis, 280, 282–283
  mystery schools, 282
  Nephthys, 280–281
  Osiris, 280, 282–283
  Seth, 280–281, 282, 283
  Sphinx, 281
  symbols for fixation and passion, 280–281
  visible and invisible world, 279
8-wing, 206
Eightfold Path tradition, 261
Eliot, T.S., 104
emotional armor, 104
emotional crises, what to pay attention to in, 176–177
emotional escalation phase, 158
emotional maturity, as a characteristic of self-management, 128
emotionally charged thoughts, 89
empathy
  increasing capacity for, 130
  panel interviews and, 70
energetic attuning, 171
energy
  about, 95–96
  attentiveness and, 42–44
enlightenment, 238
The Enneads (Plotinus), 90, 294–295
Enneagram Germany, 316
Enneagram Holland, 315
Enneagram Institute, 275
Enneagram Professional Training Program (EPTP), 273
Enneagram USA, 316
Enneagram Worldwide, 273

Enneagrams. *see also specific topics*
  about, 11–13, 23
  applying to daily life, 303–308
  benefits of, 16–19, 23–24
  development of, 255–257
  opinions on, 13–14
  origins of, 255–257
  pioneers of, 260–266
  practical applications for, 19
  symbol versions, 258–266
  tests, 61–63
  using as a tool, 28
The Enneagram (Palmer), 309, 310
The Enneagram at Work, 316
The Enneagram at Work: Towards Personal Mastery and Social Intelligence (Nathans), 196
The Enneagram Field Guide: Notes on Using the Enneagram in Counseling, Therapy and Personal Growth (Bartlett), 180–181, 310
The Enneagram Institute, 317
The Enneagram Journey, 317
The Enneagram: Nine Faces of the Soul (Rohr and Ebert), 310
The Enneagram: Understanding Yourself and the Others in Your Life (Palmer), 66
Enneagram@work, 316
envy, as a passion, 92, 98, 328
EPTP (Enneagram Professional Training Program), 273
equanimity, as a higher virtue, 246
escalation phases, of conflict, 158
esoterics, 290–291
Essential Enneagram: The Definitive Personality Test and Self-Discovery Guide (Daniels and Price), 311
establishing contact, 170
Euclid, 284
evolution, 213
Example icon, 6
exoterics, 290–291
experiences
  broadening, 192–193
  importance of, 30–31
external attribute, 88

external properties, 26

external support, as a condition of personality development, 214

F

Facets of Unity: The Enneagram of Holy Ideas (Ali), 275

faith
  as a sacred idea, 250
  Type 6 and, 334

fakir, path of the, 217

fantasy world, 90–91

fear
  about, 54–55
  as a passion, 92, 99, 333

feedback
  giving, 153–156
  receptivity to, as a characteristic of self-management, 128

feeling, 104

The Fifth Discipline: The Art and Practice of the Learning Organization (Senge), 306

fight or flight strategy, 107

first-level learning, 205

5-wing, 206

fixations
  about, 79–81
  Egyptian symbols for, 280–281
  letting go of, 228–235

flattery
  Providers and, 82
  as a reaction, 81
  Type 2 and, 322

flowing meditation, 221

follow up, 169

Fontana, David, 221
  The Meditation Handbook, 312

forces, underlying driving, 42–49, 59

forgetting yourself, Type 9 and, 340

foundation, necessity of a healthy, 174–188

4-wing, 206

Fox, Matthew
  Original Blessing: A Primer in Creation Spirituality, 243, 244

freedom, as a sacred idea, 250

Freud, Sigmund, 104, 166, 197, 262, 266

G

Geb (god), 279

getting started, 56–59

gifts, 245–248

gnosis, 292–293, 298

God's Will Be Done (Bakhtiar), 268–270

The Golden Verses, 290

Gospel of Truth, 298

greed, as a passion, 92, 99, 330–331

Greek philosophers
  about, 283
  acousticians, 288
  cradle of wisdom, 284–285
  The Enneads, 90, 294–295
  esoterics, 290–291
  exoterics, 290–291
  gnosis, 292–293, 298
  mathematical harmony in music and scale, 287–288
  mathematicians, 288
  number theory, 286–287
  Plato, 46, 283, 291–292, 299
  Plotinus, 90, 284, 294–295
  Pythagoras, 263, 283–291

Gregory I, Pope, 89

Grinder, John, 243

grounding yourself, 170–171

growth mechanisms
  letting go of fixations, 228–235
  using type mechanisms as tools, 226–228

guided meditation, 244

Gündel, Jürgen
  Das Enneagram: Neun Weisen, die Welt zu Sehen, Neun Typen der Persönlichkeit, 313

The Provider (Type 2) *(continued)*
  conflicts and, 160, 161
  fear as a passion in, 100
  feedback and, 155
  flattery and, 82, 322
  as a heart type, 116–117
  higher self and, 249, 322, 324
  histrionic personality disorder and, 199
  humility as a higher virtue, 323–324
  interventions and, 152
  issues related to, 187
  learning and, 193
  letting go of fixations, 229–230
  lower self and, 322
  moving from vices to virtues, 246–247
  personal development strategies, 323
  personality disorders and, 198
  pride as a passion in, 97, 322–323
  reactivity and, 227
  strengths of, 121, 323
  stress type/relaxation point, 209
  suppression and, 105
  in therapeutic situations, 182, 184–185
psychological elements, 19–22
psychology, positive, 188
psychospiritual integration, 211–214, 273
Purgatorio (Alighieri), 92
Pyramid Texts, 282–283
Pythagoras, 262, 283–291

Q

questionnaires, 62
Quispel, Gilles
  The Hermetic Gnosis Through the Centuries, 292
Quran, 261

R

raja yoga, 261
rapport, 170
rational escalation phase, 158
rationalization, as a defense mechanism, 106
Re (god), 279

reactions, 81, 105
reactivity
  about, 226–228
  interaction patterns and, 167–168
Ready, Romilla
  Neurolinguistic Programming For Dummies, 16, 171
reality, 71, 240
receiving, 240–241
receptive, being, 239, 241
Reclaiming Judaism as a Spiritual Practice: Holy Days and Shabbat (Milgram), 271
reconstruction, 193–194
recruitment, Enneagrams and, 307
reflection, as a condition of personality development, 214
regression, 196
Reifrath, Wilfried
  Wie Anders Ist der Andere?, 311
relationship definitions, 146–148
relationships, Enneagrams and, 305
relaxation points, 208
Remember icon, 6
remembering, as an activity of the head center, 78–79
The Republic (Plato), 46
resentment
  Perfectionists and, 82
  as a reaction, 81
  Type 1 and, 320
resources
  recommended, 309–313
  seminars, 315–317
  training courses, 315–317
  workshops, 315–317
responsibility, as a characteristic of self-management, 127–128
revenge
  Bosses/Protectors and, 84–85
  as a reaction, 81
  Type 8 and, 337
RHETI (Riso-Hudson Enneagram Type Indicator), 276
Ridhwan School, 275

right action
  as a higher virtue, 246
  Type 9 and, 341
Riso, Don Richard, 202, 275–276
Riso-Hudson Enneagram Type Indicator
    (RHETI), 276
Rohr, Richard, 92, 271–272
  The Enneagram: Nine Faces of the Soul, 310
Rose of Leary model, 172–173
royal yoga, 261
rule of threes, 49–52

S

sacred ideas, 250
Saint John of the Cross, 241
  The Dark Night of the Soul, 242
Saint Teresa of Avila, 241
Sarmoung, 261
SAT (Seekers after Truth), 265, 274
scale, mathematical harmony in, 287–288
scared work, Type 7 and, 336
schizoid personality disorder, Type 5 and, 200
schools and movements
  about, 3, 267–268
  Addison, Howard Avruhm, 270–271
  Ali, Hamid, 274–275
  Bakhtiar, Laleh, 268–270
  Christian perspective, 271–272
  Daniels, David, 3, 40, 61, 75, 212, 273–274, 311
  diamond approach, 274–275
  Hudson, Russ, 202, 275–276
  Kabbalah, 203, 216–217, 270–271
  levels of development, 275–276
  Maitri, Sandra, 274–275
  Milgram, Goldie, 271
  Nathans, Hannah, 54–55, 168–169, 196, 249,
      270–271
  oral tradition, 273–274
  Palmer, Helen, 3, 75, 92, 211, 213, 273–274
  Riso, Don Richard, 202, 275–276
  Rohr, Richard, 92, 271–272, 310
  Sufi Enneagram, 268–270

second-level learning, 238
The Secret Book of James, 297
SEDIG (Stanford Enneagram Discover Inventory
    and Guide) test, 61, 311
Seekers after Truth (SAT), 265, 274
*Seeking and Soaring: Jewish Approaches to Spiritual
    Direction* (Milgram), 271
selective perception, 13
self-acceptance, as a condition of personality
    development, 214
self-awareness
  about, 63
  as a condition of personality development, 214
self-consciousness, as a characteristic of
    self-management, 127
self-development, 15–17
self-effacement
  Mediators and, 85
  as a reaction, 81
self-management
  about, 18, 175
  Enneagrams and, 304
  mastering, 126–131
self-motivation, as a characteristic of
    self-management, 127–128
self-observation
  about, 45
  as a condition of personality development, 214
self-protection strategies, 104
self-reflection, 56, 193–194
seminars, 315–317
Senge, Peter
  *The Fifth Discipline: The Art and Practice of the
      Learning Organization,* 306
serenity, as a higher virtue in Type 1, 321
Seth, 280–281, 282, 283
7-wing, 206
sharing knowledge, 65–71
silent meditation, 221
sincerity, in Type 3, 326
six A's of conversations, 168–173
6-wing, 206
skills, compensating, 192
slothfulness, as a passion, 92, 101, 340

About the Author

Jeanette van Stijn was educated as an Enneagram trainer by Helen Palmer and David Daniels in the Enneagram Professional Training Program (EPTP) at their Enneagram Worldwide training institute in California, where she was initially associated as a supervisor and also later as a lecturer. For this she received additional training from Helen Palmer and David Daniels and is the only person in the Netherlands who is authorized to pass along their method. Together with Hannah Nathans, Jeanette van Stijn founded the Enneagram Stichting Nederland (ESN), which appointed the two founders as honorary members.

Before Jeanette was introduced to the Enneagram, she acquired a broad professional background through her education and work experience. The common theme was always to promote the further development of individuals and organizations: How do you bring out the best in people? How can you help people bring out the best in themselves?

Jeanette completed her first course of studies at the Higher Hotel School in The Hague (at that time called College of Business Administration.) The hospitality industry is an industry for and by people, in which the management of people is central. During her second course of studies at the Vrije Universiteit Amsterdam in the field of Cultural Anthropology (Culture, Organization, and Management), she worked as an organizational consultant. She has been an independent entrepreneur since the age of 27.

During her work as an organizational consultant, Jeanette's focus shifted: People played an increasingly central role, and she developed more and more into a coach, trainer, and mediator. The importance of the Enneagram grew rapidly in her activities and her work with people. In 2003, Jeanette decided to focus only on people and the Enneagram. She left her well-established organizational consultancy and started two new activities:

With the company Reflexxi, Jeanette offers readings, coaching, and training with the Enneagram. With Enneagram Nederland, she offers training according to the Helen Palmer/Enneagram Worldwide method and many other seminars and workshops on the Enneagram for open enrollment.

Dedication

Everyone who is or was part of my life has contributed to the person I am today. Every encounter, short or long, intense or superficial, pleasant or less pleasant, has left its traces in me. They have contributed to the lessons I learned and still need to learn. They have brought me to where I am today and made me the person I am now. They have become a lasting, indelible part of myself. I dedicate this book to all the people I have met along the way, and I thank them.

Author's Acknowledgments

I warmly thank "my guys" — this book wouldn't exist without them. Hard to believe how much support I received for my very first book! I retreated to our family's boat for almost two months to create this book. During that time, my husband held down the fort at home and spent valuable, intensive time with our sons. It was wonderful to take breaks on Sundays, when they visited my boat and we set sail. Then I was always especially productive on Mondays.

Just as warmly, I want to thank my favorite aunt, Miek; she was always available on the phone with wise words, advice, and consolation. My friend Alexandra deserves just as much gratitude. How strange that our paths crossed for the second time. Without her, this book would definitely never have been written. She helped me move from my interior world back to the outside world. Alexandra was also always available for me by phone, with friendship and professional advice. As my most eager and consistent reader, she gave me many pointers in the right direction.

I would also like to thank all those who have been my companions on this journey of inner work, and especially two people with whom I have a Pythagorean friendship, thanks to our journey together: Charlotte Krop and Hannah Nathans. (Thank you, Charlotte, for always reminding me of the way of the heart and inspiring me to take it. Thank you, Hannah, for being an inexhaustible fountain of knowledge, experience, and insight, and for the joy I derived from being able to drink so much from it. Thank you for your friendship.)

I would like to thank the John Wiley & Sons, Inc., which made it possible to now also have this book available in English-speaking countries.

I thank my neighbors on the docks: for relaxation, a glass of wine, and conversations in between. Kees, I hope you can see that there is a happy ending, because that's what you asked for every time.

Finally, I'd like to thank my family. Occasionally, I may have been a bit distracted or crabby, and you were always there for me.

Publisher's Acknowledgments

Acquisitions Editor: Tracy Boggier

Senior Managing Editor: Kristie Pyles

Senior Project Editor: Paul Levesque

Copy Editor: Becky Whitney

Technical Editor: Pamela Michaelis

Production Editor: Tamilmani Varadharaj

Cover Image: © Peter Hermes Furian/ Shutterstock

Leverage the powe

Dummies is the global leader in the reference category and one of the most trusted and highly regarded brands in the world. No longer just focused on books, customers now have access to the dummies content they need in the format they want. Together we'll craft a solution that engages your customers, stands out from the competition, and helps you meet your goals.

Advertising & Sponsorships

Connect with an engaged audience on a powerful multimedia site, and position your message alongside expert how-to content. Dummies.com is a one-stop shop for free, online information and know-how curated by a team of experts.

- Targeted ads
- Video
- Email Marketing
- Microsites
- Sweepstakes sponsorship

20 MILLION
PAGE VIEWS
EVERY SINGLE MONTH

15
MILLION
UNIQUE
VISITORS PER MONTH

43%
OF ALL VISITORS
ACCESS THE SITE
VIA THEIR MOBILE DEVICES

700,000 NEWSLET
SUBSCRIPT
TO THE INBOXES OF

300,000 UNIQUE INDIVIDUALS
EVERY WEEK

# of dummies

Custom Publishing

Reach a global audience in any language by creating a solution that will differentiate you from competitors, amplify your message, and encourage customers to make a buying decision.

- Apps
- Books
- eBooks
- Video
- Audio
- Webinars

Brand Licensing & Content

Leverage the strength of the world's most popular reference brand to reach new audiences and channels of distribution.

For more information, visit dummies.com/biz

PERSONAL ENRICHMENT

Staying Sharp
9781119187790
USA $26.00
CAN $31.99
UK £19.99

Facebook
9781119179030
USA $21.99
CAN $25.99
UK £16.99

Guitar
9781119293354
USA $24.99
CAN $29.99
UK £17.99

Investing
9781119293347
USA $22.99
CAN $27.99
UK £16.99

Beekeeping
9781119310068
USA $22.99
CAN $27.99
UK £16.99

Digital Photography
9781119235606
USA $24.99
CAN $29.99
UK £17.99

Meditation
9781119251163
USA $24.99
CAN $29.99
UK £17.99

Pregnancy
9781119235491
USA $26.99
CAN $31.99
UK £19.99

Samsung Galaxy S7
9781119279952
USA $24.99
CAN $29.99
UK £17.99

iPhone
9781119283133
USA $24.99
CAN $29.99
UK £17.99

Crocheting
9781119287117
USA $24.99
CAN $29.99
UK £16.99

Nutrition
9781119130246
USA $22.99
CAN $27.99
UK £16.99

PROFESSIONAL DEVELOPMENT

Windows 10
9781119311041
USA $24.99
CAN $29.99
UK £17.99

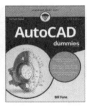

AutoCAD
9781119255796
USA $39.99
CAN $47.99
UK £27.99

Excel 2016
9781119293439
USA $26.99
CAN $31.99
UK £19.99

QuickBooks 2017
9781119281467
USA $26.99
CAN $31.99
UK £19.99

macOS Sierra
9781119280651
USA $29.99
CAN $35.99
UK £21.99

LinkedIn
9781119251132
USA $24.99
CAN $29.99
UK £17.99

Windows 1
978111931056
USA $34.00
CAN $41.99
UK £24.99

SharePoint 2016
9781119181705
USA $29.99
CAN $35.99
UK £21.99

Fundamental Analysis
9781119263593
USA $26.99
CAN $31.99
UK £19.99

Networking
9781119257769
USA $29.99
CAN $35.99
UK £21.99

Office 2016
9781119293477
USA $26.99
CAN $31.99
UK £19.99

Office 365
9781119265313
USA $24.99
CAN $29.99
UK £17.99

Salesforce.com
9781119239314
USA $29.99
CAN $35.99
UK £21.99

Coding
978111929332
USA $29.99
CAN $35.99
UK £21.99

Learning Made Easy

ACADEMIC

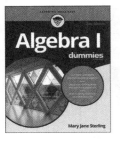

9781119293576
USA $19.99
CAN $23.99
UK £15.99

9781119293637
USA $19.99
CAN $23.99
UK £15.99

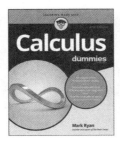

9781119293491
USA $19.99
CAN $23.99
UK £15.99

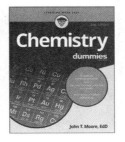

9781119293460
USA $19.99
CAN $23.99
UK £15.99

9781119293590
USA $19.99
CAN $23.99
UK £15.99

9781119215844
USA $26.99
CAN $31.99
UK £19.99

9781119293378
USA $22.99
CAN $27.99
UK £16.99

9781119293521
USA $19.99
CAN $23.99
UK £15.99

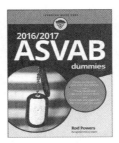

9781119239178
USA $18.99
CAN $22.99
UK £14.99

9781119263883
USA $26.99
CAN $31.99
UK £19.99

Available Everywhere Books Are Sold

dummies.com

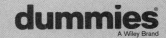

A Wiley Brand

Small books for big imaginations

9781119177173
USA $9.99
CAN $9.99
UK £8.99

9781119177272
USA $9.99
CAN $9.99
UK £8.99

9781119177241
USA $9.99
CAN $9.99
UK £8.99

9781119177210
USA $9.99
CAN $9.99
UK £8.99

9781119262657
USA $9.99
CAN $9.99
UK £6.99

9781119291336
USA $9.99
CAN $9.99
UK £6.99

9781119233527
USA $9.99
CAN $9.99
UK £6.99

9781119291220
USA $9.99
CAN $9.99
UK £6.99

9781119177302
USA $9.99
CAN $9.99
UK £8.99

Unleash Their Creativity

dummies.com

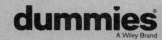